Fundamentals of Applied Multidimensional Scaling
for Educational and Psychological Research

Cody S. Ding

Fundamentals of Applied Multidimensional Scaling for Educational and Psychological Research

 Springer

Cody S. Ding
Department of Education Science and Professional Program
University of Missouri-St. Louis
St. Louis, MO, USA

Center for Neurodynamics
University of Missouri-St. Louis
St. Louis, MO, USA

ISBN 978-3-319-78171-6   ISBN 978-3-319-78172-3   (eBook)
https://doi.org/10.1007/978-3-319-78172-3

Library of Congress Control Number: 2018935924

Printed on acid-free paper

This Springer imprint is published by the registered company Springer International Publishing AG part of Springer Nature.
The registered company address is: Gewerbestrasse 11, 6330 Cham, Switzerland

Preface

Since I have been conducting research in education and psychology using multidimensional scaling (MDS) models for many years, I read quite a few books as well as some classical articles on MDS. My experiences with these readings are that writings on this topic are often very technical and esoteric, which make it hard to relate to the current research needs in education or psychology. I gradually develop an urge to write a book on MDS that is more understandable and relevant to the current research setting. This is my first effort.

In this round of writing, I focus on MDS concepts that I deem to be more relevant to current research in education or psychology. I try to convey MDS concepts in more understandable terms and focus on aspects of MDS that may be more potentially useful to readers. Although I put some technical aspects of the MDS (such as equations) in a few chapters, they are simple for the purpose of making the discussion more complete. Readers can skip these sections without losing the main ideas of the topic. I made each chapter as short as I can to only cover main points so that readers can focus on the fundamentals. Of course, this is done at the risk of omitting many potentially helpful materials.

MDS has not been often employed in education or psychology research in recent years. Although I did not cover everything that can be done with MDS analysis, I did indicate some potential research that can be done via MDS. I provided some examples of MDS analyses so that readers can get some ideas, with the hope that this could pique reader's interest. MDS analysis has its limitations but it can certainly be useful. Thus, the book is intended for students or researchers who want to know more about MDS but not so technical. The book is not a textbook in a technical sense since it does not teach or show readers how to perform MDS analysis. However, the book provides a comprehensive view of fundamentals of MDS so that readers can understand what MDS is and can do.

This book is intended as a research reference book for graduate students and researchers to get fundamental ideas of multidimensional scaling (MDS) and how this particular analytic method can be used in applied settings. Some of the major problems with the content of existing MDS books are that the discussion on MDS (1) tends to be very technical, (2) covers many topics that are less relevant to current practices in educational or psychological research, and (3) uses language or examples that are less common in today's research setting. As such, graduate students or researchers are not likely to view MDS as a viable method for studying issues at hand.

Before 1985 or so, there were many publications on MDS. But then it somehow fell out of fashion. Today MDS is offered as part of materials on multivariate analysis, usually as a chapter. However, one chapter is not nearly close to covering some unique aspects of MDS, particularly regarding the applications of this method to research in education and psychology. I do not expect dramatic changes in its popularity, but I do believe MDS as a method can offer some interesting applications to research and this is not a popularity contest. This book is an effort to make MDS more accessible to a wider audience in terms of the language and examples that are more relevant to educational research and less technical so that the readers are not overwhelmed by equations and do not see any applications. In addition, it discusses some new applications that have not previously been discussed in MDS literature. My philosophy is that methods are just methods, not bad or good, and it all depends on how you use them and for what purpose. Using popularity to assess the value of academic books will limit the spread of knowledge. In addition, MDS is not one method, but rather it comprises a family of methods that can be used for different purposes.

This book can also be used as a supplemental book for advanced multivariate data analysis on the topic of MDS, which is typically one chapter in such a book of multivariate data analysis for graduate students. As mentioned previously, the main impetus for writing this proposed book is that I hope to have a book that is not so technical for graduate students and researchers who are not interested in the technicality of MDS. I have read quite a few books on MDS and I am struggling with thoughts of why and what these materials in the books are useful for, although they are informative from a purely academic perspective. Therefore, the book is more of response to my own desire to have a book in which I can see the relevancy of MDS in actual research settings. The book does not have exercises or discussion questions since my goal is to have readers learn some fundamentals and start using MDS via available software programs. If they do want to know more technical aspects of MDS, they can always refer to books by Davison (1983) or Borg and Groenen (2005), for example. There is no need for me to replicate what they have already done.

St. Louis, MO, USA   Cody S. Ding

Contents

Part I
Basics of MDS Models

Describe basic and fundamental features of MDS models pertaining to applied research applications.

Chapter 1
Introduction

Abstract Discuss fundamental ideas of MDS, particularly MDS as a data visualization tool in the context of big data is highlighted. Similarities and differences between MDS, factor analysis, and cluster analysis are discussed.

Keyword MDS · Visualization · Factor analysis · Cluster analysis

In this chapter, we mainly discuss the concept of multidimensional scaling in the current psychological or education research context. We also discuss some differences and similarities among multidimensional scaling, factor analysis, and cluster analysis. The goal of such a discussion is to have readers obtain a better sense of the concept of multidimensional scaling in relation to other conceptually similar methods, particularly in the language that is more relevant to current educational and psychological research.

1.1 What Is Multidimensional Scaling

In much of the quantitative and statistical literature, multidimensional scaling (MDS) is often referred to as a technique that represents the empirical relationships of data as a set of points in a geometric space, typically in two or higher dimensional spaces. Specifically, multidimensional scaling represents a family of statistical methods or models that portray the structure of the data in a spatial fashion so that we could easily see and understand what the data indicate. This may be the reason that MDS tends to be viewed as a data visual technique, and sometimes it is considered with respect to mapping technique. The unifying theme of different MDS models is the spatial representation of the data structure. In this regard, MDS can be considered as one analytic tool of data visualization in the context of big data.[1] In the context of data visualization, MDS models can be used to investigate a wide range of issues in education and psychology such as perception of school

---

[1] Big data means that there are lots of data being collected. Visualization is one method for big data analysis.

© Springer International Publishing AG, part of Springer Nature 2018
C. S. Ding, *Fundamentals of Applied Multidimensional Scaling for Educational and Psychological Research*, https://doi.org/10.1007/978-3-319-78172-3_1

climate by various age groups of students, changes in achievement, sensitivity of psychological measures, or individual differences in mental health, to name a few. Moreover, it can also be employed for the purpose of hypothesis testing, like that in structural equation modeling. Although MDS is a powerful tool of studying various behavioral phenomena, it appears to be underused in current educational and psychological research.

In the literature, MDS has been defined in slightly different ways. For example, Davison (1983) defined MDS as a method for studying the structure of stimuli (i.e., variables) or individuals. Borg and Groenen (2005) defined MDS as a technique of representing distances between objects (or variables) in a multidimensional space. In a nutshell, MDS can be defined as a family of analytical methods that use the geometric model (typically in the form of a distance equation) for analysis of inter-relationships among a set of variables, people, or combination of variable and people (such as in preference analysis) so that the latent structure of data can be visualized for meaningful interpretation. A distance equation could be the Euclidean distance, the city-block distance, or the Minkowski distance. Thus, an MDS analysis involves employment of a specific model of study, for instance, how people view things in different ways.

More specifically, multidimensional scaling is carried out on data relating objects, individuals, subjects, variables, or stimuli to one another. These five terms are sometimes used interchangeably, which may cause some confusion. Objects, variables, or stimuli usually refer to inanimate things, such as variables or test scores; individuals and subjects refer to people. Given the distance measures between variables, MDS models produce a solution that consists of a configuration of patterns of points representing the variables in a space of a small number of dimensions, typically in two or three dimensions. For this reason, it is also called small space analysis (SSA). The following example illustrates this point. This example represents a group of students who take a given reading test five times over a two-month period. The distance matrix of these score is:

$$
D = \begin{bmatrix}
0 & & & & \\
1 & 0 & & & \\
2 & 1 & 0 & & \\
3 & 2 & 1 & 0 & \\
4 & 3 & 2 & 1 & 0
\end{bmatrix}
$$

This distance matrix can be thought of as giving information about how similar or dissimilar these test scores are to each other over time. MDS model takes this information and represents these test scores as a point in space, which is shown in Fig. 1.1 In this two-dimensional space, as shown in Fig. 1.1, the more similar the test scores are, the closer they lie to each other. The pattern of points that most accurately represents the information in the data is the MDS solution or configuration.

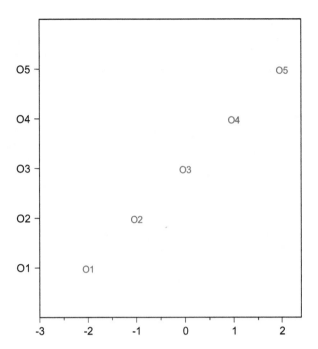

Fig. 1.1 A hypothetical example of a configuration of five reading test scores

In this example, these five reading test scores have a linear configuration, indicating the linear increase of reading achievement over time. As Tukey (1977) says: "A picture is worth a thousand words."Thus, a picture of the data is produced that is much easier to assimilate (visually) than a matrix of numbers, particularly if such a matrix of number is large. It may also bring out features of the data that were obscured in the original matrix of coefficients (i.e., dissimilarity coefficients).

This example, although based on fictitious data, allows a number of points to be noted:

1. MDS is primarily concerned with representation, in this case with the production of a simple and easily assimilated geometrical picture where distances are used to represent the data.
2. MDS models differ in terms of the assumptions they make about how important the quantitative properties of the data are. In the example above, it is in fact only the rank order of the data percentages, which is matched perfectly by the distances of the configuration. This is an example of ordinal scaling or, as it is more commonly termed in MDS literature, non-metric scaling.
3. A wide range of data and measures can be used as input, as will be discussed in Chap. 2. Any data that can be interpreted as measures of similarity or dissimilarity are appropriate for MDS scaling analysis.

Traditionally, there are following issues that we must consider in using multidimensional scaling:

1. *The data*, the information to be represented (discussed further in Chap. 2);
2. *The transformation* how data should be related to the model, such as basic non-metric MDS model or metric MDS model (discussed in Chap. 3).
3. *The model* how the solution should be interpreted, such as individual differences model or basic scaling model (more on this in later chapters), as giving information about the relationships between the variables.
4. The sample size required for an MDS analysis does not need to be large: it can range from a few people to a few hundred. Since the MDS analysis is more of a descriptive (except for maximum likelihood MDS) and does not involve significance testing, the interpretation and accuracy of the analysis results are not tied to the sample size. Thus, the MDS analysis can be used for studies based on the single-case design such as an investigation of the response of a small group of individuals to a treatment. However, if one wants to make a generalization based on the people in the study, a representative sample is required.
5. MDS models (except for maximum likelihood MDS) do not have distributional requirements such as normality of the coordinates. But the maximum likelihood MDS assumes that the coordinates are normally and independently distributed and each object or variable can have the same variance or different variances (discussed in Chap. 7).

1.2   Differences and Similarities Between MDS, Factor Analysis, and Cluster Analysis

Before we start further discussion on MDS models, it is imperative to discuss differences and similarities between MDS, factor analysis, and cluster analysis. Without a clear conceptual understanding of what MDS models are all about, particularly in relation to these methods, practitioners may have difficulty in utilizing MDS for their work, thus impeding further developments of MDS models in psychological and educational research. In light of this and to remain consistent with the applied orientation of the book, this discussion is focused more on conceptual grounds rather than mathematical aspects.

1.2.1   MDS and Factor Analysis

Conceptually, factor analysis is a technique that discovers latent relationships among a set of variables. The objective is to explain *a number of* observed variables, (*m*), by a set of latent variables or factors (*f*), where (*f*) is much smaller in number than (*m*). The hypothesis is that only a few latent factors suffice to explain most of the variance of the data. In other words, the relationships among the observed variables exist because of the underlying latent variables. Likewise, the objective of

MDS is to reveal geometrically the structure of data in fewer dimensions. Like MDS, factor analysis yields a quantitative dimensional representation of the data structure. Both have been used to study dimensionality among variables. It is often the case that the term *factor* and *dimension* are used interchangeably in factor analysis literature. Because of this similarity, it is not a surprise that factor analysis and MDS are viewed as very similar if not the same.

Studies have been done to compare the two techniques (e.g., Davison 1985). The differences between the two may be summarized as follows: (1) factor analysis yields more dimensions than does MDS; (2) factor analysis typically represents linear relationships among variables, whereas MDS can represent both linear and nonlinear relationships; (3) MDS is traditionally used more often as a data visualization tool than factor analysis, which is typically a measurement technique of finding a set of latent variables that connect observed variables together; and (4) MDS can employ a variety of kinds of data such as preference ratio data, whose values are coded between 0.0 and 1.0, indicating the degree to which a variable in a variable pair is preferred. But factor analysis usually analyzes the correlation matrix, whose values indicate similarities between variables. Therefore, the applications of MDS can be more diverse than that of factor analysis. For example, MDS preference analysis can be used to study individuals' preferences to a set of coping behaviors (e.g., prefer shouting to talking with friends), whereas factor analysis usually is used in studying how a set of coping behaviors measures a particular coping construct (e.g., withdrawal coping).

The take-home message of the differences between these two methods is that factor analysis is focusing on latent variables that represent some constructs such as anxiety or depression, while MDS analysis is more in line with Network Analysis (McNally et al. 2015), where behaviors (as assessed by variables) are best construed as a system embodied in networks of functionally interconnected fashion. Thus, the configuration of relation between variables is mereological – part to whole – rather than causal as in factor analysis (Borsboom and Cramer 2014; Guyon et al. 2017). For example, typical example used in illustrating MDS analysis is to show the relation between the 50 states as a map. Accordingly, the map is mereological: parts (i.e., 50 states) to whole (i.e., the United States). There is no underlying causal relation between states and the country called the United States; states are part of it. Moreover, MDS as a network analysis is more exploratory, that is, empirically discovered rather than formed by theories. Thus, the difference is ontological as in factor analysis versus mereological as in MDS analysis.

1.2.2 MDS and Cluster Analysis

Another closely related method to MDS is cluster analysis (Kruskal 1977). Traditional cluster analysis, such as hierarchical cluster analysis, is employed to identify individuals who share similar attributes (e.g., high risk adolescents).

While MDS can be used in the same way, Davison (1983) pointed out three differences between MDS and cluster analysis. First, relationships between the observed distance matrix and model derived distance matrix in cluster analysis cannot be expressed in linear or even monotone fashion as in MDS. Second, dimensions in cluster analysis are typically represented in a tree diagram of many simple two-valued dimensions to represent data. As such, the number of dichotomous dimensions needed to represent the data structure become large in practice. Third, MDS defines clusters of individuals in terms of continuous dimensions rather than in either-or fashion. Thus, we can describe a group of individuals who possess more of one attribute (e.g., depression) than the other (e.g., anxiety) rather than having that attribute (e.g., depression) or not. In addition to these three differences, MDS is a model-based approach, while traditional cluster analysis is not. Recently, some researchers have developed model-based cluster analysis (Fraley and Raftery 2007). However, a key difference between model-based cluster analysis and MDS remains in that MDS represents cluster in terms of dimension rather than ina dichotomous fashion.

1.3   Conclusion

In this chapter, we discuss what the MDS models are and their fundamental utilities. We also summarize some fundamental differences between MDS, factor analysis, and cluster analysis. One take-home message is that MDS is not simply a data-reduction method. MDS can be used for many other purposes in education and psychological applications such as the longitudinal study of achievement, treatment preferences, or hypothesis testing of behavioral likings, as we will see in the later chapters.

References

Borg, I., & Groenen, P. J. F. (2005). *Modern multidimensional scaling: Theory and applications* (2nd ed.). New York, NY: Springer.
Borsboom, D., & Cramer, A. O. J. (2014). Network analysis: An integrative approach to the structure of psychopathology. *Annual Review of Clinical Psychology, 9*, 91–121. https://doi.org/10.1146/annurev-clinpsy-050212-185608.
Davison, M. L. (1983). *Multidimensional scaling*. New York: Wiley.
Davison, M. L. (1985). Multidimensional scaling versus components analysis of test intercorrelations. *Psychological Bulletin, 97*(1), 94–105.
Fraley, R. C., & Raftery, A. (2007). Model-based methods of classification: Using the mclust software in chemometrics. *Journal of Statistical Software, 18*(6), 1–13.

Guyon, H., Falissard, B., & Kop, J.-L. (2017). Modeling psychological attributes in psychology – An epistemological discussion: Network analysis vs. latent variables. *Frontiers in Psychology, 8*, 798. https://doi.org/10.3389/fpsyg.2017.00798.

Kruskal, J. B. (1977). The relationship between multidimensional scaling and clustering. In J. V. Ryzin (Ed.), *Classification and clustering* (pp. 17–44). New York, NY: Academic.

McNally, R., Robinaugh, D. J., Wu, W. G. Y., Wang, L., Deserno, M. K., & Borsboom, D. (2015). Mental disorders as causal systems: A network approach to posttraumatic stress disorder. *Psychological Science, 3*, 836–849.

Tukey, J. W. (1977). *Exploratory data analysis.* Reading, MA: Addison-Wesley.

Chapter 2
Data Issues in MDS

Abstract Data is the first step in process of any statistical analysis. Since MDS has a bit different terms associated with data concepts and it can be confusing, I try to discuss the data used for MDS with terms that are more understandable or relevant to the common research setting.

Keyword Distance measures · Measurement conditionality · Number of ways · Number of mode

In this chapter, we discuss some essential features of data that are typically associated with MDS analysis. Some data are unique to MDS analysis such preference ratio or binary choice data. In addition, some terms used in describing MDS data are a bit confusing. Here we attempt to explain these terms as clearly as a layperson can understand. If we can better understand these features of data, we are more likely to use the MDS analysis in our research or data practices. We also discuss a MDS program that can perform various types of MDS analysis.

2.1 A Look at Data

MDS can be used for various analyses, and therefore different types of data can be involved. Young (1987) provided a thorough discussion of data for MDS models, as did some other authors (e.g., Borg and Groenen 2005; Davison 1983). In here, we will discuss those aspects of data that are most relevant to MDS in the current research context.

Several types of data lend themselves to analysis by multidimensional scaling. Behavioral scientists have adopted several terms relating to data, which often are not familiar to others. Typically, variables can be classified according to their "measurement scale". The four scales that are commonly mentioned in the literature are the nominal scale, the ordinal scale, the interval scale, and the ratio scale. For MDS models, any type of data can be converted into proximity measures as an input for

MDS analysis. Traditionally, the data used in MDS analysis are typically called proximity measures. The term, *proximity*, is vague, however, since it can indicate similarity data as well as dissimilarity data. For this reason, in this book we use a specific term for a particular kind of data. For instance, if distance matrix is to be used, we will refer to such data as distance data or measure (c.f., dissimilarity or proximities). The most common measure of the relationship of one variable (stimulus, etc.) to another is a distance measure (i.e., distance coefficient). It measures the "dissimilarity" of one object to another, where the distance, δ_{ij}, between the two objects is measured. If the data are given as similarities, s_{ij}, such as correlation coefficients, some monotone decreasing transformation will convert them to dissimilarities or distance coefficients.

$$\delta_{ij} = 1 - s_{ij}$$

$$\delta_{ij} = c - s_{ij} \text{ where c is for some constant}$$

$$\delta_{ij} = \sqrt{2\left(1 - s_{ij}\right)}.$$

MDS analyses assume that distance measures are given. How one collects these distance measures is a problem that is largely external to the MDS models. However, because distance measures are obviously needed and because the way these distance measures are generated has implications for the choice of an MDS model, we discuss some of these issues here.

2.2 Data Source

Traditionally, the data used in MDS analysis usually come from direct judgment of certain stimuli with respect to some attribute. For example, participants are asked to judge which car's color is brighter or to judge which two schools are similar with respect to certain characteristics such as friendliness or orderliness. Such judgment data are generated via four types of judgment tasks: magnitude estimation, category rating, graphic rating, and category sorting. Currently, the judgment data in education or psychology (except for some experimental studies) are not so common because of the practical problems (e.g., time constraints or willingness to participate) and the participant's ability and willingness to perform the various tasks.

Typical data commonly used in today's research is data generated by questionnaires or surveys using a Likert-type scale metric such as from 1 to 4, with 1 being *not at all* and 4 being *always* with respect to a certain event or trait (e.g., how often do you feel happy?). This type of data is typically not discussed in traditional MDS literature; however, data produced by a Likert-type scale can be easily converted into either a distance data matrix by averaging across all participants or individual distance matrices, one for each participant. Such data are called indirect proximity measures in the MDS literature. A distance matrix based on indirect proximity data generated from surveys or questionnaires are often used in today's research setting, which may be more common than direct judgment. Thus, the input data for MDS are more likely to be indirect data rather than direct judgment data.

There are various measures of proximity (similarity or distance), and Table 2.1 shows a list of common distance or similarity measures that can be computed based on the different levels of measurement.

Moreover, the data based on rating data using a rating scale can also directly be used as input for MDS preference analysis since this kind of data can be considered to represent individual's preference or inclination judgment toward a certain trait. For example, data from rating on item "*I shared with other students*" on a scale metric of 1–5, with 1 being *most preferred* and 5 being *least preferred* can be used as liking data to examine the preferred behaviors of students or individuals. MacKay and Zinnes (2014) provided discussion of this and the other kinds of preference data for MDS preference analysis. Here, we briefly discuss some of these data sources for MDS analyses.

A common preference data type is liking rating, as typically generated by Likert-type rating scale in a survey or questionnaire, where each respondent rates his/her preference or liking with respect to a particular attribute or statement. For example, in a coping survey with the scale of *1–5*, with 1 being most likely to use and 5 being least likely to use, an individual responding to a statement "*I always get angry when I have a problem*" with 1 may indicate his/her preference to this type of coping style. You can think of a liking rating as a judgment about the distance of an object (e.g., item or statement) from your ideal point (i.e., preference or liking). As mentioned previously, liking ratings are the most commonly used indirect judgment data type.

Binary preferential choice data consist of 0's and 1's, with 0 being not-preferred and 1 being preferred, and are usually entered as a lower-half matrix without a diagonal. An example of binary choice matrix is:

$$
\begin{array}{l}
0 \\
0\ 0 \\
1\ 00 \\
1\ 11\ 1 \\
0\ 01\ 0\ 1 \\
0\ 10\ 0\ 1 \\
1\ 01\ 0\ 1\ 1\ 0
\end{array}
$$

Since diagonal entries are missing, the first row corresponds to the second object or item. Thus, the 1 in the third row indicates the individual prefers to the fourth object or item over the first one. Each participant has a binary choice matrix.

$$
\begin{array}{llllll}
0.97 \\
0.74 & 0.34 \\
1.19 & 2.02 & 5.34 \\
1.99 & 1.13 & 1.99 & 1.07 \\
1.38 & 1.16 & 3.17 & 0.74 & 0.87 \\
0.89 & 1.51 & 3.11 & 0.80 & 0.81 & 0.625
\end{array}
$$

Table 2.1 List of measures of proximity (similarity or dissimilarity)

Symbol	Definition or description
v	The number of variables or the dimensionality
x_j	Data for observation x and the jth variable, where j = 1 to v
y_j	Data for observation y and the jth variable, where j = 1 to v
w_j	Weight for the jth variable
W	The sum of total weights. No matter if the observation is missing or not, its weight is added to this metric
$\overline{x}$	Mean for observation x $$\overline{x} = \sum_{j=1}^{v} w_j x_j / \sum_{j=1}^{v} w_j$$
$\overline{y}$	Mean for observation y $$\overline{y} = \sum_{j=1}^{v} w_j y_j / \sum_{j=1}^{v} w_j$$
$d(x,y)$	The distance or dissimilarity between observations x and y
$s(x,y)$	The similarity between observations x and y
Methods accepting all measurement level:	
GOWER	Gower's similarity $$s(x,y) = \sum_{j=1}^{v} w_j \delta_{x,y}^j d_{x,y}^j / \sum_{j=1}^{v} w_j \delta_{x,y}^j$$ $\delta_{x,y}^j$ is computed as follows: For nominal, ordinal, interval, or ratio variable, $\delta_{x,y}^j = 1$ For asymmetric nominal variable, $\delta_{x,y}^j = 1$ if either x_j or y_j is present $\delta_{x,y}^j = 0$ if both x_j and y_j are absent For nominal or asymmetric nominal variable $d_{x,y}^j = 1$ if $x_j = y_j$ $d_{x,y}^j = 1$ if $x_j \neq y_j$ For ordinal, interval, or ratio variable $d_{x,y}^j = 1 - \mid x_j - y_j \mid$
DGOWER	1 minus Gower d(x,y) = 1 − s(x, y)
Methods accepting ratio, interval, and ordinal variables	
EUCLID	Euclidean distance $$d(x, y) = \sqrt{(\sum_{j=1}^{v} w_j ((x_j - y_j)^2) W / (\sum_{j=1}^{v} w_j)}$$
SQEUCLID	Squared Euclidean distance $$d(x, y) = (\sum_{j=1}^{v} w_j ((x_j - y_j)^2) W / (\sum_{j=1}^{v} w_j)$$

(continued)

Table 2.1 (continued)

Symbol	Definition or description
COV	Covariance similarity coefficient $s(x, y) = \sum_{j=1}^{v} w_j \left(x_j - \bar{x}\right) - \left(y_j - \bar{y}\right) / vardiv$, where $vardiv = v$ if VARDEF $=$ D $= v - 1$ if VARDEF $=$ DF $= \sum_{j=1}^{v} w_j$ if VARDEF $=$ WEIGHT $= \sum_{j=1}^{v} w_j - 1$ if VARDEF $=$ WDF
CORR	Correlation similarity coefficient $s(x, y) = \dfrac{\sum_{j=1}^{v} w_j \left(x_j - \bar{x}\right)\left(y_j - \bar{y}\right)}{\sqrt{\sum_{j=1}^{v} w_j \left(x_j - \bar{x}\right)^2 \sum_{j=1}^{v} w_j \left(y_j - \bar{y}\right)^2}}$
DCORR	Correlation transformed to Euclidean distance as sqrt(1–CORR) $d(x, y) = \sqrt{1 - s(x,y)}$
SQCORR	Squared correlation $s(x, y) = \dfrac{\left[\sum_{j=1}^{v} w_j \left(x_j - \bar{x}\right)\left(y_j - \bar{y}\right)\right]^2}{\sum_{j=1}^{v} w_j \left(x_j - \bar{x}\right)^2 \sum_{j=1}^{v} w_j \left(y_j - \bar{y}\right)^2}$
DSQCORR	Squared correlation transformed to squared Euclidean distance as (1–SQCORR) $d(x,y) = 1 - s(x,y)$
L(p)	Minkowski (Lp) distance, where p is a positive numeric value $d(x,y) = \left[\left(\sum_{j=1}^{v} w_j \left|x_j - y_j\right|^p\right) W / \sum_{j=1}^{v} w_j\right]^{1/p}$
CITYBLOCK	L_1 $d(x,y) = \left(\sum_{j=1}^{v} w_j \|x_j - y_j\|\right) W / \left(\sum_{j=1}^{v} w_j\right)$
CHEBYCHEV	L_∞ $d(x,y) = \max_{j=1}^{v} w \# x_j - y \#$
POWER(p,r)	Generalized Euclidean distance, where p is a nonnegative numeric value and r is a positive numeric value. The distance between two observations is the rth root of sum of the absolute differences to the Pth power between the values for the observations: $d(x,y) = \left[\left(\sum_{j=1}^{v} w_j \left|x_j - y_j\right|^p\right) W / \sum_{j=1}^{v} w_j\right]^{1/r}$

Note. The symbols and formula described here are based on the document from SAS (SAS Institute Inc 2008)

Preference ratio data are the comparison of two objects (i.e., a ratio) and are usually entered as a lower-triangle matrix without diagonal entries. An example of the preference ratio data is:

Unlike binary choice data without the diagonal entries, the number in the first row corresponds to the preference ratio of the first to the second object. Thus, the 1.99 in fourth row indicates the individual prefers the first object over the fifth object almost twice as much. Typically, preference ratio data are generated using graphic rating scales.

2.3 Data Design

One distinct feature of data used in MDS analysis comes from data theory stipulated by Coombs (1964) and Young (1987), which involves the shape of the data (i.e., number of ways and number of mode) and measurement conditionality. These features are a bit unique to MDS analysis and we often encounter them in traditional MDS literature. Specifically, number of ways indicates the number of factors involved in collecting data (e.g., different or same people, how many variables, or different situations). This idea of number of ways is somewhat similar to that of number of factors in analysis of variance (ANOVA). In MDS, number of ways implies the factors that can produce variations in the data. For example, if one participant is asked to rate differences among five coping behaviors, then this is a one-way data design since one participant does not produce variation but five coping behaviors are a source of variation in rating. On the other hand, if three participants are asked to judge the differences among five coping behaviors, this is a 2-way data design since now different participants produce variations along with five coping behaviors. Thus, two-way data take the form of a matrix consisting of rows and columns. However, two-way data only indicates that it may be represented in a single matrix, and it does not say anything about whether the matrix is square or rectangular, symmetric or asymmetric.

The number of modes, on the other hand, indicates the layout of the data in terms of data being either square or rectangular. A typical data layout of two-way one-mode is a square and symmetric data matrix such as correlation matrix or distance matrix, where the rows and columns may refer to the same set of objects. If rows and columns refer to two distinct objects, then the data have two modes, where layout is a person (row) by variable (column) rectangular data matrix. Thus, the data can be described together with respect to number of ways and modes. A correlation or distance matrix averaged over a group of individuals is a two-way one-mode data; but if we have several correlation or distance data matrices, one for each individual, the data will still be two-way one-mode data. The commonly seen data layout from questionnaires or survey instruments is two-way two-mode data layout, with two-way being participants and variables and two-mode being rectangular.

2.4   Data Conditionality

Measurement or data conditionality refers to measurement characteristics of data (Young 1987). There are four types of measurement conditionality: unconditional, matrix-conditional, row-conditional, and general-conditional. MDS models explicitly take into consideration data having different measurement characteristics by fitting the data in a least square sense and maintaining the measurement characteristics of the data via optimal scaling of the observed data. Thus, richness of the data can be captured and maintained by employing an appropriate MDS model based on measurement characteristics. Specifically, matrix-conditional data occurs when each participant has his/her own distance matrix when she responds to a set of items with a scale of, say, 1–10 in a questionnaire. It is likely that one participant's response of '6' may not be considered to be the same as another participant's response of '6'. In fact, it is quite likely that they do not use the scale in the same way, as we may observe. Thus, the measurement characteristics are conditional on participants, with each participant having his/her own matrix and serving as a partition of the data, thus matrix-conditional when we have multiple matrices. One possibly interesting application is to use such data measurement characteristics to study different response styles like acquiescent response style. So far, however, MDS has not been used to study such an issue.

On the other hand, the row-conditional data refers to a data layout in which each row of data cannot be compared with one other. For example, a '4' in a first row of data has no bearing on a '4' in a second row (or any other rows). A response of a '4' in the first row merely indicates that a participant provides a rating of '4' on a particular item. Two '4's in the different rows do not indicate the same degree of similarity or dissimilarity. Thus, each row of each individual's data serves as a partition of data, thus row-conditional.

Both matrix-conditional and row-conditional data are traditionally discussed in the context of similarity judgment by participants using a particular judgment tool, such as magnitude estimation or to rank the similarity among sets of stimuli or objects. Data obtained through such type of collection techniques are not commonly seen in most of current research settings. However, a new habit of thinking can be developed with respect to how we conceptualize our data. For example, the data we commonly encounter today are person by variable multivariate data matrix, called column-conditional data. In column-conditional multivariate data each column represents a variable and rows represent people. Thus, measurement characteristics are within columns of the data matrix, the first column representing gender, second column achievement status, third income, and so forth, with each variable having its own measurement level. But one can also view such multivariate data matrices as matrix- or row-conditional. Consider an example in which a group of five participants responds to ten anxiety items on a scale of 1–6. If we are willing to make an assumption that each participant has his/her own internal standard with respect to anxiety level, and one participant's response of '3' on a particular anxiety item may indicate a different level of anxiety from another participant's response of '3' on the same item, then we can say that the meaning of measurements is conditional on each participant's response matrix. Thus, we can analyze the data as matrix-conditional data when we convert the data into distance matrix, one for each participant and preserve the original characteristics of measurement. On the other hand, we can also think of this 5 by 10 data matrix as row-conditional data if we are willing to assume that the response of one participant has no relationship with any other participants, and we cannot compare between participants, then we could analyze the data as row-conditional data. Historically, few multivariate data have been thought of in such ways and analyzed accordingly using the appropriate MDS model.

The third measurement conditionality is called unconditional data. Unconditional data occur when we think the response to a particular item is comparable across participants, which leads to one partition of the data. Accordingly, we can analyze one data matrix averaged across all participants. For example, a correlation matrix or distance matrix obtained from a group of participants is a typical unconditional data.

The fourth measurement conditionality is general-conditional data. Perhaps a better term should be situation-conditional data. General-conditional data occur when the same data are collected under different situations. As an example, a psychologist is interested in client's perception of different treatments over a period of time. A different treatment will be used each day and data for each day are generated. Since the treatment that generates the data each day is different, she could view the data as being partitioned into subsets, with one partition for each day. Such data can be analyzed as general-conditional data. To the best of my knowledge, no studies have been conducted in such a fashion.

2.5   Some Implications

Thinking about these different kinds of data structures opens up many possibilities for data analysis. A special strength of MDS is its ability to handle all these different kinds of data structures. In contrast, the commonly used analytic techniques such as hierarchical linear modeling or structural equation model typically use column-conditional data and do not take into consideration the other measurement characteristics. Theoretically, the strength of considering the measurement characteristics in our analysis is that it will force us to think more carefully about the different aspects of the data, which will have implications for our interpretations of the findings. These aspects may include, for example, what data say and what assumptions about the data we are willing to make. Of course, we need to further investigate the potential utility of MDS analysis when we make different assumptions about the multivariate data. For example, we do not typically have data generated from direct judgment or rating tasks such as having students rate similarity among a group of teachers with respect to helpfulness. Instead, we could have data generated from a Likert-type scale in assessing student perception of their teacher's helpfulness. Then it is possible that the data possess certain measurement characteristics so that appropriate MDS model can be used to provide a better exploratory, predictive, or explanatory power for the study under inquiry. Certainly, more research is needed in this regard.

Conversely, another line of research could be conducted using MDS models with respect to measurement characteristics. For example, in column-conditional multivariate data, we take it for granted that one individual's response of '3', on a scale of 1–6 for an item is the same as another individual's response of '3' for the same item. MDS analysis could help to investigate whether such measurement characteristic presents in the data. If not, it may not be appropriate to analyze data by aggregating over individuals since such an indirect measurement does not keep individual data intact and may fail to detect systematic individual differences in the data. Thus, MDS models may be used as a measurement tool for identifying if we have different response styles represented in our sample.

2.6 MDS Computer Programs

Over the years, quite few computer programs have been developed to perform MDS analysis, but many of them are not so easily available. The most commonly used MDS analysis software programs can be found in either *SPSS*, *SAS*, or R. There are also many other stand-alone programs that can perform particular types of MDS analysis. For example, *MULTISCAL* or *PROSCAL* can be used for maximum likelihood MDS analysis. Many other programs are quite scattered in various places. A piece of good news is Coxon and his associates (Coxon et al. 2005) developed a computer program called *NewMDS(X)*, which put together various stand-alone MDS analysis programs into one place. The *NewMDS(X)* program, thus, greatly increases the accessibility of different MDS analysis programs and facilitates the applications of MDS models for educational and psychological research. In Table 2.2, I briefly describe some of the available programs in the *NewMDS(X)* to provide readers with a flavor of what can be done by these programs. The detailed description of all programs can be found in the *New MDS(X)* manual (Coxon et al. 2005).

2.7 Conclusion

In this chapter, we focus on main features of data that are associated with MDS analysis. It discusses the type of distance measures that can be used, data types, and some terminologies that may cause confusions when working with MDS models. It is hoped that such a discussion can help readers to more easily relate their research issues in hand to MDS analysis. Although common choice of statistical analysis is often based on popularity of some methods such as structural equation modeling or multilevel modeling, MDS can contribute or be complementary to our understanding of human behaviors from a multi-methods perspective, particularly with respect to data visualization.

Table 2.2 A brief description of some programs in the *NewMDS(X)*

Program name	Brief description
MINIRSA	It performs multidimensional unfolding analysis using internal mapping via the distance model. The analysis provides rectangle space analysis or internal analysis of two-way data in a row-conditional format of distance data.
MINISSA	It performs the basic non-metric MDS analysis of two-way symmetric matrix of distances, with matrix conditional.
MRSCAL	It stands for metric scaling, which performs internal analysis of two-way data of a lower triangle distance measure by a Minkowski distance function. It can perform an MDS analysis by group (e.g., by male and female) and the configuration for each group can be compared by *PINDIS* analysis (see below).
PARAMAP	It stands for parametric mapping, which provides internal analysis of either a rectangle (row-conditional) or square symmetric two-way distance data by a distance model.
PREFMAP	It stands for preference mapping. It performs external analysis of two-way, row-conditional data.
PROFIT	It stands for property fitting, which performs external analysis of a configuration by mapping each participant into the configuration as a vector.
MDPREF	It stands for multidimensional scaling preference scaling. It provides internal analysis of two-way preference for either row-conditional data or a set of paired comparisons matrices.
INDSCAL	It provides individual differences analysis, as that can be done by *PROXSCAL* or *ALSCAL* in *SPSS* or proc MDS in *SAS*.
PINDIS	It stands for procrustean individual differences scaling. It can be used to compare configurations from different groups or compare models with different numbers of dimensions. It can be used for hypothesis testing in a sense.
TRISOCAL	It stands for triadic similarities ordinal scaling, which performs internal analysis of triadic distances by a Minkowski distance model. The basic idea is that the participants are asked to make judgments of similarities of objects or items by considering a group of three objects or items at a time.

References

Borg, I., & Groenen, P. J. F. (2005). *Modern multidimensional scaling: Theory and applications* (2nd ed.). New York, NY: Springer.

Coombs, C. H. (1964). *A theory of data*. New York, NY: Wiley.

Coxon, A. P. M., Brier, A. P., & Hawkins, P. K. (2005). *The New MDSX program series, version 5*. Edinburgh/London: New MDSX Project.

Davison, M. L. (1983). *Multidimensional scaling*. New York: Wiley.

MacKay, D. B., & Zinnes, J. (2014). *PROSCAL* professional: A program for probabilistic scaling: www.proscal.com

SAS Institute Inc. (2008). *SAS/STAT® 9.2 User's Guide*. Cary, NC: SAS Institute Inc.

Young, F. W. (1987). Multidimensional scaling: History, theory, and applications. In R. M. Hamer (Ed.), *Multidimensional scaling: History, theory, and applications*. Hillsdale, NJ: Lawrence Erlbaum Associates.

Chapter 3
The MDS Models: Basics

Abstract Fundamental concepts of MDS models are discussed. Since MDS includes a family of different models and various terms are used to describe these models as well as their corresponding elements, I explain these models and their associated terms using more understandable language.

Keyword MDS models · Vector representation · Metric model · Non-metric model · Preference model · Unfolding model · Individual differences model

As I mentioned in Chap. 1, multidimensional scaling is a family of analytical techniques, consisting of many different models, each of which has its own uniqueness but also overlaps to some degree with each other in terms of what each model can accomplish. In this chapter, we discuss fundamentals of these models. Specific applications of these models will be discussed in later chapters of the book. For now, it is important to know what these models are and their fundamental concepts, which provide a foundation for later discussion and applications. For any MDS analysis, there are three aspects that need attention. The first one is the data, which give empirical information on how the objects or variable and persons relate to each other. This refers to the number of ways, number of mode, and measurement conditionality, as we discussed in Chap. 2. However, usual multivariate data format (i.e., row represents person and column represents variable or object) commonly encountered may need to be transposed so that the row represents variable or object and column represents person or object attributes. This is an important aspect to be noted when working with some of the MDS models using a particular software such as SAS (Statistical Analysis System). Typically, distance measure between variables is used as input data for MDS analysis, including preference data (also distance measure between preferred objects). The detailed aspects of the data were discussed in Chap. 2.

The second aspect is the model, which usually is the Euclidean distance model as basic MDS model. We may need to use other distance models such as Gower distance matrix when the level of measurement is nominal rather than ordinal or interval. The aim of the MDS analysis is to turn distance data into a set of coordinates

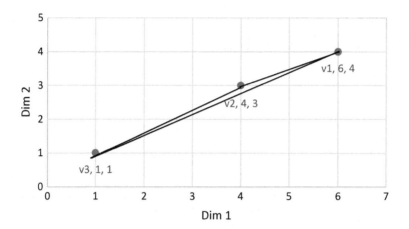

Fig. 3.1 A spatial representation of distance based on the coordinates

or spatial configuration as the model estimated Euclidean distances. The solution (also called the final configuration) consists of an arrangement of points in a small number of dimensions (typically two or three) so that the estimated distance between the points matches the observed distances between the variables as closely as possible.

The third is the transformation, which is the rescaling that may legitimately be performed on the original data to bring them into closer conformity to the model. This is usually referred to as the 'level of measurement' of the data. Kuhfeld et al. (1987) discussed various transformations for some of the MDS models. The type of transformation determines what kind of MDS model used in the analysis.

In the following sections of the chapter, we discuss in detail some fundamental aspects of MDS analyses and MDS models.

3.1   Model: Coordinates and Distance

An MDS model is typically a geometric or spatial model that represents distances among a set of variables. Consider the following matrix with three variables:

$$X = \begin{bmatrix} 6 & 4 \\ 4 & 3 \\ 1 & 1 \end{bmatrix}$$

If we consider this matrix as a set of coordinates in a two-dimensional space, we can obtain the following plot as shown in Fig. 3.1. The distance between any pair of variables can be computed based on this matrix. For example, distance between variables 1 and 2 is Euclidean distance:

$$d_{1,2} = \sqrt{(6-4)^2 + (4-3)^2} = \sqrt{4+1} = 2.236$$

R codes for compute distance between these three variables based on this data matrix is

```
library(psych)
m = matrix(c(6,4,4,3,1,1), nrow = 3,ncol = 2, byrow = TRUE)
dist(m, method = "euclidean", diag = FALSE, upper = FALSE, p = 2)
```

Distance between variables 1 and 3 is:

$$d_{1,2} = \sqrt{(6-1)^2 + (4-1)^2} = \sqrt{25+9} = 5.83$$

Thus, the matrix of distance among variables can be computed based on this coordinate matrix. In this case, the distance matrix is:

Variable	1	2	3
1	0		
2	2.24	0	
3	5.83	3.61	0

This set of distances indicates the relationships between these variables. For example, variables 1 and 3 are more dissimilar than variables 1 and 2 since the distance between variables 1 and 3 are larger.

In actual research situation, we usually do not have a set of coordinate matrix among variables available to us. What we often have is a raw data matrix with a dimension of n x v, where n is number people and v is number of variables. This is what we called column-conditioned data or multivariate data that are collected from survey instruments or some experiments. In order to geometrically represent the relationships among these variables, we need to first convert this multivariate raw data matrix into distance matrix. The job of MDS model is to represent the relationships between variables based on the distance matrix as accurately as possible in a geometric space so that we can visualize the latent relationships among these variables. From this discussion, we can state the following:

1. Distance matrix contains the information about variance and covariance among the variables. Such a distance matrix is applied to the data in an MDS analysis to turn the information into certain geometric representations in k dimensional space so we may understand the underlying structure of the data for a better description, prediction, or explanation.
2. MDS models represent the latent variable analysis because the relationships among variables are indicated by a set of latent coordinates estimated from the observed distance matrix. Coordinates of each corresponding variable are latent variables, representing latent structure of the data.

3. Given the coordinates, it is easy to compute the estimated distance among variables, as we have seen in Fig. 3.1. However, estimating coordinates given distance among variables is quite challenging because a set of distance can give a rise to a different set of coordinates.
4. The accuracy of the MDS model in representing the relationships between variables is assessed by comparing distance estimated from the MDS model to the observed distance. The smaller the discrepancy, the more accurate the representation is. We will further discuss this point in Chap. 4.

As we discussed in Chap. 2, there are different ways to compute distances among variables. A very general MDS model is represented by the Minkowski distance equation, which is:

$$d_{ij}^p = \left(\sum_{k=0}^{m} \left| x_{ik} - x_{jk} \right|^p \right)^{1/p} \tag{3.1}$$

where d_{ij}^p is distance between point i and j, m is number of dimensions, x_{ik} and x_{jk} are the coordinate of points i and j on dimension k, and p is the Minkowski exponent, which may take any value not less than 1. In words, Eq. 3.1 indicates that the distance between a pair of points or variables in m-dimensional configuration X is equal to the sum of the difference between two coordinates raised to a specific power, p.

The most common distance coefficients used in education and psychology is Euclidean distance, a special case of Minkowski distance, which is defined as:

$$d_{ij} = \sqrt{\sum_{k=0}^{m} \left(x_{ik} - x_{jk} \right)^2} \tag{3.2}$$

This equation defines the distance d_{ij} as the square root of the sum of squared differences between coordinates in k dimensional space. In this book, the distance implies Euclidean distance unless specified otherwise since Euclidean distance is more commonly encountered in psychology or education.

In addition to the common properties of distance, as discussed by Davison (1983), four definitional characteristics of Euclidean distance are stated by Tversky and Krantz (1970), which further clarifies the assumptions implicit in the use of the distance model. We did not describe these characteristics since they are not fundamental to applied MDS analysis.

3.2 Vector Representation of the Distance in a Geometric Space

So far, we discussed the spatial representation of relationships among variables as indicated by the distance. However, we can also represent such relationships using vectors in a m space. The vector representation of the same coordinate data matrix above, which again is

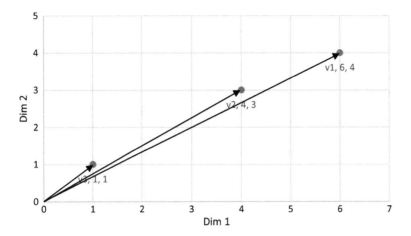

Fig. 3.2 Vector representation of distances

$$X = \begin{bmatrix} 6 & 4 \\ 4 & 3 \\ 1 & 1 \end{bmatrix}$$

and it is shown in Fig. 3.2. The scalar products measure of distance between the variables are produced by forming the major product moment matrix, A = XX', which in this case is:

$$A = \begin{bmatrix} 6 & 4 \\ 4 & 3 \\ 1 & 1 \end{bmatrix} \begin{matrix} 6 & 4 & 1 \\ 4 & 3 & 1 \end{matrix} = \begin{matrix} 52 & 36 & 10 \\ 36 & 25 & 7 \\ 10 & 7 & 2 \end{matrix}$$

The entries in the product moment matrix can be considered as follows: the diagonal entry gives the squared length of the vector draw from the origin to the point i (call it l_i^2). It indicates the direction and weight the variable gives to each dimension. The longer the length, the more weight. In the current example, all three variables point toward the same direction, suggesting the saliency for each dimension is about the same. However, variable 1 has more weight ($l_1 = \sqrt{52} = 7.2$) than variable 2 ($l_2 = \sqrt{25} = 5$) and 3 ($l_3 = \sqrt{2} = 1.4$), suggesting that variable 1 is more of indicator of dimensions 1 or 2, while variable 3 is less of relevancy to dimension 1 or 2.

On other hand, the symmetric off-diagonal elements give the scalar product (i.e., covariance) between vector i and j, which is related to the angular separation between the vectors. It indicates how different the variables are. In the current case, the angular separation between three variables is small, suggesting that they are not so different, although variable 1 has more weight or relevancy. For example, in this case, we can compute the angular separation by cosine as follows:

$$\cos\left(x_{ij}\right) = \frac{a_{ij}}{l_i l_j}$$

For variables 1 and 2, the cosine is

$$\cos\left(x_{12}\right) = \frac{a_{12}}{l_1 l_2} = \frac{36}{7.2^* 5} = 1^0$$

The application of vector model will be more evident in MDS preference analysis, as discussed later in this chapter. For now, it suffices to know what vectors represents and what they mean.

3.3 Metric Model

As we mentioned previously, the essential task of MDS models is to find geometric representation of latent structure of data given the observed distance matrix. That is, MDS maps observed distance coefficients δ_{ij} into corresponding MDS model estimated distances d_{ij} in a representation function of

$$f : \delta_{ij} \rightarrow d_{ij} \# X$$

where the particular choice of *function* specifies the different MDS model. The function defines how the original variables are transformed to maximize the fit to the model and it represents a set of transformations used in MDS analysis. Thus, an MDS model is a statement that observed distance matrix, after some transformation f, are equal to model estimated distances among points of a configuration X, which can be expressed as:

$$f\left(\delta_{ij}\right) = d_{ij} \# X$$

The earliest MDS models are metric models, which state that observed distance is linearly or proportionally related to model estimated distance:

$$f\left(\delta_{ij}\right) \rightarrow a + b^* \delta_{ij} = d_{ij} \# X$$

The parameters a and b are free and can be chosen such that the equation holds. The two main MDS methods are **classical scaling** and **least squares scaling**. The classical scaling is also known as **Torgerson's metric model** or interval MDS model. The other names used for metric model include classical metric scaling, Torgerson scaling, or Torgerson-Gower scaling.

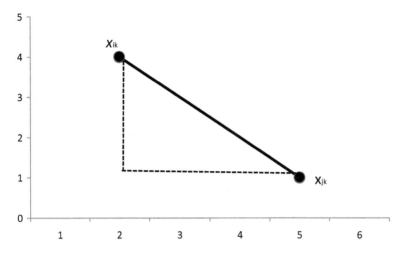

Fig. 3.3 Euclidean distance (solid line) between two points in a two-dimensional configuration X

3.3.1 Torgerson's Metric Model

One of the first metric MDS models is Torgerson's metric model (Torgerson 1952). Young and Householder (1941) showed how the configuration of points in a Euclidean space can be found from a matrix of distances between points such that original distances are preserved. Torgerson (1952) brought the subject to popularity using the technique for scaling. In Torgerson's metric model, observed distance δ_{ij},which is computed directly from the data, is assumed equal to distances d_{ij}in Euclidean space, that is:

$$\delta_{ij} = d_{ij} = \sqrt{\sum_{k=0}^{m} \left(x_{ik} - x_{jk} \right)^2} \tag{3.3}$$

Figure 3.3 illustrates the Euclidean distance in a two-dimensional configuration X.

Torgerson showed that when the observed distance δ_{ij} is double-centered (i.e., distance with both row and column means removed, also called row-standardized and column-standardized), this double-centered distance matrix δ_{ij}^{*} is the products of coordinates in k dimensional space as follows:

$$\delta_{ij}^{*} = \sum x_{ik} x_{jk} \tag{3.4}$$

This δ_{ij}^{*} is called **disparity** or **scalar product matrix** since it is the sum of products between two coordinate values. The value of double-centered distance can be from 0 to $\pm\infty$, although the original value of distance ranges from 0 to $\pm\infty$. This is the case even if the raw data are standardized. Torgerson's model is called metric MDS model because it requires the observed distance data be proportional to or linearly related to model-derived or estimated distances in a Euclidean space.

To be of practical use, a configuration of points or latent coordinates, needs to be found based on a set of the observed distances. The idea is to produces a configuration of points from the observed distance matrix via an algebraic reconstruction method so that the relationships among variables can be explained by latent coordinates. Suppose a distance matrix D is doubly centered to produce matrix B, which is product moment matrix. That is, B is an inner product moment matrix, which can be defined as

$$B = X_d X_{d'}^T$$

where X_d and $X_{d'}$ are doubly centered matrix of observed distances among variables. Eigenvalue decomposition of B will produce the latent coordinates among variables. The procedures for classical scaling are:

1. Compute the distance matrix D based on data.
2. Double centering D by $-1/2(\delta^2_{jk} - \delta^2_{ik} - \delta^2_{ij})$ to form B.
3. Eigenvalue decomposition of B to obtain eigenvalue, l, and eigenvector, v, associated with B.
4. Specify desired number of dimensions.
5. The coordinates of the points between variable in an m dimensional space are given by

$$x_{ij}^2 = l_j^{1/2} v_{ij}$$

It is worth mentioning that centering the variables has the geometric effect of moving the origin of the space (0,0) to the centroid (center of gravity) of the points defined by the means of the variables, but it does not affect the distances in any way. In addition, in MDS analysis, regardless of types of MDS model used, the configuration is typically centered and standardized, which means that the sum of coordinates of each dimension is zero and the variance is one.

3.3.2 Metric Least Square Model

Given that observed distance is linearly or proportionally related to model estimated distance, metric least squares scaling finds a configuration mapping observed distance to model estimated distance by minimizing a loss function, S, with possibly a linear transformation of observed distances. It is an iterative numerical approach (method of steepest descent) taken to minimize Sammon's loss function (Sammon 1969), which is defined as:

$$S\left(d_{ij}, \delta_{ij}\right) = \Sigma\Sigma\left(\delta^{-1}_{ij}\left(d_{jk} - \delta_{ij}\right)^2_{ik}\right) / \Sigma\Sigma\delta_{ij} \qquad (3.5)$$

In the numerator of S, the squared difference between the observed distance δ_{ij} and the model estimated distance d_{ij} is weighted by δ^{-1}_{ij} so that smaller distances have more weight in the loss function than larger ones. The denominator, $\Sigma\Sigma\delta_{ij}$, is a normalizing term making S scale free.

A simplified view of the metric least square scaling algorithm is as follows:

1. Assign points to arbitrary coordinates in m dimensional space.
2. Compute Euclidean distances among all pairs of points, to form the δ matrix.
3. Compare the δ matrix with the model estimated d matrix by evaluating the stress function. The smaller the value, the greater the correspondence between the two.
4. Adjust coordinates of each point in the direction that best maximally stress.
5. Repeat steps 2 through 4 until S (called stress) value will not get any lower.

3.4 Non-metric Model

The chief difference between metric and non-metric MDS models is how the observed distances are assumed to be related to the model-derived distances. In metric MDS models, the observed distances are assumed to be linearly or proportionally related to model-derived distances, as we discussed previously. This assumption tends to be restrictive. Non-metric models, proposed by Shepard (1962), are assumed that the observed distances are monotonically related to the model-derived distances; that is, the model-derived distances only need to reflect the rank order of the observed distances. Coxon (1982) called this ordinal rescaling of the data since the data are rescaled or transformed to be close to the model. However, it should be noted that in practice, the differences between metric and non-metric MDS are not that important (Borg and Groenen 2005), and the results from both types of analyses tend to be similar rather than different, with non-metric MDS models providing a better fit to the data.

Non-metric models have the following form:

$$\delta_{ij} = f\left(d_{ij}\right) = f\left(\sqrt{\sum_k \left(x_{ik} - x_{jk}\right)^2}\right) \qquad (3.6)$$

where f is a monotone function, including linear, power, exponential, and logarithmic functions. δ_{ij} is observed distance; d_{ij} is model estimated distance. Non-metric MDS algorithm computes estimated d_{ij} based on model coordinate estimates x_{ik} and x_{jk} such that the rank order of estimated d_{ij} is as close as possible to the rank order of the observed distance, δ_{ij}. Thus, in essence, this model is the same as the metric model, differing only in the assumption of how the observed data should be related to the model estimated distances.

There are two monotone transformation functions discussed in the MDS literature. One is *strong monotonic* (Guttman 1968) relationship between observed distance and model estimated distances. In this transformation, if distance between one pair of variable is less than another then the corresponding distances must be in the same order. That is, if $\delta_{ij} < \delta_{kl}$ then $d_{ij} < d_{kl}$

A second one is a *weak monotonic* (Kruskal 1964) relationship between observed data and model estimated distances. That is, $\delta_{ij} < \delta_{kl}$ then $d_{ij} \leq d_{kl}$. Thus, weak monotonicity only requires that no inversions in order should happen between the observed data and model estimated distance. That is, that if $\delta_{ij} < \delta_{kl}$ then it should never be the case that $d_{ij} > d_{kl}$, but d_{ij} may be equal to d_{kl}, even when $\delta_{ij} < \delta_{kl}$. In this case, the transformation function moves upward (even vertically upward) but it may never move downward.

In an actual research data, some values will not be distinct; that is, at least some values will be the same. The question is: should equal distances be fit by equal disparities?

There are two approaches to address the question, referred to as the *primary* and the *secondary* approach to ties. Primary approach treats ties as indeterminate and allows fitting values either to preserve the equality or replace it by an inequality, given that in doing so the goodness of fit is improved. On the other hand, in the secondary approach, ties in the data are required to be retained in the fitting values; that is, the secondary approach tied data are treated as being genuinely equivalent.

Which approach to use? As suggested by Coxon et al. (2005), in general, the primary approach to ties should be used, especially if there is a fairly large number of distinct values in the data. The secondary approach can badly misrepresent the structure. Moreover, when the data from a scale containing a very limited number of ordered categories, secondary approach may distort all information. For this reason, some MDS programs use the primary approach to tied data in obtaining a solution, while others offer the choice of primary or secondary approach.

Given that there is transformation involved, three sets of parameters are estimated by Eq. 3.6. The first is coordinate estimates x_{ik} and x_{jk}, which represents the configuration of variables in the geometric space. The second is estimated distance d_{ij}, which is computed from coordinate estimates. The third set of parameters is called the **rank images** of data, also known as **disparities, pseudo-distances, fitted distances,** or **transformed proximities**. These five terms may be used interchangeably and that may cause some confusion. In this chapter, we use the term *disparities* and designate it as δ_{ij}. Why do we need this third set of parameters? It turns out that disparity δ_{ij} is calculated in such a way that: (1) it is monotonically related to the observed distance and (2) it is as closely fit to the estimated distance d_{ij} as possible. It acts like a middle man, bringing the data and the model estimates as close as possible. That is, disparities are based on the transformed variables. Thus, it is this δ_{ij} that is used in measure of model fit, which will be discussed in Chap. 4.

3.5   Individual Differences Models

In the sections above, we presented and discussed two kinds (metric or non-metric) of basic MDS models (may be also known as classical scaling), which form the foundation of the other kinds of MDS models. But as we mentioned above, the difference between metric and non-metric is not crucial and non-metric analysis produces a better fit. Therefore, we do not specifically differentiate these two.

Beyond the basic MDS model, one of the models is individual differences models (may be also known as weighted MDS), which take into account of individual differences in latent structure of variables. As indicated by Cox and Cox (2001), there were two basic approaches to address individual differences. The first was to average across over all individuals and the second to compare results individual by individual.

3.5.1   Weighted Euclidean Model or INDSCAL

In the literature of MDS analysis, one common individual differences model is called the **weighted Euclidean model** or INDSCAL (Carroll and Chang 1970), and the other one is called **generalized weight Euclidean model** or the three-mode model (Tucker 1972). INDSCAL is also the name of the computer program that performs weighted Euclidean model. Weighted Euclidean model can be considered as a special case of generalized weighted Euclidean model and it is used more in practice. Thus, we focus on weighted Euclidean model in this chapter.

In metric or non-metric MDS models, the configuration estimated from the observed distances represents average configuration across all individuals, this is called group configuration. However, we also want to know how individuals differ with respect to the group configuration; that is, we not only want to know about nomothetic information, we also want to know about idiographic information. Each participant has his or her own configuration, x_{iks}, in relation to the group configuration, x_{ik}. Such an idiosyncratic configuration x_{iks} is related to the group configuration x_{ik} in the form:

$$x_{iks} = x_{ik} w_{ks} \tag{3.7}$$

where w_{ks} is the value that indicates the variation in the dimensional configuration across individuals. In other words, it is the weight for participant s along dimension k, indicating dimensional importance or salience given by an individual. The idiosyncratic configuration for participants can be expressed as:

$$\delta_{ijs} = \sqrt{\sum \left(x_{iks} - x_{jks} \right)^2} = \sqrt{\sum w_{ks}^2 \left(x_{ik} - x_{jk} \right)^2} \tag{3.8}$$

As in metric or non-metric MDS models, in addition to parameter estimates of coordinate x_{ik} and x_{jk}, estimated distance d_{ij}, and the *disparities* δ_{ik} , two more sets of parameters are estimated: (1) weight w_{ks}, which quantifies the differences among participants' rating along the k dimensions and (2) participants' coordinate estimates x_{iks} and x_{jks}.

Essentially, weighted Euclidean model comprises two spaces: a group stimulus space and individuals or subjects space, both of chosen dimension k. Configuration in the group stimulus space represents the objects or stimuli and forms an "underlying" configuration. The individuals are represented as vectors in the subject space, and the coordinates of each individual are weighted to give the weighted Euclidean distances between the points in the stimulus space. The acronym INDSCAL indicates INdividual Differences SCALing.

MacCallum (1977) concluded that INDSCAL was susceptible to the assumption that individuals perceive the dimensions of the group stimulus space to be orthogonal. To overcome this problem, Carroll and Chang (1972, March) generalized their INDSCAL model to the IDIOSCAL model (Individual DIfferences in Orientation SCALing). The IDIOSCAL model thus allows the group stimulus space to be manipulated, with various rotations and dilations of axes being allowed. Carroll and Wish (1973) give a good account of models which arise from IDIOSCAL using a suitable choice of w_{ks}. Specifically, when w_{ks} is restricted to being a diagonal matrix, IDIOSCAL reduces to INDSCAL. Furthermore, there are *Carroll-Chang decomposition of* w_{ks}, which uses the spectral decomposition of w_{ks}, and *Tucker-Harshman decomposition of* w_{ks} to aid interpretation. Tucker's 3-mode model (Tucker 1972) is the IDIOSCAL model with the weight matrix, w_{ks}, decomposed by a set of $p \times p$ "core" matrices. If all the core matrices were diagonal, then analysis produces an INDSCAL type solution.

3.5.2   *The Tucker-Messick Model*

Tucker (1960) suggested that averaging over individuals loses much information regarding the individual responses. He suggested placing the distance into a matrix, D, with rows indicating all the $\frac{1}{2}n(n-1)$ possible variable-pairs and columns indicating the N individuals. Then, the singular valued decomposition (SVD) of D is found to approximate D such that $D = U_p \Lambda_p V_p^{\mathrm{T}}$. The matrix $\mathbf{U}_p$ gives the principal coordinates in a space for the pairs of variables, the matrix $\Lambda_p V_p^{\mathrm{T}}$ gives the principal coordinates in a space for the individuals.

We do not discuss this model in detail since it has not been easily accessible via any available software, which limits its applications. We simply indicate that there is such a model, which may be useful in some time.

3.5.3 PINDIS

The PINDIS model (Procrustean INdividual Differences Scaling) was developed along the lines of the older methods of individual differences scaling where scaling for each individual is carried out separately and then an overall comparison is made (Borg 1977; Lingoes 1977; Lingoes and Borg 1978).The model was developed after INDSCAL. Cox and Cox (2001) provided a detailed discussion. Basically, PINDIS assumes that a scaling has been carried out for each individual matrix by some method (regardless types of MDS model), producing individual configuration matrix X_i. The configurations X_i are then compared using Procrustes analysis. The procedure includes (1) all the N configurations X_i are centered at the origin and then dilated to have mean squared distance to the origin equal to unity; (2) the X_2 configuration is rotated to the X_1,configuration giving the first estimate of Z; (3) X_3 is rotated to Z and then a weighted average of Z and X_3 gives the next estimate of Z; (4) this process is repeated until all the X_i configurations have been used; (5) the N configurations are each rotated to Z and a goodness of fit index calculated; (6) the average of the newly rotated X_i configurations gives the next updated estimate of the centroid Z, and the goodness of fit index is recalculated; (7) this procedure is repeated until converges. The resulting Z is the centroid configuration.

This procedure of PINDIS produces the basic model, designated as P_0 model. That is, the centroid configuration Z is the group stimulus space, and only the rigid rotations (admissible transformation) is performed to rotate the individual configurations X_i to the centroid Z from the subject space. However, the other types of transformation can also be performed, which allows non-admissible transformation. The hierarchy of models is as follows, with the basic model always providing the poorest fit and the last model the best. Choice of model is made by assessing the improvement in fit made by going from one model to another in the hierarchy.

1. Basic model, P_0: Rigid rotations only.
2. Dimension weighting, P_1: The dimensions of the group stimulus space are weighted and then rotated.
3. Idiosyncratic dimension weighting, P_2: The weighting of dimensions of the group stimulus space can be different for each individual.
4. Vector weighting, P_3: Each variable in the group variable space is allowed to be moved along the line through the origin to the variable before rotation occurs.
5. Vector weighting, individual origins, P_4: This is the same as modelP_3, except that the origin of Z for each individual can be moved to an advantageous position.
6. Double weighting, P_5: This allows both dimensional and vector weighting.

For now, it suffices to be familiar with these concepts. In Chap. 9, we will apply these concepts to applications in the context of assessing configural similarity and hypothesis testing.

3.6   Preference or Unfolding Models

In MDS literature, MDS preference or unfolding models are treated separately. Specifically, MDS preference models typically involve vector modeling in which individuals' preference is indicated by vector with respect to its length and direction. In contrast, MDS unfolding models involve ideal points in which individuals' preference or ideal is indicated by points in the configuration. In a sense, the ideal point can be considered as preference. Thus, in this book, I use the term MDS preference or unfolding models interchangeable in our conceptual discussion; that is, either vector or ideal point model represents individuals' preference. However, I will also discuss how to use vectors or ideal-points to indicate preference in order to be consistent with the MDS literature.

The idea of MDS preference models is very appealing for studying individual differences, particularly in the case of single or multiple subject(s) design in which we would like to see how individuals respond to a particular treatment or a learning method as measured by a set of measurement items. Coombs (1950) first introduced the J scale and I scale in the unidimensional non-metric unfolding model. The J scale shows a line upon which points are placed for the n individuals together with the v variables, while I scale simply indicates each individual's preference ordering of variables. The basic concept of MDS preference models is that the distance model (i.e., ideal-point model or unfolding) can be used to represent both the variables (called real objects) and the participants as points (called ideal points or objects) in a geometric space. Thus, the MDS solution will consist of a configuration of v variable points and a configuration of s participant points in the same space. The closer a participant's point (i.e., ideal point or object) to the variables' point (i.e., real object) in the space, the more ideal or preferred the variable is by the participant. For this reason, it is called ideal-point model. The variables typically represent some behaviors (e.g., drinking) or constructs (e.g., anxiety). The large distance, therefore, indicates the less preference to a behavior. To put it another way, a large distance between a real object and an ideal point indicates that the real object has a high disutility.

In the basic metric model, the preferences are represented as

$$\delta_{is} = d_{is} = \sqrt{\sum \left(x_{ik} - x_{sk} \right)^2} \tag{3.9}$$

where δ_{is} is estimated distance quantifying the degree of participant s preference for item i, that is, dislike for item i. x_{ik} is the location of item i along dimension k. x_{sk} is the participant's ideal or preference location along dimension k. The model implies that the participant's preference is manifested by comparing item location to his or her ideal location in the same geometric space. The preference models differ from individual differences model (i.e., weighted Euclidean model) because in preference models, participant space and item space are in the same space, whereas in weighted Euclidean model there are two separate dimensional configurations, one for participants and another for stimuli or variables.

There are two types of preference models, internal and external (Carroll 1972), and both have metric and non-metric form. For internal preference models, the model provides parameter estimates of item coordinates, participant ideal points, and a fit measure. For external preference models, the item coordinates are assumed to be known from either theory or previous analysis. The model provides parameter estimates of participant ideal points and a fit measure for each participant. Because external preference models involve known item coordinates, it sometimes can be used to test a particular hypothesis about preference.

According to Davison (1983), external preference models includes four preference models: the vector model, the simple Euclidean model, the weighted Euclidean model, and the general Euclidean model. The vector model is a linear model, while the other three models are distance models (therefore nonlinear models). These models can be estimated using standard multiple regression methods. The estimates of various participant ideal points are regression coefficients or variants of regression coefficients. The input data for external preference analysis are pre-specified item coordinates that are based on either theory or previous analyses and observed data (such as liking ratings) indicating participant preference.

In the following sections, we present these preference models in more technical details for the purpose of completeness. Readers who are not interested in these technical aspects of the models can skip these sections. These materials are mainly based on Davison (1983).

Vector model is a linear model. That is, participant's ideal point is linearly or monotonically related to item scale value along the dimension k. It can be expressed as:

$$\delta_{is} = \sum b_{ks} x_{ik} + c_s \tag{3.10}$$

where b_{ks} is linear regression weight or coefficient (i.e., ideal point), indicating participant's preference; c_s is a constant for each participant. In words, Eq. 3.10 indicates an individual's preference, as measured by distance between an item and individual, δ_{is}, is equal to individual's ideal point, b_{ks}, times item's location, x_{ik}, plus a constant.

The simple Euclidean model suggests that the more an item resembles a participant's ideal point along each dimension, the more the participant likes it. All dimensions are assumed to be equally salient to the participants. The model is:

$$\begin{aligned}
\delta_{is} &= \sum w_s^2 \left(x_{ik} - x_{sk} \right)^2 + c_s \\
&= w_s^2 \sum x_{ik}^2 + \sum b_{ks} x_{ik} + c_s
\end{aligned} \tag{3.11}$$

This model provides participant's ideal point coordinate estimate, x_{sk}, participant's dimension weight, w_s^2, and a fit measure. This model indicates that participant's ideal point is curvilinearly (i.e., single-peaked) related to item scale value. In words, Eq. 3.11 says that an individual's preference, as measured by distance between an item and individual, δ_{is}, is measured by three quantities: (1) item's location, x_{ik}, times participant's dimensional weight, w_s, which is equal across all dimensions, (2) individual's ideal point, b_{ks}, times item's location, x_{ik}, and (3) a constant, c_s.

The weighted Euclidean model differs from simple Euclidean model only in that the dimensional salience varies across participants rather than assumed to be the same across the participants. Thus the model is

$$
\begin{aligned}
\delta_{is} &= \sum w_{ks}^2 \left(x_{ik} - x_{sk} \right)^2 + c_s \\
&= \sum w_{ks}^2 x_{ik}^2 + \sum b_{ks} x_{ik} + c_s
\end{aligned}
\tag{3.12}
$$

The model provides parameter estimates of participant's ideal point, b_{ks}, participant's dimension salience weights, w_{ks}^2, and a fit measure. In words, Eq. 3.12 says that an individual's preference, as measured by distance between an item and individual, δ_{is}, is measured by three quantities: (1) item's location, x_{ik}, times participant's dimensional weight, w_{ks}, that is different across all dimensions, (2) individual's ideal point, b_{ks}, times item's location, x_{ik}, and (3) a constant.

The fourth external preference model is the general Euclidean model, also called three-mode model (Tucker 1972). This model is the most general model of all MDS preference models, as can be seen in Eq. 3.13:

$$
\begin{aligned}
\delta_{is} &= \sum w_{ks}^2 \left(x_{ik} - x_{sk} \right)^2 + \sum_{k,k'} w_{ks} w_{k's} r_{kk's} \left(x_{ik} - x_{sk} \right) \left(x_{ik'} - x_{sk'} \right) + c_s \\
&= \sum w_{ks}^2 x_{ik}^2 + \sum b_{ks} x_{ik} + \sum_{k,k'} b_{kk's} x_{ik} x_{ik'} + c_s
\end{aligned}
\tag{3.13}
$$

where $r_{kk's}$ indicates the correlation between dimensions. This model allows the interaction between dimensions and provides parameter estimates of participant's ideal point location, x_{sk}, participant's dimension salience weight, w_{ks}, and participant dimensional interaction, $r_{kk's}$. If $r_{kk's} = 0$, then we have a weighted Euclidean model. That is, the difference between Eqs. 3.13 and 3.12 is Eq. 3.13 quantifies the interaction between dimensions, as measured by correlation between dimensions in participant's weight, $b_{kk's}$, and items' coordinates, $x_{ik} x_{ik'}$.

As mentioned above, I used term preference and unfolding interchangeably in our conceptual discussion. However, to be consistent with the MDS literature, I will discuss how to use vector or ideal-point models to represent individuals' preference or ideal.

3.6.1   Vector Representation of Preference

The vector representation of preference consists of a configuration of v variable points in a particular number of dimensions (typically two dimensions) and n vectors that represent the n individuals' set of preference ranks or ratings of variables or objects. The original data of preference rating of objects by individuals is called "first-score matrix". The matrix of preference scores estimated by the model is called the "second-score matrix". The purpose of the vector model is to obtain a variable or object configuration X and individual preference vectors Y so that the discrepancy between the original 'first-score' data and the estimated 'second-score' values is as small as possible. For a non-metric MDS analysis, the monotonically transformed data will be compared to the estimated values.

The purpose of the preference model is to represent both the variables and the individuals in a common or 'joint space'. When we use vector model, we mainly focus on following aspects:

1. How well the individual's preferences can be accommodated by the model and represented in the common space. This can be assessed by the correlation between first-score matrix (or optimally transformed data) and second-score matrix to measure the goodness of fit. In addition, the absolute length of a vector is arbitrary, but the relative lengths of the vectors indicate fit, with the squared lengths being proportional to the communalities; that is, variance accounted for by the principal components.
2. How well the variables are clustered or grouped. Look for regions in the configuration that contain clusters of variable points and determine what attributes the variables have in common. Variable points that are tightly clustered in a region of the configuration represent variables that have the same preference patterns across the individuals.
3. How the vectors relate to each other, since the main purpose may be to examine individual differences in a set of rankings/ratings. Individual differences between preferences are indicated in the vector model by angular separation (discussed in Sect. 3.2). On the one hand, the direction in which a vector points indicates the manner in which the individual mixes or trades off the characteristics of the objects in producing her preferences, and this is measured by the cosine of the angle that the vector makes with the dimensions of the space.
4. If we are interested in how one individual vector relates to another, we inspect the angular separation between them; that is, the correlation or cosine of the angle between the two preference vectors. In inspecting a vector model solution, the first point of interest is how the individual preference vectors are distributed in the configuration. If the vector ends are located in a small sector or region, this indicates high consensus or agreement in individuals' preferences, whereas the more unevenly they are distributed round the circle, the greater the disagreement. The differences in preferences, suggested by small sectors with a high density of vector ends and empty sectors between sectors, may suggest existing of distinguishably different 'points of view' or perspective. If these are different groups of individuals, we may also want to know whether the average direction differs significantly between the groups. Statistical tests and procedures for analyzing directional data have been developed and are available.

The external form of this analysis, i.e. where the stimulus configuration is obtained separately and remains fixed while the preference vectors are estimated. This form of analysis can be used for hypothesis testing.

The following hypothetical example illustrates results of the preference vector model and ideal-point model. In this example, we have 10 individuals rate their preferences on a set of five behaviors: reading, writing, tv watching, drinking, and playing sports. The rating data looks like the following:

Obs	read	write	tv	drink	sport
1	3	5	2	1	2
2	4	3	5	2	3
3	3	4	1	1	2
4	4	3	3	2	3
5	5	3	4	2	3
6	4	4	1	1	3
7	4	5	4	1	2
8	4	3	4	2	1
9	3	4	2	1	1
10	5	3	3	1	3

The higher score indicates a higher level of preference by individuals. The vector model analysis can be conducted using SAS *MDPref* procedure. However, the multivariate data format (i.e., individual by variable matrix) needs to be transposed so that the row represents variables and columns represent individuals (i.e., variable by individual matrix) using this procedure, as we mentioned previously. The input data look like the following:

NAME	COL1	COL2	COL3	COL4	COL5	COL6	COL7	COL8	COL9	COL10
Read	3	4	3	4	5	4	4	4	3	5
Write	5	3	4	3	3	4	5	3	4	3
Tv	2	5	1	3	4	1	4	4	2	3
Drink	1	2	1	2	2	1	1	2	1	1
Sport	2	3	2	3	3	3	2	1	1	3

The analysis results using preference vector model is typically shown visually. Figure 3.4 shows the results.

The following assessments can be made based on the plot:

1. The correlation between first-score matrix (i.e., original rating values) and the second-score matrix (i.e., rating values estimated from the model) is 0.88, indicating that the individual's preferences can be accommodated by the model relatively well (we want this correlation to be above 0.95 for a very good model). This moderately good model may be due to the fact that in this hypothetical data, individuals' preferences are not so well fit with the behaviors measured here.
2. The variables are not well clustered or grouped since there are no particular regions in the configuration that contain clusters of variable points. Thus, it is hard to determine what attributes the variables have in common and accordingly variables do not have the same preference patterns across the individuals.
3. It seems that there are three closely related vectors (i.e., three groups), as indicated in the vector model by angular separation between vectors. Individual 2, 5, and 8 show preference between TV watching and reading; individual 4, 7, and 10 show preference for reading; and individual 1, 3, 6, and 9 show

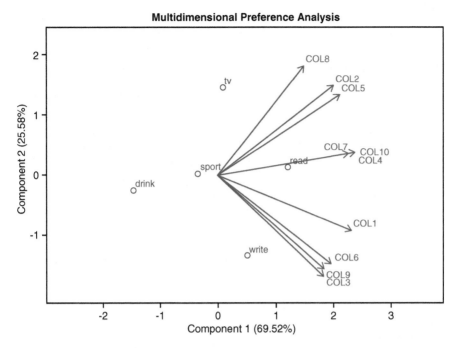

Fig. 3.4 Individual preference in vector model, with points representing behaviors and vectors representing individual preference

preference between reading and writing. Their preference is assessed by the direction in which a vector points indicates the manner in which the individual mixes or trades off the characteristics of the behaviors in producing her or his preferences.

3.6.2   *Distance (Point-Point) Representation of Preference*

The basic idea of distance representation (unfolding model) is that the distance of points in a space is used to represent their empirical dissimilarity. Given a set of distances it is always possible to reconstruct the configuration of points that generated them, and this is exactly what MDS model tries to accomplish, as we discussed previously. However, such a recovered configuration is not unique because several aspects of configuration are arbitrary and may be changed with any transformation. In particular, the actual size or scale of the configuration and the origin of the space are arbitrary. Moreover, the orientation of the axes may be changed and reflected at will. The origin and axes simply provide a convenient framework to locate the points. Thus, it is only the relative distance between points that has significance in interpreting a distance model solution.

When we have ranking or rating data that represent individuals' preference, the distance model can be used to represent both the variable or objects and the individuals as points in the same configuration. The solution consists of a configuration of v variables points and n individual points where each individual is represented as being at a 'maximal' or 'ideal' "point, located in such a way that the distances from this individual point to the variable points are in maximum agreement with the individual's ranking or rating of preference on a set of behaviors or ideas. The model estimates both sets of points simultaneously. The non-metric distance model is best known under the title of 'unfolding analysis', developed by Coombs (1964).

Substantively, the position of the 'ideal point' is interpreted as the one point in the configuration where the individual's preferences decrease in every direction. This is often called a 'single peaked preference function'since it assumes that there is only *one* point of maximum preference for each individual. Typically, the variable points located at the center of the configuration correspond to the most popular or preferred behaviors, and the least preferred behaviors or ideas are located at the periphery or the outside of a configuration. For this reason, variable points in the central part of a configuration are normally the most stable, while those at the periphery can usually be moved around fairly freely without affecting the goodness of fit.

Thus, if a behavior is sufficiently not preferred, it can be located virtually anywhere on the periphery or at an extreme distance from the center, so long as it is at a maximum distance from the ideal points.

In contrast to vector model of preference, the properties of the point-point (distance) model of preference assumes single peakedness; that is, each individual has one single point of maximum preference and that preference decreases (symmetrically) from this point. Moreover, if the distance model holds, then each behavior must be preferred most by at least one individual. This is why in SPSS *PrefScal* analysis module, there is an index that assesses the inter-mix of variable points and individual ideal points.

Distance model of preference can also be used in some confirmatory (hypothesis testing) fashion via external models. In such an analysis, variable or behavior configuration is obtained separately or pre-specified and remains fixed while the 'individual 'or property points are estimated. We can test whether certain behaviors are more preferred based on theory or previous knowledge. So far, no empirical studies have been done in this regard, but it is worthwhile to pursue.

Figure 3.5 shows the individual preference as ideal points based on the same data as used in Fig. 3.3. The results are the same: Individual 2, 5, and 8 show preference between TV watching and reading; individual 4, 7, and 10 show preference for reading; and individual 1, 3, 6, and 9 show preference between reading and writing. Here we only try to illustrate how distance model is used to represent individual preference.

3.6.3 *Single-Ideal Point Model*

In typical preference or unfolding MDS models, the analysis produces a configuration of both variables (i.e., object space) and individuals (i.e., ideal points space). As Borg (2005) indicated, what is important is how ideal and variable points are

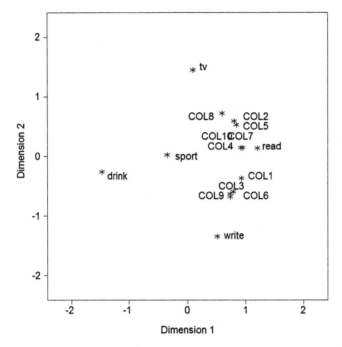

Fig. 3.5 Individual preference in distance model, with points representing both behaviors and individual preference (labeled as COL)

distributed throughout the space relative to each other. The best configuration is one that has a distribution of ideal points and object points that are thoroughly mixed. In other words, we want real object points and ideal points are evenly spread throughout the space. Substantively, this implies that we have individuals with many different preference patterns, so each object is someone's first choice.

MacKay et al. (1995) proposed a probabilistic MDS single-ideal point model (MDS-SIP), which requires a single-ideal solution to be estimated. The theoretical framework of the MDS-SIP model can be traced to Thurston (1928) and Coombs (1950). The model is initially used to represent a rectangular matrix of preferences by i individuals for v objects or variables as distances between i ideal point and v actual objects or variables. MDS-SIP model can be viewed as another way to model ipsative change. As an unfolding model, a single-ideal solution represents both individuals and behaviors as a point in the same Euclidean space. With the assumption of dependent sampling and that all individuals share the same latent MDS space, the model estimates one ideal point and n points that represent actual items or variables across all individuals at a given time, as discussed by MacKay (2007). Hence, it is called single-ideal point model. The distance relation between the single-ideal point and behaviors provides information about the preference structure of the individuals at that time point in such a way that individuals are closer to the behaviors they prefer. The model estimates the coordinates of the single-ideal point and objects across all individuals in the same latent space. Thus, an MDS single-ideal point model is a spatial model that maps the observed preference or disutility (also called disliking) data into the latent MDS space. As such, the model estimates latent coordinates to

Table 3.1 Hypothetical rating data of 20 individuals on four behaviors

Singing	Drinking	Reading	Writing
4	2	3	4
3	2	3	6
3	1	6	4
6	2	3	6
3	2	4	5
3	1	4	4
3	2	3	4
4	1	5	4
3	2	3	4
4	1	5	4
6	2	3	4
6	2	3	4
3	1	5	4
3	1	3	4
3	2	3	4
5	2	5	6
6	1	3	4
6	2	4	4
3	1	5	4
3	1	4	4

represent both individuals' ideal point and the points of actual behaviors using the rating or ranking data that describe individual's liking/preference or disliking with regard to a set of behaviors at a particular time. In other words, the preference rating or ranking data provide information about individuals' latent ideal or typical behavior choice with respect to a set of behaviors, and the estimated coordinates are latent spatial structure or configuration that includes both individuals' ideal point and the points of actual behaviors.

Table 3.1 shows a hypothetical example of liking/preference rating data of 20 individuals on four behaviors (e.g., singing, drinking, reading, and writing) at a given time, using a rating scale of 1 (*most preferred*) to 6 (*least preferred*).

Figure 3.6 shows the results of the model estimated coordinates (i.e., project preference rating data into MDS latentspace) of individuals' ideal point and the points of these four behaviors based on the data.

As can be seen in Fig. 3.6, behavior 2 (e.g., drinking) is most preferred behavior since it is the closest to the ideal point, while other three behaviors are least preferred. Thus, the preference of individuals for an item or object at a time t is an inverse function of the distance between the point that represents the actual objects and the ideal point that represents the individuals at a particular time point. A large distance between an object and an ideal point indicate that the object has high disutility (i.e., less liked or preferred). In other words, individual respond negatively to an actual object (a variable or item) when the attitude or behavior represented by the object or item does not closely reflect the attitude or behavior of the individual at

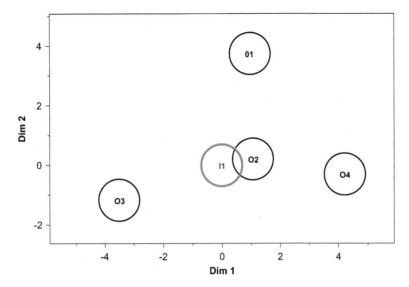

Fig. 3.6 Hypothetical example of estimated ideal point and points of four behaviors based on the data in Table 3.1. O1-Singing, O2-Drinking, O3-Reading, O4-Writing, and I1-the ideal point

that time. In the MDS single-ideal point model, such disagreement occurs when the individual is located too far away from the object. On the other hand, individuals respond positively to actual items or objects that have locations similar to their own. Across time, the distance between the ideal point and the points of actual behaviors may change, suggesting a developmental difference in preferred or typical behaviors. Such changes in distance between the ideal point and the actual objects are reflected in the configuration of these points at a given time.

Let us now consider some technical aspects of MDS-SIP model, and readers can skip this section.

In the probabilistic MDS single-ideal point model, the ideal point and actual items are represented not by points but by distribution (shown as a circle in Fig. 3.6), as proposed by Mackay and his associates (MacKay 2007; MacKay and Zinnes 1986; Zinnes and MacKay 1983). As shown in Fig. 3.6, the preferred behavior at time t is presented by the distances between unobserved coordinates of actual objects and ideal point in a latent k dimensional space. Such distances can be defined as

$$d_{ij(t)} = \sqrt{\sum_{k-1}\left(x_{ik(t)} - x_{jk(t)}\right)^2} \tag{3.14}$$

where $d_{ij(t)}$ is the distance random variable between ideal point i and actual items or variables j at time t with $d_{ij(t)} \sim N(\delta_{ijk(t)}, \sigma^2_{ijk(t)})$, and $\delta_{ijk(t)} = \mu_{ik(t)} - \mu_{jk(t)}$ and $\sigma^2_{ijk(t)} = \sigma^2_{ik(t)} + \sigma^2_{jk(t)}$. $x_{ik(t)}$ or $x_{jk(t)}$ are coordinates that are assumed to be normally and independently distributed with mean (i.e., centroid) of $\mu_{(t)}$ and variance of $\sigma^2_{(t)}$ at time t, be it actual or ideal. The variance $\sigma^2_{(t)}$ can be assumed equal (i.e., isotropic, as in Fig. 3.6) or unequal (i.e., anisotropic) at a given time for ideal point or actual objects on each dimension k in a Euclidean space. The goal of the analysis is to estimate the mean location $\mu_{(t)}$ and variance of $\sigma^2_{(t)}$ of coordinates for each time point. In order to obtain the parameter estimates $\mu_{(t)}$ and $\sigma^2_{(t)}$, one needs to specify the probability function of the distance random variable d_{ij}, which depends on the variance structure and sampling properties. The detailed discussion of how a probability MDS single-ideal point model is derived and estimated may be found in MacKay and his associates (MacKay 1989, 2007; MacKay and Zinnes 1986; Zinnes and MacKay 1983; Zinnes and MacKay 1992).

The model fit with respect to kinds of variances assumed in the data can be tested using information criterion statistics, such as consistent Akaike information criterion (CAIC) (Bozdogan 1987), Bayesian information criterion (BIC) (Schwarz 1978), or log-likelihood ratio tests. Technically, for the ideal point i or actual item j, there is a corresponding k-dimensional random vector X_j that has an x variate normal distribution with mean vector u_j and covariance matrix Σ_j. Individuals' choices are assumed to be based on values sampled from the X_j distributions. If an individual has a consistently preferred behavior, then we expect the diagonal elements of the covariance matrix Σ_j to be small. However, if the individual does not have a consistently preferred behavior or there are more measurement errors at a particular time, the diagonal elements of the Σ_j are expected to be large.

The practical significance of testing the structure of the variance is that it allows us to assess the degree of heterogeneity of individuals' behaviors at each time of measurement. For example, individuals with a general anxiety disorder may perceive a positive event in more different ways (i.e., not so consistent with a larger variance) than they do for a negative event (i.e., more consistent with a smaller variance). A psychologist might have an interest in knowing if such a pattern of variability may change as a result of interventions so that the effectiveness of the treatment program can be evaluated. Thus, when variability in preferred behavior exists, or when there are measurement errors inherent in single-items of an instrument, it is desirable to take such variability or measurement errors into consideration (MacKay et al. 1995).

3.7 The MDS Model Using Maximum Likelihood Estimation

The MDS models discussed so far are the least-squares MDS models except for MDS-SIP; that is, the model parameter estimation procedures are based on least-squares principle, with model-data fit measures being minimization between model estimated distances and observed (or transformed) distances. The least-squares MDS models are more commonly used in current practices in education or psychology. Such a usage is encouraged by readily available analytical procedures such as *PROXSCAL*, *PREFSCAL*, and *ALSCAL* in *SPSS* (SPSS Inc. 2007) or Proc MDS in *SAS* (2010).

However, the MDS models can also be estimated using maximum likelihood method. The primary research work was done by Ramsay (1977), Takane (1978) and his associates (Takane and Carroll 1981), and MacKay and Zinnes (1983). As of this writing, two software programs can provide maximum likelihood MDS analysis. One is Ramsay's *MULTISCAL* (Ramsay 1977) and the other one is called *PROSCAL*(MacKay and Zinnes 2014). The maximum likelihood MDS models are basically metric and are concerned with statistical inference. It is assumed that the distance data are erroneous rather than error-free so that confidence region for items or participants (for weighted models) is provided in the estimation procedures. Thus, statistical tests between pairs of models can be conducted based on estimated standard errors. Such an approach changes multi-dimensional scaling from a descriptive method into an inferential one so that we can specifically test the appropriate dimensionality, the proper MDS model, and the error model. That is, a chosen MDS model assumes a specific nature of error model that influences the data. If the nature of error model reflects the actual error processes in reality, the significance test of the MDS model is meaningful. Therefore, the choice of error models becomes crucial in conducting maximum likelihood MDS analysis. In Ramsay's work, error in distance can be assumed to be normally distributed (additive model) or lognormally distributed (multiplicative model). In MacKay and Zinnes' work, error in stimuli or items rather than distances are normally distributed.

The loss function in *Multiscale* of Ramsay (Ramsay 1977)is based on the sum of the squared difference of the logarithm of the observed distances and the model estimated distances; that is,

$$\# \, X = \sum_{i<j} \left[\log\left(\delta_{ij}\right) - \log\left(d_{ij}\right) \right]^2 \tag{3.15}$$

This loss function or error is used in a *maximum likelihood* (ML) framework. The likelihood is the probability that we find the data given X. This probability is maximized in MLMDS analysis. For ML estimation, we need to assume independence among the residuals and a *lognormal* distribution of the residuals.

Since both maximum likelihood MDS programs have extensive manuals, those who are interested in specific aspects of maximum likelihood MDS can consult the manual for how the different maximum likelihood MDS models with error terms are defined and specified. we do not provide detailed descriptions in this book since these topics are quite technical and not fundamental to understand MDS analysis in most applied settings. It suffices to know that maximum likelihood MDS can provide a useful way to conduct psychological analyses. For example, we could test hypothesis of instrument sensitivity with respect to different symptoms or different population. We could also test the dimensionality, single-ideal vs. multiple-ideal points model, or equal vs. unequal variance models. Few empirical studies so far have employed maximum likelihood MDS model to examine any substantive issues.

3.8   Conclusion

In this chapter, we discussed fundamentals of basic MDS models most frequently encountered in actual research settings or literature. The discussion focused on the conceptual level without too much technical detail. It is important for us to have some basic understanding of these models so that we know what each MDS model is all about. In later chapters, we will present actual analyses using these models in the context of educational or psychological research.

References

Borg, I. (1977). Some basic concepts of facet theory. In J. C. Lingoes (Ed.), *Progressively complex linear transformations for finding geometric similarities among data structures* (pp. 65–102). Mimeo.

Borg, I., & Groenen, P. J. F. (2005). *Modern multidimensional scaling: Theory and applications* (2nd ed.). New York, NY: Springer.

Bozdogan, H. (1987). Model selection and Akaike's information criterion (AIC): The general theory and its analytical extensions. *Psychometrika, 52*(3), 345–370.

Carroll, J. D. (1972). Individual differences and multidimensional scaling. In R. N. Shepard, A. K. Romney, & S. Nerlove (Eds.), *Multidimensional scaling: Theory and applications in the behavioral sciences* (Vol. I). New York, NY: Academic Press.

Carroll, J. D., & Chang, J. J. (1970). Analysis of individual differences in multidimensional scaling via an N-way generalization of "Eckart-young" decomposition. *Psychometrika, 35*, 238–319.

Carroll, J. D., & Chang, J. J. (1972, March). *IDIOSCAL (Individual Differences in Orientation Scaling): A generalization of INDSCAL allowing idosyncratic reference systems as well as analytic approximation to INDSCAL.* Paper presented at the The Psychometric Society, Princeton, NJ.

Carroll, J. D., & Wish, M. (1973). Models and methods for three-way multidimensional scaling. In R. C. Atkinson, D. H. Krantz, R. D. Luce, & P. Suppes (Eds.), *Contemporary developments in mathematical psychology.* San Francisco, CA: W. H. Freeman.

Coombs, C. H. (1950). Psychological scaling without a unit of measurement. *Psychological Review, 57*(3), 145–158.

Coombs, C. H. (1964). *A theory of data.* New York, NY: Wiley.

Cox, T. F., & Cox, M. A. A. (2001). *Multidimensional scaling* (2nd ed.). Boca Raton, FL: Chapman & Hall/CRC.

Coxon, A. P. M. (1982). *The user's guide to multidimensional scaling.* London: Heinemann Educational Books.

Coxon, A. P. M., Brier, A. P., & Hawkins, P. K. (2005). *The New MDSX program series, version 5.* Edinburgh: London: New MDSX Project.

Davison, M. L. (1983). *Multidimensional scaling.* New York: Wiley.

Guttman, L. (1968). A general non-metric technique for finding the smallest co-ordinate space for a configuration of points. *Psychometrika, 33*, 469–506.

Kruskal, J. B. (1964). Nonmetric scaling: A numerical method. *Psychometrika, 29*, 28–42.

Kuhfeld, W., Young, F. W., & Kent, D. P. (1987). New developments in psychometric and market research procedures. *SUGI, 12*, 1101–1106.

Lingoes, J. C. (1977). *Progressively complex linear transformations for finding geometric similarities among data structures.* Mimeo.

Lingoes, J. C., & Borg, I. A. (1978). A direct approach to individual differences scaling using increasingly complex transformations. *Psychometrika, 43*, 491–519.

MacCallum, R. C. (1977). Effects of conditionality on INOSCALand ALSCALweights. *Psychometrika, 42*, 297–305.

MacKay, D. B. (1989). Probabilistic multidimensional scaling: An anisotropic model for distance judgments. *Journal of Mathematical Psychology, 33*, 187–205.

MacKay, D. B. (2007). Internal multidimensional unfolding about a single-idea--A probabilistic solution. *Journal of Mathematical Psychology, 51*(5), 305–318.

MacKay, D. B., Easley, R. F., & Zinnes, J. L. (1995). A single ideal point model for market structure analysis. *Journal of Marketing Research, XXXII*, 433–443.

MacKay, D. B., & Zinnes, J. (2014). *PROSCAL* professional: A program for probabilistic scaling: www.proscal.com.

MacKay, D. B., & Zinnes, J. L. (1986). A probabilistic model for the multidimensional scaling of proximity and preference data. *Marketing Science, 5*, 325–344.

Ramsay, J. O. (1977). Maximum likelihood estimation in multidimensional scaling. *Psychometrika, 42*, 241–266.

Sammon, J. W. (1969). A nonlinear mapping for data structure analysis. *IEEE Transportation & Computing, 18*, 401–409.

SAS Institute. (2010). *SAS/STAT(R) 9.22 user's guide*. Cary, NC: SAS Institute Inc..

Schwarz, G. (1978). Estimating the dimension of a model. *Annals of Statistics, 6*(2), 461–464.

Shepard, L. (1962). The analysis of proximities: Multidimensional scaling with an unknown distance. I and II. *Psychometrika, 27*, 323–355.

Inc, S. P. S. S. (2007). *SPSS Statistics 17.0: Command syntax reference*. Chicago, IL: SPSS Inc..

Takane, Y. (1978). A maximum likelihood method for nonmetric multidimensional scaling: I The case in which all empirical pairwise orderings are independent-theory. *Japanese Psychological Research, 20*, 7–17.

Takane, Y., & Carroll, J. D. (1981). Nonmetric maximum likelihood multidimensional scaling from directional rankings of similarities. *Psychometrika, 46*, 389–405.

Thurstone, L. L. (1928). Attitudes can be measured. *American Journal of Sociology, 33*, 529–554.

Torgerson, W. S. (1952). Multidimensinoal scaling: I. Theory and method. *Psychometrika, 17*(4), 401–419.

Tucker, L. R. (1960). Intra-individual and inter-individual multidimensionality. In H. Gulliksen & S. Messick (Eds.), *Psychological scaling: Theory and applications* (pp. 155–167). New York: Wiley.

Tucker, L. R. (1972). Relations between multidimensional scaling and three-mode factor analysis. *Psychometrika, 37*, 3–27.

Tversky, A., & Krantz, D. H. (1970). Dimensional representation and the metric structure of similarity data. *Journal of Mathematical Psychology, 7*, 572–596.

Young, G., & Householder, A. S. (1941). Note on multidimensional psychophysical analysis. *Psychometrika, 6*, 331–333.

Zinnes, J. L., & MacKay, D. B. (1983). Probabilistic multidimensional scaling: Complete and incomplete data. *Psychometrika, 48*, 24–48.

Zinnes, J. L., & MacKay, D. B. (1992). A probabilistic multidimensional scaling approach: Properties and procedures. In F. G. Ashby (Ed.), *Multidimensional models of perception and cognition* (pp. 35–60). Hillsdale, NJ: Lawrence Erlbaum Associates.

Chapter 4
Model Selection and Interpretation

Abstract Concepts of MDS model fit are discussed, along with various fit indices. Interpretation of MDS solutions is explained; particularly I highlight the point that MDS is a visual tool using a two-dimensional space and interpretation should focus on clustering patterns of the MDS solution.

Keyword MDS fit indices · Interpretation · Clustering pattern

In Chap. 3 we discussed various MDS models, with focus on the basic ideas of these models. In this chapter, we continue this discussion of MDS models but focus on how do we assess the fit of a MDS model to the data, the factors that may impact the model-data fit, and how we interpret the results from MDS analysis.

4.1 Assess Model Fit

Like many other model-based analytical techniques, MDS also adopts the habit of using fit measures, which is typically called badness-of-fit measures since the higher the badness-of-fit measures, the worse the fit. The fit measure is typically called *Stress* value, which minimizes the fit discrepancy between the model-derived distances and the observed distances. This discrepancy is called error, as in most statistical models. In addition, there are other types of model fit measures that are used in preference MDS models and maximum likelihood MDS analysis.

Some common badness-of-fit measures used in MDS models include the following:

Kruskal's STRESS formula one (S_1) and STRESS formula two (S_2):

$$S_1 = \sqrt{\frac{\sum\left(\hat{\delta}_{ij} - d_{ij}\right)^2}{\sum d_{ij}^2}} \qquad (4.1)$$

$$S_2 = \sqrt{\frac{\Sigma\left(\hat{\delta}_{ij} - d_{ij}\right)^2}{\Sigma\left(d_{ij} - \bar{d}\right)^2}} \tag{4.2}$$

where $\hat{\delta}_{ij}$ is disparities (distance based on optimally transformed data); d_{ij} is model estimated distance, and $\bar{d}$ is mean of model estimated distances. The numerator of Eqs. 4.1 and 4.2 is squared error, indicating the sum of differences between the observed distance (after transformation) and model-derived distance. The denominator in Eqs. 4.1 and 4.2 is normalizing factor (NF). By normalizing raw stress in the numerator, it is possible to compare configurations by making stress independent of the size or scale of the configuration, and standardizing its value between 0 (perfect fit) and 1 (worst possible fit). Thus, S_1 and S_2 differ in the normalizing constant used in the denominator. It has been suggested that when the data are preferences, S_2 is a better choice for the fit measure (Takane et al. 1977).

It should also be noted that the numerator of Eqs. 4.1 and 4.2 is a measure of *Raw Stress*, which is the sum of squares of differences between the model distances and disparities (of optimally transformed data). Kruskal's S_1 is also called normalized stress value. When it is squared, S_1^2 shows the proportion of the sum of squares of the δ_{ij} that is *not* accounted for by the model estimated distances.

We should also repeat here again that minimizing *Stress* value always requires finding an optimal configuration in a given dimensionality m. In order to achieve such an optimal configuration, we transform observed distances into approximated distance (i.e., disparities, as discussed in Chap. 3) by using either linear or monotone regression (other transformation can also be used if appropriate). There are two types of disparities. One is Kruskal's disparities, $\hat{\delta}$, (called d-hat), which is based on weak monotone transformation. As mentioned in Chap. 3, weak monotone transformation allows tied points to be untied using primary approach to ties. A second one is Guttman's rank-image disparities, $\hat{\delta}^*$, (called d-star), which is based on strong monotone transformation using secondary approach to ties. A strong monotone transformation does not allow unequal data to be fitted by equal disparities. Regardless which type of disparities used, the fit measures are based on the "approximated distances", "pseudo-distances", or *disparities* with respect to model estimated distances.

The other fit measures mentioned in the MDS literature include:

Young's S-STRESS formula one and two:

$$SS_1 = \sqrt{\frac{\Sigma\left(\hat{\delta}_{ij}^2 - d_{ij}^2\right)}{\Sigma d_{ij}^2}} \tag{4.3}$$

$$SS_2 = \sqrt{\frac{\sum\left(\hat{\delta}_{ij}^{2} - d_{ij}^{2}\right)}{\sum\left(\delta_{ij}^{2} - \bar{d}^{2}\right)^{2}}}$$

(4.4)

Tucker's congruence coefficient

$$c = \frac{\sum_i x_i y_i}{\sqrt{\sum_i x_i^2 \sum_i y_i^2}}$$

(4.5)

Coefficient of monotonicity:

$$u = \frac{\sum \hat{\delta}_{ij} d_{ij}}{\sqrt{\left(\sum \hat{\delta}_{ij}^{2}\right)\left(\sum d_{ij}^{2}\right)}}$$

(4.6)

Coefficient of alienation:

$$k = \sqrt{1 - u^2}$$

(4.7)

Tuck's congruence coefficient (c) between two variables X and Y is the correlation of these variables about their origin or "zero", not about their means, as in Pearson's correlation coefficient. As correlation coefficient, the congruence coefficient is always between -1 and 1. As can be seen in Eqs. 4.5 and 4.6, Tuck's congruence coefficient is the same as coefficient of monotonicity, as sometimes called. On the other hand, coefficient of alienation is akin to stress, and in some cases, it is identical to it. Coefficient of alienation k is strictly monotonic with stress, which measures the extent of residual variance not explained from the fitted monotone regression.

The *Stress* value, which indicates loss function, can be visualized using Shepard diagram. It plots model-estimated distance or disparities on y-axis against observed distance on the x-axis. In essence, it is just a scatter plot between two variables. If the line is on the diagonal, it indicates the perfect fit. Otherwise, it indicates certain degree of loss or badness-of-fit. Figure 4.1 shows such an example.

In Fig. 4.1, we get an overall impression of the scatter around the representation function. There is quite a bit of scatter around the monotone regression curve. In addition, we see that there are no real outliers, although some points contribute relatively much to *Stress*. In addition, some MDS analysis programs also provide scatter plots of observed distance vs. the disparities or disparities vs. the model estimated distance, as shown in Fig. 4.2. Using another method, we can also inspect the residual or error matrix to find out which pair of variables makes greatest contribution to the mismatch between the model and the data.

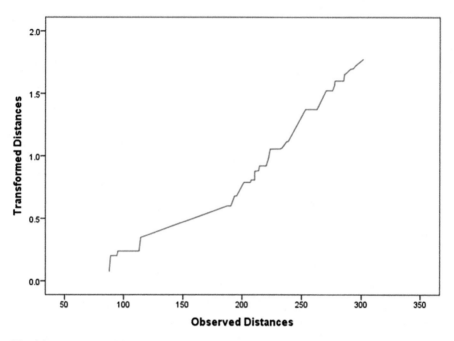

Fig. 4.1 An example of Shepard diagram

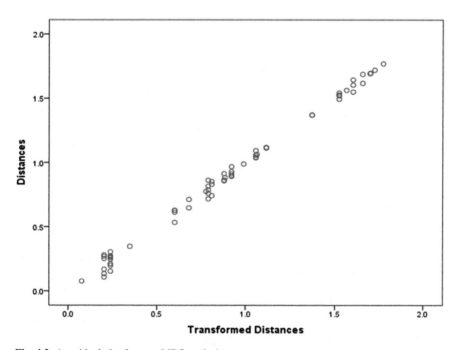

Fig. 4.2 A residual plot from an MDS analysis

There are a few noteworthy points about Stress value.

1. *Stress* value goes down as number of dimensions goes up, given the number of variables used in the analysis.
2. *Stress* value goes up as number of variables increases, given the number of dimensions.
3. The *Stress* value can be used in the following way to determine the proper number of dimensions for interpretation.

   (a) *Stress* value does not decrease more than 5% as the number of dimensions increases. Typically, squared *Stress* value (such as Kruskal S_1) can be interpreted as the percentage of variance in the disparities that cannot be explained by the model. For example, if squared Stress value is 0.10, then we can say that 90% of variance in the disparities that can be explained by the model.
   (b) Kruskal (1964) suggested that the following rule of thumb for *Stress* value:

   0.20 = poor, 0.10 = fair, 0.05 = good,
   0.025 = excellent, and 0.00 = perfect.

However, this suggestion may not be useful since in actual research setting the change in *Stress* value is very small between m vs. $m + 1$ number of dimensions, making it difficult to determine proper number of dimensions.

4. Guttman (1968) suggested the use of the coefficient of alienation k, which is closely related to *Stress*. He indicated that the coefficient of alienation k should be less than 0.15 for an acceptably precise MDS solution in typical non-metric MDS analysis.

In addition to this set of basic fit measures used in MDS analysis, Busing et al. (2005b) suggested additional fit measures used for preference MDS distance model via *PREFSCAL*, a MDS unfolding analysis module within SPSS. We use an example to demonstrate these fit measures based on internal preference modeling. In this example, a 12-item instrument of the Life Orientation Test (LOT) (Scheier et al. 1994) that was developed to assess generalized optimism versus pessimism was administered to a group of students. The responses were coded along a 5-point Likert-type scale, ranging from "strongly disagree" to "strongly agree." The items were scored so that high values indicate optimism (i.e., a large distance from pessimism). Examples of items include "*In uncertain times, I usually expect the best.*" "*If something can go wrong for me, it will.*" or "*I'm always optimistic about my future.*" In a sense, these items assessed adolescents' attitudinal preferences towards life.

A two-dimensional MDS preference distance model was specified in *SPSS PREFSCAL* module. The algorithm converges to a solution after 130 iterations, with a penalized stress (marked final function value) of 0.72. The *PREFSCAL* procedure yielded the following fit indices:

Iterations		130
Final Function Value		0.716
Badness of fit	Normalized stress	0.088
	Kruskal's stress-I	0.296
	Kruskal's stress-II	0.817
	Young's S-stress-I	0.390
	Young's S-stress-II	0.643
Goodness of fit	Dispersion accounted for	0.912
	Variance accounted for	0.622
	Recovered preference orders	0.927
	Spearman's rho	0.741
	Kendall's tau-b	0.618
Variation coefficients	Variation proximities	0.453
	Variation transformed proximities	0.568
	Variation distances	0.467
Degeneracy indices	Sum-of-squares of DeSarbo's Intermixedness indices	0.058
	Shepard's rough nondegeneracy index	0.729

There are a few things to be noted about this output. First, please notice how some of these fit measures are related to each other.

1. Normalized Stress is equal to squared Kruskal's Stress-I, that is, $0.088 = .296^2$
2. Dispersion Accounted For (DAF), also referred to as the sum-of-squares accounted for (SSAF), is equal to 1 - Normalized Stress, that is, $1 - S_1^2$, 0.1– 0.912 = 0.088. It is also equal to Tucker's congruence coefficient:

$$c = \frac{\sum_i x_i y_i}{\sqrt{\sum_i x_i^2 \sum_i y_i^2}} .$$

As Busing et al. (2005a) indicated, the function values of normalized raw Stress, SSAF or DAF, and Kruskal's Stress-I are insensitive to differences in scale and sample size, and these values are suitable for comparing models with different dimensional solutions.

Second, Variance accounted for (VAF) is equal to the square of correlation coefficient and is calculated over all values regardless of the conditionality of the analysis. Recovered preference orders (RFO) indicate proportion of preference ordering of variables that is accounted for by the model.

Third, the variation proximities, variation transformed proximities, and variation distances indicate variability in these data. They should be close to each other, indicating the solution provides discrimination between variables.

Fourth, the sum-of-squares of DeSarbo's intermixedness indices (DeSarbo et al. 1997) are a measure of how well the points of the different set (i.e., object points and person points) are intermixed. The closer to 0, the more intermixed the solution. In here the intermixedness is 0.059, indicating that the solution is well intermixed. Shepard's rough nondegeneracy index (Shepard 1974), which assesses

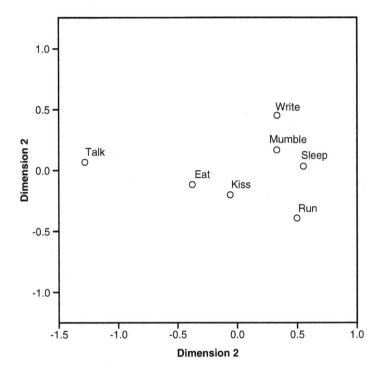

Fig. 4.3 Configuration of seven behaviors

the percentage of distinct distances, is 0.729, indicating 73% of distinct distances. Taken together, the results indicate the solution was not degenerate; that is, the points along the dimensions were distinctly separated.

4.2   Interpretation

Interpretation of MDS solution is a bit tricky in that it does not have a clear consensus regarding the ways in which the configuration should be interpreted. Traditionally, configuration from MDS solution is interpreted based on dimensions, that is, the meaning of dimensions according to how the variables are related to each dimension. Figure 4.3 shows a hypothetical example of MDS analysis of seven behaviors using the basic non-metric MDS model.

What we can tell from this configuration is that behavior *Talk* is away from the rest of behaviors, which are more about private behaviors. Thus, Dimension 1 may represent private vs. open behaviors, while Dimension 2 does not have a clear interpretation. In fact, this hypothetical example illustrates an important point about MDS analysis. That is, MDS analysis usually provides a visualization of relationships among variables in a two-dimensional space. The interpretation of this configuration is mainly based on the cluster of variables rather than based on dimensional interpretation, as we traditionally do. Although a higher dimension may be needed in some cases, we chiefly attempt to identify meaningful latent structure among variables and visualize it in a two-dimensional space.

There is one exception to this practice. In recent years, MDS models have been used in profile analysis (Davison et al. 1996; Ding 2006). In such an application, as discussed in Chap. 10, each dimension represents a typical profile, and there may be more than two profiles. Thus, the focus of the MDS analysis is not on visualization of latent structure but rather on typical behaviors manifested by individuals. In Chap. 10 we will provide application of MDS analysis for such a purpose and a further discussion on this topic.

4.3   Transformation of Configuration

Euclidean distances in MDS models between two points are invariant with respect to transformation of distance points so that dimensionality does not change. The transformation includes rotation, translation, reflection, or dilations. Specifically, a rotation can be thought as a rotation of the dimensions about their origin, and such a rotation may be needed to aid interpretation of the dimensions. On the other hand, translation involves re-location of origin or zero points of coordinate (i.e., adding a constant to all of the coordinates on each dimension); dilation involves multiplying the coordinates by a constant; reflection involves reversing the sign of each coordinate of dimensions. The implication of these concepts is that seemingly different dimensional configurations may be identical to each other due to the possibility of rotation, translation, dilation, or reflection of dimensions. Thus, interpretation of dimensions can be aided by taking these transformations into consideration. In this regard, Procrustean analysis of MDS solution may provide a way to assess the degree to which the seemingly different configurations are essentially the same so that the interpretation of the findings is not affected. In Chap. 9, we will discuss how to assess configuration similarities in detail. For now, it suffices to realize that the potential transformation of a configuration may affect the interpretation, and we need to be careful about and acknowledge this issue.

4.4   Conclusion

In this chapter, we discussed various fit measures in deciding the proper number of dimensions to use for interpretation. Although the list is not exhaustive, it represents commonly used fit indices in MDS analysis and should be sufficient for common MDS analysis in educational and psychological research.

Interpretation of MDS solutions is quite subjective. Although MDS literature provides some extensive discussion with respect to interpretation, the fundamental approach is to inspect salient patterns among variables in a two-dimensional space. This chapter offered a general picture of model fit measures and interpretation of MDS solutions. In later chapters, more specific issues of model fit and interpretation are further discussed in the context of actual analysis using a specific MDS model.

References

Busing, F. M. T. A., Groenen, P. J. K., & Heiser, W. J. (2005a). Avoiding degeneracy in multidimensional unfolding by penalizing on the coefficient of variation. *Psychometrika, 70*(1), 71–98.

Busing, F. M. T. A., Heiser, W. J., Neufeglise, P., & Meulman, J. J. (2005b). *PREFSCAL: Program for metric and nonmetric multidimensional unfolding, including individual differences modeling and fixed coordinates (Version 14)*. Chicago, IL: SPSS Inc.. Retrieved from http://publib. boulder.ibm.com/infocenter/spssstat/v20r0m0/index.jsp?topic=%2Fcom.ibm.spss.statistics. help%2Fsyn_prefscal.htm.

Davison, M. L., Gasser, M., & Ding, S. (1996). Identifying major profile patterns in a population: An exploratory study of WAIS and GATB patterns. *Psychological Assessment, 8*, 26–31.

DeSarbo, W. S., Young, M. R., & Rangaswamy, A. (1997). A parametric multidimensional unfolding procedure for incomplete nonmetric preference/choice set data. *Marketing Research, 34*(4), 499–516.

Ding, C. (2006). Multidimensional scaling modelling approach to latent profile analysis in psychological research. *International Journal of Psychology, 41*(3), 226–238.

Guttman, L. (1968). A general non-metric technique for finding the smallest co-ordinate space for a configuration of points. *Psychometrika, 33*, 469–506.

Kruskal, J. B. (1964). Nonmetric scaling: A numerical method. *Psychometrika, 29*, 28–42.

Scheier, M. F., Carver, C. S., & Bridges, M. W. (1994). Distinguishing optimism from neuroticism (and trait anxiety, self-mastery, and self-esteem): A re-evaluation of the Life Orientation Test. *Journal of Personality and Social Psychology, 67*, 1063–1078.

Shepard, R. N. (1974). Representation of structure in similarity data: Problems and prospects. *Psychometrika, 39*, 373–421.

Takane, Y., Young, F. W., & De Leeuw, J. (1977). Nonmetric individual differences multidimensional scaling: An alternating least squares method with optimal scaling features. *Psychometrika, 42*, 7–67.

Part II
Specific MDS Model and Its Applications

Describe each specific MDS models and its applications for education and psychology

Chapter 5
MDS Analysis Using Basic MDS Model

Abstract Use of basic MDS model is explained. Examples are provided. How the basic model is estimated is discussed, although readers can skip this part. Interpretation of results from basic MDS analysis is further explained, including decision on number of dimensionality.

Keyword Data structure · Estimation · Dimensionality · Interpretation

In previous chapters, we discussed the fundamental concept of applied MDS analysis, the data input for MDS analysis, various MDS models, model fit assessment, and interpretation. Given this essential background information about MDS, we are ready to discuss in more detail the analysis performed using these models. Some of these concepts discussed in the previous chapters are expanded for better understanding. In this chapter, we discuss the analysis using basic MDS model; that is, the analysis using non-metric MDS model.

The materials in this chapter are organized as follows. We first present an example in educational or psychological research. Then we discuss the data input, the model, the estimation, model fit, and interpretation.

5.1 An Illustrative Example: Study Item Structure

Experiential avoidance is the phenomenon that occurs when a person is unwilling to remain in contact with particular private experiences and takes steps to alter the form or frequency of these experiences or the contexts that occasion them, even when these forms of avoidance cause behavioral harm. Experiential avoidance has been implicated in a wide range of clinical problems and disorders, from substance abuse to suicide. Ruminative worry tends to occur because it functions to avoid greater arousal and distress (Borkovec et al. 1999; Wells and Papageorgiou 1995), even though it does not help worriers actually deal with the instrumental situation.

Given the importance of experiential avoidance to some of the new behavior therapies, a research instrument is needed to begin to explore this concept of experiential avoidance. Specifically, it should be possible to develop a broad self-report

Table 5.1 Fit measures for
basic non-metric MDS
solution

Normalized raw stress	0.0005
Stress-I	0.022
Stress-II	0.048
S-stress	0.001
Dispersion accounted for (D.A.F.)	0.999
Tucker's coefficient of congruence	0.999

measure of experiential avoidance that clusters items focused on various aspects of the experiential avoidance concept. As such, Acceptance and Action Questionnaire (AAQ) was designed to assess a high need for emotional and cognitive control, avoidance of negative private events, inability to take needed action in the face of private events, and forms of cognitive entanglement (Bond and Bunce 2003; Hayes et al. 2004). Since its conception, it is the most frequently used measure of experiential avoidance, with versions of nine or 16 items (Hayes et al. 2004).

Although the AAQ is widely used, it has shown problems with its factor structure and internal consistency in various settings (Chawla and Ostafin 2007). Due to the broad item content of the different related constructs, it is unclear whether the AAQ measures one overarching construct or a multidimensional construct (Chawla and Ostafin 2007). For example, the nine-item AAQ showed a one-factor solution (Hayes et al. 2004), while the 16-item AAQ showed a two-factor solution of EA, consisting of willingness and overt action (Bond and Bunce 2003). Furthermore, internal consistency of the scale is often low, which is probably a result of the complex items (Bond et al. 2011).

Due to these problems, Bond et al. (2011) further revised AAQ into AAQ-II with 10 items. However, the authors found a two-factor solution for a 10-item scale. Notably, the second factor consisted of only the three positively worded items on the scale, thus suggesting that the second factor resulted from a method effect and did not represent a second substantive dimension. Thus, the final AAQ-II consists of 7 items. The confirmatory factor analysis suggests a good model fit of one factor structure, only after allowing error terms to be correlated for two items.

As Kline (2010) suggested, correlated error term may indicate extra factor in the data. Thus, it is possible that the AAQ-II assesses different dimensions of the experiential avoidance rather than one dimension, although experiential avoidance is an overarching theme or factor. To further examine the item structure of the AAQ-II, we use the non-metric MDS analysis. One key difference between MDS and exploratory factor analysis is that the general factor bears no effect in MDS model; thus, the possible general factor due to highly correlated items may not interfere with the identification of various aspects of experiential avoidance, as assessed by the AAQ-II item.

Based on the data from 652 undergraduate students, we conducted basic non-metric MDS analysis using SPSS *Proxscal* module (Data Theory Scaling System Group n.d.). The MDS solution indicates a good fit to the data, as indicated by the fit indices in Table 5.1.

The results of the analysis are shown in Fig. 5.1. As can be seen in Fig. 5.1, there are clearly three distinct item clusters, suggesting a possible multifaceted construct of experiential avoidance. In the following section, we discuss how such an MDS solution arrives and the related issues with respect to estimation and interpretation.

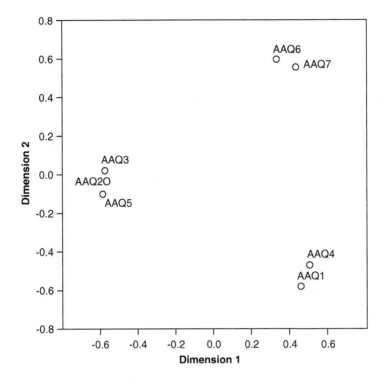

Fig. 5.1 Item structure of the AAQ-II

Table 5.2 Euclidean distance matrix for the example of experiential avoidance

23.124
23.0368 20.3387
17.6852 23.0368 22.9930
25.4081 20.4834 19.7016 24.8841
24.0650 21.1652 22.0065 22.3703 22.6004
23.6634 24.2113 23.7060 20.4623 23.7164 20.1643

5.2   Basic MDS Analysis

When we mention basic MDS analysis, we mean the non-metric MDS analysis for identifying or examining the latent structure of data in a two-dimensional space. The main results from such an analysis are the visualization of data structure and the model fit indices. The data input of the analysis is typically distance matrix such as Euclidean distance measure, δ_{ij}, computed based on the rating data from the questionnaire. For the example of experiential avoidance, the Euclidean distance matrix is shown in Table 5.2.

As we mentioned in Chap. 2, there are different kinds of distance coefficients or measures. The use of different distance matrix as a data input needs to be justified. Typically, Euclidean distance is most used distance coefficient measure in educational and psychological research.

The model used in basic MDS is the simple Euclidean distance model as described in Chap. 3. Sometimes the analysis using such a model is also called *smallest space analysis* (SSA). For example, in NewMDS(X) program package, there is a procedure (called MiniSSA-N) that performs this type of analysis. As mentioned in Chap. 3, this model uses the disparities or pseudo-distance rather than actual or observed distance; that is, the data δ_{ij} will be interpreted by the model as being 'distance-like', not as actual distances but as approximate or estimate of actual distance based on the optimally transformed data. Thus, the distance is more like transformed distance based on transformation procedure. The aim of the basic MDS analysis is to turn such data into a set of genuine Euclidean distances. The solution (also called the 'final configuration') consists of points in a two-dimensional space located so that the model estimated distance between the points matches the observed distances between the items or variables as closely as possible. In basic MDS model, the ordinal or monotonic transformation is used since the model assumes that only the rank order of the items in the data matrix contains significant information. For this reason, non-metric MDS is sometimes referred to as 'ordinal rescaling analysis' (Sibson 1972) since the distances of the solution should, as far as possible, be in the same rank order as the original data after the transformation.

5.2.1   Data Transformation

How does the model perform the ordinal or monotonic transformation? There are two types of transformations (weak or strong monotonicity) and two approaches (primary or secondary approach to ties), as mentioned in Chap. 3. We repeat this information again for an easy access. These methods have something to do with how the tied (equal) data are dealt with. For weak monotonicity (Kruskal 1964), if one data point (e.g., 4) is smaller than another (e.g., 7), then the corresponding distance can be in the same rank order or be equal, but never in the reversed order. That is,

$$\text{if } \delta_{ij} < \delta_{kl} \text{ then } d_{ij} \leq d_{kl}$$

Since the transformation of observed distance involves disparities, then this relationship becomes:

$$\text{if } \delta_{ij} < \delta_{kl} \text{ then } \hat{\delta}_{ij} \leq \hat{\delta}_{kl}$$

that is, weak monotonicity allows unequal data to be fitted by equal disparities in the monotone transformation function (i.e., monotonic regression). In addition, the disparity values, $\hat{\delta}_{ij}$, have the useful property of being as close as possible to the corresponding model estimated distances. This means that, over all the points of the configuration, the sum of the squared differences between the model estimated distances d_{ij} and the corresponding disparities $\hat{\delta}_{ij}$ is as small as possible. For this reason, the MDS solution is a least square solution.

For strong monotonicity (Guttman 1968), if one data point (e.g., 4) is smaller than another (e.g., 7), then the corresponding distance must be in the same rank order. That is, if $\delta_{ij} < \delta_{kl}$ then $\hat{\delta}_{ij} < \hat{\delta}_{kl}$. Because of this reason, $\hat{\delta}_{ij}$ is called rank image estimates. It should be noted that a MDS solution usually has poor fit index if strong monotonicity transformation is chosen. Thus, it is necessary to pay attention to which form of monotonic regression is being used.

In addition to the form of transformation, we also need to pay attention to the ties in the data (i.e., the same value), which is also common. There are two ways to solve this issue. One is to allow ties in the data to be either equal or not equal. This is called primary approach. Another is to retain ties in the data to be tied, which is called secondary approach. In this case, tied data are treated as being truly equivalent. When there are small numbers of ties in the data, primary approach to tie should be used since secondary approach to ties can misrepresent the data structure. However, what values count as tie or the same is hard to judge, particularly in psychological term. In our example data in Table 5.2, quite a few distance values only differ in decimal places, but it is easier to consider them to be different.

Taken together, the monotonicity criterion (weak vs. strong) and the approach to ties (primary vs. secondary) produce somewhat different effects on the ordinal information (order inequalities or equalities) in the data, and the monotonic function has a slightly different form in each of these four cases. As we have mentioned in Chap. 4, the differences between the model estimated distance and its corresponding 'pseudo-distance' ($d_{ij} - \hat{\delta}_{ij}$) serves as a fit index of how the model estimated distance departs from the disparities required to preserve an ordinal relation with the data. If the required ordering is preserved, then the difference will be zero. Alternatively, the difference can be looked on as the residual from monotone regression (i.e., the difference between the estimated distance and an ordinal rescaling of the data.

5.2.2 Finding the MDS Solution

How does the basic non-metric MDS analysis actually work? Given a set of data, how does one find a configuration of points in Euclidean space where the rank-order of the distances from the estimation best matches the rank order of the observed data? In a sense, this becomes a latent variable analysis in which the latent variables are coordinates in a geometric space for each variable, and we try to find such a set of latent coordinates (i.e., latent configuration) that best represents the data. In order to find the configuration, a typical analytic approach is by an iterative process, which is simple in theory but can be complex in implementation of the estimation procedures. There are variations in the estimation process, and here we show the one that is discussed by Davison (1983). The basic iterative steps involve the following:

1. **Create an initial configuration**.

There are different ways to create an initial configuration. We describe some of them.

1. Torgerson's class metric MDS (metric initial configuration).

   (a) specify a specific number of dimensions, e.g., two dimensions.
   (b) first calculate distance matrix from the data.
   (c) convert it into scalar products, that is, double-centered distance matrix, δ^*_{ij}.
   (d) perform principle component analysis on the double-centered distance matrix based on the Torgerson's classic scaling equation $\delta^*_{ij} = XX`$. This will be the best estimate of an initial configuration in a least square sense.

Thus, this initial configuration is closely related to principal components analysis and Eckart-Yeung singular value decomposition. It generally produces a fairly good initial estimate of the solution, unless the configuration of points forms some highly non-linear shape.

2. User-defined starting configuration.

We can provide an initial configuration, usually either based on a priori grounds or from a similar study, which is thought to be close to the final configuration.

3. Random start.

As the name suggests, the initial configuration may be formed simply by allocating random numbers to the $n \times r$ coordinates, or by positioning the points regularly at unit intervals along the dimensions of the initial configuration.

4. Simplex start.

We place the variables in the configuration all at the same distance of each other and taking one iteration to improve this high-dimensional configuration, followed by a dimension-reduction operation to obtain the user-provided maximum dimensionality specified.

5. Quasi non-metric initial configuration

   (a) the data are first reduced to rank order by jettisoning all non-ordinal information.
   (b) a ranks matrix from these data is formed, which is similar to scalar products and a   strict monotone function of data.
   (c) a principal components analysis is performed on the ranks matrix.

2. **Standardize distance and coordinate estimates**

   After the initial configuration, the first iteration starts by first standardizing the current distance estimates and coordinate estimates based on the initial configuration or previous iteration. The distance and configuration estimates are standardized by multiplying them by the same constant so that the coordinate estimates are on the same scale as the distance. The distance is standardized in such a way so that the sum of squares of the distance equals to 1.00. The standardization of distance serves to reduce the likelihood of a degenerative solution.

3. **Nonmetric estimation**

Based on standardized distance, disparities are computed so that they constitute a monotone transformation of the original distance. In each iteration, each disparity is set to equal to the corresponding distance estimates from the previous iteration. There is a series of steps involved in this process, including ranking the data, dealing with ties in the data by creating blocks and re-arranging them. After all these steps, the disparities will satisfy the weak monotonicity function since the data points are regressed onto the distance estimates.

4. **Metric estimation**

Using the disparities, the estimated distance, and the estimated coordinates from the previous iteration, a new set of coordinates is obtained, which is use to compute the new distance estimates. Disparities remain unchanged in this process. Fit measure such as *Stress* value is computed. This ends the first iteration, and after standardization of the new coordinates and distance estimates, the second iteration starts.

5. **Iteration**

The Steps 2–4 iterate until a pre-specified criterion of improvement in fit is met. This process is called gradient methods in which iteration continues until a set of coordinate estimates and disparities have been found to satisfy the solution equations.

5.2.3 Assessing a MDS Solution

Numerical analytic technique of gradient methods can produce several sets of parameter estimates (i.e., coordinates and disparities) for several configurations (i.e., from one to three dimensions). We are looking for ones that have the lowest value of the fit measure such as *Stress* value, which should correspond to the global minimum. Of course, it is hard to know whether the solution corresponds to the global minimum rather than local minimum. It has been suggested that using multiple random start as an initial configuration can reduce the likelihood of local minimum.

Another issue to watch for in the solution is degenerative solution, in which the number of distinct coordinate points in the configuration is small compared to the number of variables used in the analysis, that is, some coordinate points collapse onto a single point. Thus, we need to ensure that coordinates points in the configuration are unique.

The third issue in the analysis is issue of lack of convergence, which is relatively easy to deal with. We can increase the maximum number of iterations to reach convergence. But this problem could be due to local minimum or a degenerative solution. Thus, we need to be careful about what this issue entails.

5.3 Dimensionality and Interpretation of a MDS Solution

5.3.1 Dimensionality

The issue of dimensionality in MDS analysis is always a challenging one. There are various discussions on this issue. A common suggestion is that we ran a set of solutions, say, from one-dimensional to six-dimensional solutions, and then examine the various fit measures. A solution that corresponds to the best fit measure may be the solution of the choice. As we discussed in Chap. 2, there are suggestions regarding what would be the best fit values to guide the choice of the dimensionality.

However, experiences in working with MDS suggests that fit measures (e.g., *Stress value*) can only serve as a guideline rather than a decision rule. The original intent of MDS analysis is to view complex data structure in a low dimensional space. What constitutes a low dimensional space? Given the limited capacity of human mind to visualize objects in more than three dimensions on a piece of paper or a computer screen, it is reasonable to expect that we should be able to view the data structure in two- or three-dimensional space without too much difficulties, usually in a two-dimensional space. Thus, unless there is a special need calling for more than a three-dimensional solution, a two-dimensionality is what we need to view the data structure, and in most cases, that should be sufficient.

One possible exception is that when we use MDS models for profile analysis and growth analysis, we can go to dimensionality that is more than three. We will discuss this particular application of MDS analysis in a later chapter.

5.3.2 Interpretation

There are two major approaches for interpreting the MDS solutions. One is what I called "cluster-pattern approach." In this approach, the interpretation of the MDS solution is chiefly based on the patterns of points in the configuration; that is, we mainly look for patterns in the configuration that make sense for the study under inquiry. No statistical methods can substitute substantive knowledge on the subject. Usually, we do not interpret the whole configuration, but rather to identify patterns within parts of it (i.e., regional density). Therefore, we need to resort to our knowledge to determine what the MDS solution really indicates and interpret the findings accordingly.

The second approach of interpretation can be called "dimensional interpretation approach." In this approach, the interpretation is made according to what each dimension indicates. Traditionally this is the approach we use. For this approach, the common practice in the interpretation of MDS solution is to examine the point of variables along each dimension and then interpret the meaning of each dimension according to what variables cluster around it. This way of interpreting MDS solution follows that of factor analysis. This may be one of the reasons why MDS and factor analysis are viewed as the same method. Although such interpretation is possible, it should not be considered as the main focus or the only way of interpreting the solution. MDS is a visualization method in that we make inferences based on what we see rather than based on statistical values or tests, although such statistical tests exist. We will discuss some of these statistical tests in Chap. 6. Pattern identification is what matters, either patterns around dimensions or patterns that have regional density. In addition, we should not rely on small differences of point locations since small differences in location may be very likely to capitalize on chances and unstable characteristics of the solution.

Another issue regarding the interpretation of a MDS solution is that interpretation of configuration of MDS analysis is affected by similarity transformation of the configuration, which includes rotation, reflection, rescaling, and translation of origin. Specifically, rotation refers to rotation of the axes; reflection refers to changing sign of scale values so that positive becomes negative and versus; rescaling refers to the configuration can be stretched or shrunk by multiplying a constant without changing the information in the configuration; translation of origin refers to the zero point of configuration can be freely located within the configuration without changing the distance. This set of similarity transformations may alter the appearance of the configuration, leading to a different interpretation. Thus seemingly different but essentially the same configuration may be interpreted differently. For example, if we change the sign of the scale values along the dimensions, the configuration may appear different from the original one, which may lead to a different interpretation of the configuration. We need to be careful about this issue, particularly when we compare two configurations across groups or time. In this regard, we can conduct Procrustes analysis to make sure that two configurations do not differ substantially. Procrustes analysis will be discussed in Chap. 9.

5.4   Applications of Basic MDS Analysis in Educational and Psychological Research

In this section, we presented two empirical studies that employed the basic MDS analysis to investigate the factor structure of Beck's Depression Inventory (BDI). The purpose is to let readers get more intuitive sense of how basic MDS analysis can be used in actual research setting. Certainly, these analyses could be extended to examine group (e.g., gender) differences in data structure or other types of configuration differences.

Cohen (2008) used basic MDS model to confirm Beck's six symptom characterization of depression based on Beck Depression Inventory-II (BDI-II). BDI-II assessed the symptom of depression along the following categories: affective, motivational, cognitive, behavioral, and physiological (or vegetative) symptoms, as well as cognitive distortions. Although there are a large number of factor analytic and principal component studies of the BDI-II, these studies only partially supported Beck's categorization.

Although factor analysis is the most widely used multivariate analysis to study behavioral phenomena, Cohen (2008) indicated several limitations of factor analytic approach to studying factor structure of the BDI-II. First, the parameters of factor analytic models are rather stringent because of a metric requirement for the measurements, multivariate normality of the items, and a linear relationship between the items and the factors. These assumptions can make it difficult to provide a coherent description of the multifaceted aspects of psychological phenomena in general, particular for depression. Second, in factor analysis each factor should include at least five variables, as suggested by Gorsuch (1983). But in the BDI-II, only one factor (cognitive distortion) had five items and the rest factors did not meet the five-item requirement, which may be one reason why the factor analytic studies did not support the BDI-II factor structure.

Thus, Cohen used MDS approach to search for relations among symptom categories of the BDI-II items. Rather than a mathematical expression of the item's loading or correlation on a factor, the MDS approach enabled us to achieve a geometric representation of order relations, emphasizing visualization of data structures that may be obscured in factor analysis solutions. Although there are several MDS programs, Cohen used Smallest Space Analysis (SSA) program, which is characterized by the robustness and step-size of its algorithm. The fit measure of the SSA solution is the coefficient of alienation, with a value of 0.2 or less indicates a good fit.

The results of the MDS analysis from Cohen's study is shown in Fig. 5.2.

From Fig. 5.2, one may easily identify Beck's six symptom categories along the horizontal dimension, which was cognitive distortions, motivational, affective symptom, cognitive symptom, behavioral symptom, and vegetative symptom. Along the vertical dimension, Cohen (2008) suggested high arousal symptoms (top) vs. low arousal symptoms (bottom), with the items in the middle portion being not-so-clear arousal level.

Based these findings, Cohen (2008) suggested that to ensure the validity of the vertical dimension, some new items related to the arousal dimension should be developed, such as items focused on attention (e.g., distractibility and to jumping from one decision to another) and items focused on sluggish thinking, forgetfulness, inability to perform mentally, lack of interest, and other symptoms that indicate slow information-processing or attention deficit.

The second empirical study using basic MDS analysis was done by Bühler et al. (2014, April 28) with respect to the item structure of the BDI-II. Although the majority of studies proposed a two-factor model of the BDI-II, with each item loading on one of two factors, Bühler, Keller, and Läge proposed the basic nonmetric MDS

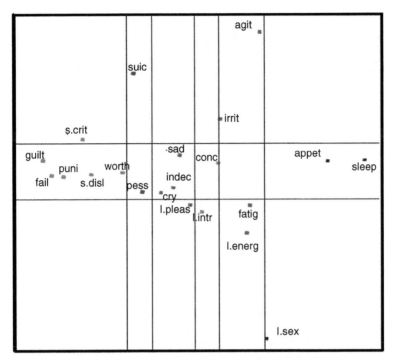

1.	sad	Sadness	12.	l.intr	Loss of Interest
2.	pes	Pessimism	13.	indec	Indecisiveness
3.	fail	Past Failure	14.	worth	Worthlessness
4.	l.pleas	Loss of Pleasure	15.	l.enrg	Loss of Energy
5.	guilt	Guilty Feeling	16.	sleep	Changes in Sleep
6.	puni	Punishment Feeling	17.	irrit	Irritability
7.	s.dis	Self-Dislike	18.	appet	Changes in Appetite
8.	s.crit	Self-Criticalness	19.	conc	Concentration Difficulty
9.	suic	Suicidal Thoughts	20.	fatig	Tiredness or Fatigue
10.	cry	Crying	21	l.sex	Loss of Interest in Sex
11.	agit	Agitation			

Fig. 5.2 MDS solution of the BDI-II symptom categorization (Adapted from Cohen's study (2008). Copyright 2007 by Elsevier. Inc. Adapted with permission)

approach to modeling the symptom structure of the BDI–II and suggested an interpretation that included systematic variability among the items with respect to the activation factor. The results of their MDS analysis is shown in Fig. 5.3, which is adapted from "Activation as an Overlooked Factor in the BDI–II: A Factor Model Based on Core Symptoms and Qualitative Aspects of Depression." by Bühler et al. (2014).

The figure clearly shows how the items from the BDI-II were patterned in a way that allow us to hypothesize the formal factor structure of the BDI-II. Based on MDS solution, Bühler et al. (2014, April 28) performed confirmatory factor analysis and indicated that the BDI–II was well represented by four factors: a G factor, a cognitive factor, a somatic factor, and an activation factor. What is interesting about

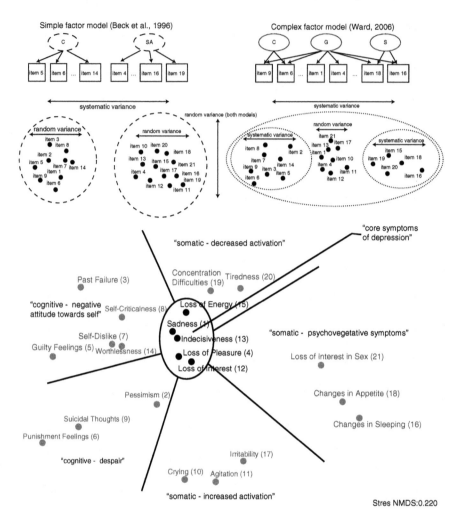

Fig. 5.3 The item structure of the BDI-II (Adapted from Bühler et al. (2014, April 28). Copyright 2007 by American Psychological Association)

Fig. 5.3 was that how MDS displayed the item structure. At the top of Fig. 5.3, items were grouped along the horizontal dimension, indicating systematic variation, while the vertical dimension was considered as random variation. The bottom of Fig. 5.3 showed a different way to interpret the item structure, that is, by how the items were grouped (i.e., regional density) in a two-dimensional space rather than by dimension. This interpretation was in direct contrast with Fig. 5.1, in which Cohen (2008) followed the dimensional interpretation approach. Thus, readers can see the different approach to interpret the MDS solution. Essentially, rather than focus on what each dimension may represent, we can examine regions of high density of items, reflecting high similarity among items, and of low density of items (i.e., separated from other items by empty or sparsely-populated region), indicating differences.

5.5 Conclusion

In this chapter we discussed the basic non-metric MDS analysis that focus on the latent configuration of variables. The take-home message is that the basic MDS analysis is a visualization method that can help us to visualize the relationships (patterns) among a set of variables under inquiry. Inferences can be made based on the patterns we see. This type of MDS analysis lays a foundation for other kinds of MDS analyses such as MDS unfolding analysis (i.e., preference analysis), confirmatory MDS analysis, or individual differences MDS analysis in that the interpretation of the results from those analyses is also mainly based on visualization of the patterns emerged from the data. The actual applications of MDS model make it clear that different ways of interpretation often provide invaluable information about local and global aspects of the configuration.

It should be pointed out now that the basic MDS analysis we discuss in this chapter is usually called internal analysis (i.e., unconstrained solutions) since the analysis only uses the observed data to generate the solution. This type of analysis is best suit for exploratory analysis. On the other hand, we can also bring prior information or knowledge into MDS analysis, which is usually called external analysis (i.e., constrained solution). In the external analysis we take the input data and relate that data to the external information (i.e., prior information). Traditionally, external MDS analysis tends to be used for the purpose of aiding interpretation. But it is quite feasible to use external MDS analysis as a method to conduct confirmatory MDS analysis. We will discuss this application in Chap. 12.

References

Bond, F., Hayes, S. C., Baer, R. A., Carpenter, K. M., Guenole, N., Orcutt, H. K., et al. (2011). Preliminary psychometric properties of the acceptance and action questionnaire–II: A revised measure of psychological inflexibility and experiential avoidance. *Behavior Therapy, 42*, 676–688.

Bond, F. W., & Bunce, D. (2003). The role of acceptance and job control in mental health, job satisfaction, and work performance. *Journal of Applied Psychology, 88*, 1057–1067.

Borkovec, T. D., Hazlett-Stevens, H., & Diaz, M. L. (1999). The role of positive beliefs about worry in generalized anxiety disorder and its treatment. *Clinical Psychology and Psychotherapy, 6*, 126–138.

Bühler, J., Keller, F., & Läge, D. (2014). Activation as an overlooked factor in the BDI–II: A factor model based on Core symptoms and qualitative aspects of depression. *Psychological Assessment, Advance online publication*. https://doi.org/10.1037/a0036755.

Chawla, N., & Ostafin, B. (2007). Experiential avoidance as a functional dimensional approach to psychopathology: An empirical review. *Journal of Clinical Psychology, 63*, 871–890. https://doi.org/10.1002/jclp.20400.

Cohen, A. (2008). The underlying structure of the Beck Depression Inventory II: A multidimensional scaling approach. *Journal of Research in Personality, 42*, 779–786. https://doi.org/10.1016/j.jrp.2007.09.007.

Data Theory Scaling System Group. (n.d.). *PROXSCAL (Version 1.0). Leiden university*. Netherlands: Faculty of Social and Behavioral Sciences.

Davison, M. L. (1983). *Multidimensional scaling*. New York: Wiley.

Gorsuch, R. L. (1983). *Factor analysis* (2nd ed.). Hillsdale, NJ: Lawrence Erlbaum Associates.

Guttman, L. (1968). A general non-metric technique for finding the smallest co-ordinate space for a configuration of points. *Psychometrika, 33*, 469–506.

Hayes, S. C., Strosahl, K. D., Wilson, K. G., Bissett, R. T., Pistorello, J., Toarmino, D., et al. (2004). Measuring experiential avoidance: A preliminary test of a working model. *Psychological Record, 54*, 553–5878.

Kline, R. B. (2010). *Principles and practice of structural equation modeling* (2nd ed.). New York, NY: Guilford.

Kruskal, J. B. (1964). Multidimensional scaling by optimizing goodness of fit to a nonmetric hypothesis. *Psychometrika, 29*, 1–27.

Sibson, R. (1972). Order invariant methods for data analysis. *Journal of Royal Statisical Society (B), 364*, 311–349.

Wells, A., & Papageorgiou, C. (1995). Worry and the incubation of intrusive images following stress. *Behaviour Research and Therapy, 33*, 579–583.

Chapter 6
Visualization of Latent Factor Structure

Abstract Illustrate how complex data structure can be visualized in a two-dimensional space using simulated data. Spatial point analysis is discussed in the context of MDS. Test of spatial randomness and clustering effect of data points is explained. Examples from real data are provided to demonstrate the points discussed.

Keywords Latent factor map · Spatial randomness · Clustering effect · The Silhouette Width index · The Dunn Index

In this chapter, we describe one particular application of basic MDS model for data visualization and discuss test of randomness of points in configuration. Although the original purpose of MDS is to visualize the data structure in a lower dimensional space (typically two or three dimensions), this aspect of MDS model has not been fully utilized in educational or psychological research as one salient aspect of the MDS analysis; that is, data visualization via MDS is not explicitly stated as an analytical tool. One question that people may be interested in knowing is whether a complex data structure can be visualized in a two-dimensional space. A complex data structure is defined in terms of number of factors underlying a set of variables or items. Traditionally, number of factors in factor analytical model is considered equivalent to number of dimensions in MDS; that is, a five-factor model in factor analysis should be represented by a five-dimension solution in MDS. Can we view such a complex factor structure in a two-dimensional space rather than a higher dimensional space? Therefore, in this chapter we focus on how MDS analysis can be used for examining latent factor structure of items in a test, questionnaire, or survey. The main goal is to show how complex factor structures of items can be legitimately visualized in a two-dimensional space. In addition, we introduce some spatial analysis methods that can be used in MDS to test spatial randomness and clustering effect of items.

© Springer International Publishing AG, part of Springer Nature 2018 75
C. S. Ding, *Fundamentals of Applied Multidimensional Scaling for Educational and Psychological Research*, https://doi.org/10.1007/978-3-319-78172-3_6

6.1   Visualization as a Formal Analytic Method

Seeing and understanding data is richer than creating a collection of equations or formula. Tukey (1980) states:

> " Ideas come from previous exploration more often than from lightning strokes. Important questions can demand the most careful planning for confirmatory analysis. Broad general inquiries are also important. Finding the question is often more important than finding the answer. Exploratory data analysis is an attitude, a flexibility, and a reliance on display, NOT a bundle of techniques, ..." (p. 23)

> "Neither exploratory nor confirmatory is sufficient alone. To try to replace either by the other is madness. We need them both." (p.23)

> "Both inchoate insight and extensive exploration (of past data) can – and should – play a role in this process of formulating the question. Science – and engineering, which here includes agriculture and medicine – DOES NOT BEGIN WITH A TIDY QUESTION. Nor does it end with a tidy answer." (p.24)

These statements from Tukey highlight the importance of data exploration by visualization and the nature of scientific inquiries. In the field of educational and psychological measurement, however, we do not often employ any visual methods as a formal technique to observe and explore factor or item structure of an instrument. Rather, we tend to use methods that employ numerical values as a way to determine the factor or item structure of a proposed instrument such as exploratory factor analysis. Sometimes, even a confirmatory approach is used to explore the factor structure via modification index in structural equation modeling to find the "best" factor model or to "test" different models without a clear stipulation of theory a prior. One reason for such a practice may be that we may not "trust" or feel comfortable with what we observe in the graph without some kind of formal "testing" with numerical values. To a lesser degree, researchers less familiar with visualization and statistics may feel that an model needs to be established before graphically displaying it (Butner et al. 2014).

Wright's (1921) innovation of path diagrams provided a method of using visual tools to generate models and equations that can be used in confirmatory analysis. Such a method helps to equip researchers with a visual tool to express their theory in graphic form and then test their model against data. However, beyond the path diagram, there have been no other visual methods that are frequently used in exploring data structure to generate testable measurement models for descriptions of human behavior and psychological processes. In this chapter we propose the use of an additional graphical representation that is capable of capturing underlying data structure in studying educational and psychological measurement instruments and then translates them into testable measurement models. This additional graphical representation can be called "*latent factor map*" that is communicated as a map of items in a two-dimensional space using multidimensional scaling (MDS). We compliment latent factor map with tests of spatial randomness and item clusters.

We argue that a latent factor map generated by MDS can aid in translating what we see or observe into a testable measurement model. First, complex and nonlinear factor structures can be represented in a two dimensional space rather than a higher one (e.g., four or more dimensions). Second, in the instrument development process, removing items that may not be relevant or appropriate is needed to construct the final instrument. However, in factor analysis, removing items may cause dramatic changes in factor loading of the remaining items, which in turn may cause change in factor structure. Latent factor map from MDS analysis, in contrast, is not subject to these changes and removing any item does not change the overall pattern of item configuration. Thus, researchers may hypothesize latent factor structures based on a latent factor map and then derive the statistical equation to test the full extent of their hypothesis.

Previous researchers (e.g., Liebovitch et al. 2011; Molenaar and Campbell 2009) have made connections between factor map and statistical models such as dynamic factor analysis (DFA; Molenaar 1985). Some researchers have directly used MDS for detecting factor structure of items (e.g., Bühler et al. 2014, April 28; Cohen 2008; Schlessinger and Guttman 1969; Schwartz 2006). One issue that may warrant further examination is whether a more complex factor structure can be depicted in a two-dimensional space, as we mentioned previously. In order to clearly see how a complex factor structure of items can be represented in two-dimensional space, we will use simulation-based data examples with clear factor structures (i.e., simple structure) to highlight the possibility of representing multifactor structure in a lower dimension, which is the original purpose of MDS analysis (Davies and Coxon 1982). Of course, the problem with using simulated simple structure data is that the data is not realistic. But I want to make a point that visualizing more than a two-factor structure in a two-dimensional space is possible. When data become messy, the latent factor map may not be as tidy as you wish. In that case, substantive knowledge is critical.

In addition, we incorporate spatial point pattern analysis into MDS, which can help test questions of whether the item pattern observed in latent factor map is random or clustered. In the following sections we discuss the idea of latent factor map generated from MDS and demonstrate how latent factor map can be used to test a specific measurement model.

6.2   Two-Dimensional Latent Factor Map Using MDS

MDS is not a new technique, and in much of the quantitative and statistical literature multidimensional scaling (MDS) is often referred to as a technique that represents the empirical relationships of data as a set of points in space, typically in two or higher dimensional space. In fact, the original purpose of MDS tends to be viewed as a data visual technique. The unifying theme of different MDS models is the spatial representation of the data structure.

However, one common myth about MDS is that is considered to be the same or similar analytical technique as factor analysis. The implications of this myth entail the following: (1) the term of the dimension and factor are used interchangeably to represent the latent constructs, (2) a dimension is assumed to have a meaning as factor does, and (3) the number of dimensions should be extracted in the same way as factors are. Thus, using MDS model as a visualization of factor structure has not been one of the main analytic tool in psychometric studies. But in this chapter, we want to highlight the point that MDS models has its own uniqueness that differentiates it from factor analysis, although these models can be used in the same way as factor analysis. One such differential feature is that in the visualization application the dimension only provides a spatial reference framework for item structure and it does not represent any substantive construct as that in factor analysis. Of course, we may provide an interpretation to each of the dimensions if we wish, but more often it will be challenging to do so if a complex data structure is depicted in a two-dimensional solution. For example, in a scatter plot where y-axis represents a dependent variable and x-axis represents an independent variable, we can know what each dimension represents. But when a four-factor structure of a set of items is displayed or mapped in a two-dimensional space, it is hard to say what each dimension represents. This point will be illustrated later in the chapter.

As suggested by Cohen (2008), visual representation of data structure may circumvent some of the issues encountered in factor analysis (i.e., exploratory factor analysis), which is a sine qua non tool for the study of complex behavioral phenomena with respect to factor structure among a set of assessment items. Some studies has been done to contrast the results from the MDS and factor analysis (e.g., Davison 1985). In general, the parameters of factor models are rather stringent: (1) a metric requirement for the measurements, (2) multivariate normality of the items, and (3) a linear relationship between the items and the factors. As Maxwell (1972) indicated, these assumptions may hinder a coherent description of the multifaceted aspects of behavioral symptomatology in general. On the other hand, MDS analysis is less demanding and a more parsimonious alternative when searching for order relations among variables, and it has been used with success to explore the factor structures of psychological inventories (e.g., Bühler et al. 2014, April 28; Cohen 2008; Läge et al. 2012; Steinmeyer and Möller 1992). According to Cohen (2008), MDS approach differed from exploratory factor analyses in (1) the manner of the analysis – geometric representation of relations based on the rank order or distance among variables and (2) the results produced – visualization of item structure in a two-dimensional space. Thus, two highly similar symptoms or behaviors are located in close proximity to each other, whereas two dissimilar symptoms or behaviors are located farther apart. In addition, the presence of a general factor has no effect on MDS solutions because of the method's relational, similarity-based approach, in which similarity is transformed to an ordered categorical scale (rank orders) (Davison 1985). Thus, high overall correlations among the items, which would constitute a general factor, are neglected in MDS analyses. This may be a very useful feature in identifying different aspects of data structure.

Using MDS to visualize factor structure is not new but it is not often employed as a viable tool for instrument development (e.g., Bühler et al. 2014, April 28; Cohen 2008). Specifically, in an MDS model variables are represented as points in Euclidian space, with interpoint distances as a measure of relationship among variables. The underlying concept of the MDS approach is that there is a strong isomorphism between distance measures among variables and a set of points in Euclidian space. The MDS approach enables us to achieve a visual representation of order relations in a two-dimensional space, rather than a mathematical expression of the item's loading on a factor. MDS emphasizes direct observation of the distance matrix and may emphasize those data structures that may be obscured in exploratory factor analysis solutions. Hence, the graphical representation of two-dimensional MDS solutions allow insight into the adequacy of factor structure, which can further be used as an empirical basis for a hypothesis-testing purpose or upon which a new factor model is constructed. In some way, MDS can be considered as a method to study association network, in which no postulation is made with respect to an underlying, latent essence that may cause the emergence of behaviors.

6.2.1   Spatial Analysis of Randomness in Configuration

In addition to the traditional MDS analytic procedures, we can incorporate the spatial analysis of point patterns to test possible clustered patterns occurring when there was attraction (i.e., association) between points in MDS configuration. Such a point-pattern analysis is drawn from spatial data analysis that is concerned with stochastic dependence between the points in a point pattern (Bivand et al. 2013). While traditional MDS analysis is more descriptive and can lead to possible hypothesis of substantive issue, the point pattern analysis can further be done to test the complete spatial randomness (CSR) versus clustered pattern in MDS configuration. The null hypothesis of CSR is that the variable locations are distributed independently at random and uniformly in the space, which implies that there are no regions or locations where the variables are more or less likely to occur and that the presence of a given variable does not modify the probability of other variables appearing closely. The basic CSR properties in MDS model include: (1) the number of locations falling in a space S has a Poisson distribution with mean $\lambda(S)$, (2) given that there are n points (i.e., items) in the specific space S, the locations of these points are identically and independently distributed and uniformly distributed inside S, and (3) the locations of two disjoint points are independent. Usually, the uniform Poisson point process (i.e., CSR) is often the 'null model' in an MDS analysis and the focus of the point pattern analysis is to establish that the data structures do not conform to a uniform Poisson process. Testing for CSR can be conducted using several statistical functions. One of them is the K function (Diggle 2003), which assesses whether the location point of the variables follows Poisson point process (i.e., CSR) or whether the location points are dependent. The CSR of the point pattern can be assessed by plotting the empirical or estimated function $\hat{k}(r)$ against the theoretical expectation $k_{\text{pois}}(r)$. The plot is produced by taking the pairs $(k(r), \hat{k}(r))$ for a set of reasonable values of the distance r, so that in the x-axis we have the values of the theoretical value of $k(r)$ under CSR and in the y-axis the empirical function $\hat{k}(r)$. When there is a clustered pattern, estimated values of $\hat{k}(r)$ will be greater than theoretical $k_{\text{pois}}(r)$ and the lines representing the estimated values of $\hat{k}(r)$ will deviate from value line of the theoretical expectation of Poisson point process. There are several estimators of $\hat{k}(r)$ such as G function, but they tend to reach the same conclusion.

6.2.2   Spatial Analysis of Clustering Effect in Configuration

While test of CSR is focused on the spatial point pattern as a whole and examines whether there are any possible clusters of item points in a particular space, it does not indicate number of the possible clusters in the space if the hypothesis of CSR is rejected. That is, we need to determine the number of point patterns that share similar characteristics (e.g., similar traits or constructs). It has been suggested that MDS and cluster analysis can be used in conjunction to detect point pattern in a space (DeSarbo et al. 1991). A plethora of clustering algorithms currently exist and deciding which clustering method to use with MDS can be a daunting task. One way to deal with this problem is to employ cluster validation methods that aim at validating the results of a set of cluster analyses and determining which clustering algorithms performs the best for a particular data. There have been various measures proposed (see a good overview by Handl et al. 2005). One of the validation measures that is appropriate for use with MDS analysis based on internal validation measures. Internal validation measures take the dataset and the clustering partition as input and use intrinsic information in the data to determine an optimal number of cluster for the data in hand based on several multiple clustering algorithms (Brock et al. 2008). Internal measures assess the compactness and separation of the cluster patterns. Specifically, compactness assesses cluster homogeneity by looking at the intra-cluster variance, while separation quantifies the degree of separation between clusters by measuring the distance between cluster centroids. The Dunn Index (Dunn 1974) and Silhouette Width (Rousseeuw 1987) are two popular measures that combine compactness and separation into one index. The Dunn Index (DI) is the ratio of the smallest distance between points not in the same cluster to the largest distance between points within the same cluster. Given m clusters in the data, DI is computed as

$$DI = \frac{\min\left[\delta\left(C_i, C_j\right)\right]}{\max\left[\delta\left(C_m\right)\right]} \tag{6.1}$$

where $\min[\delta(C_i, C_j)]$ is the smallest distance between points in cluster i and cluster j and $\max[\delta(C_m)]$ is the largest distance between points within a cluster m. The value of DI ranges from 0 to ∞, with the largest value being associated with the best number of clusters in the data.

The Silhouette Width (SW) is the average of each data or variable point's Silhouette value. SW assesses the degree of how well each data point or variable lies within its cluster. For variable i, SW is defined as

$$SW(i) = \frac{b_i - a_i}{\max(b_i, a_i)} \tag{6.2}$$

where a_i is the average dissimilarity of variable i with all other variables in the same cluster (i.e., within-cluster dissimilarity) and can be interpreted as how well variable i is assigned to its cluster. b_i is the smallest average dissimilarity of variable i to any other cluster where variable i is not a member. Since SW is a confidence width, it can also be written as:

$$SW_i = \begin{cases} 1 - a_i / b_i, & ifa_i < b_i \\ 0, & if\ a_i = b_i \\ b_i / a_i - 1, & if\ a_i > b_i \end{cases} \tag{6.3}$$

Thus, SW_i measures how tightly grouped all the data in the cluster are and assesses how appropriately the variable has been clustered. From expression 3, it is clear that

$$-1 \leq SW_i \leq 1$$

In a sense, SW_i assesses confidence in the clustering assignment of a particular variable, with well-clustered variables having values near one and poorly clustered variables having values near negative one.

The clustering algorithms the cluster validation procedure is based on include hierarchical method, also known as unweighted pair group method with arithmetic mean (UPGMA) (Kaufman and Rousseeuw 1990), k-means (Hartigan and Wong 1979), Diana, partitioning around medoids (PAM), Clara (Kaufman and Rousseeuw 1990), Fanny (Kaufman and Rousseeuw 1990), self-organizing maps (SOM) (Kohonen 1997), model-based clustering (Fraley and Raftery 2007), self-organizing tree algorithm (SOTA) (Dopazo and Carazo 1997). The clustering validation measures provide the score for the most appropriate number of clusters resulting from these clustering procedures.

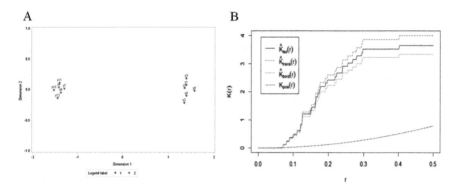

Fig. 6.1 Panel A: Two factor structure of 12 items. Panel B: K function of CSR test, which indicates that observed point pattern deviates significantly from the CSR

6.3   Illustration Based on Stimulation Data

In the following sections, we use simulation-based data of two-factor to five-factor structure to illustrate the key features we have made for latent factor map using MDS analysis: (1) complex data structure can be depicted in a two-dimensional space, (2) point pattern analysis can be used to test complete spatial randomness hypothesis, and (3) assess and validate the number of point clusters in the space. Simulation-based examples are used because they provide a clear illustration of these key features. Of course, the actual data does not always have such a clear data structure, but by knowing what a clear data structure looks like can help us to establish a standard for which we can use to compare what we have in hand. We also draw on real-world data to demonstrate the visualization of the factor structure and to test its measurement model.

In this set of simulations, we created a random data of 500 cases but with 12 items for two-factors, 18 items for three factors, 24 items for four factors, and 30 items for five factors. These factors followed a simple factor structure (i.e., each item loads only one factor and zeros on all other factors).

6.3.1   Two- to Five-Factor Structures

Figure 6.1 shows the latent factor map of the 12 items (panel A) from a MDS two-dimensional solution, which clearly suggests a pattern of two clusters among items. The K function test suggests the clustered pattern in the space, as shown in panel B of Fig. 6.1 where the value of estimated K function is greater than the value of theoretical random Poisson process. As shown in panel A of Fig. 6.1, the items in each cluster correspond well with the items that define each factor. Cluster validation measures based on hierarchical, k-means, and PAM clustering algorithm indicated a two-cluster patterns with *DI* and SW value being maximized for the two-cluster solution. Table 6.1 shows *DI* and *SW* value based on three clustering algorithms for two- to five-factor structure. As can be seen at top of Table 6.1, two-factor structure

Table 6.1 Cluster validation index of factor structure from MDS two-dimensional solution

Two cluster pattern (12 items)		Number of clusters				
Validation index	Clustering algorithm	**2**	3	4	5	6
Dunn	Hierarchical	**6.57**	0.47	0.49	0.73	0.74
	K-means	**6.56**	0.47	0.50	0.73	0.54
	PAM	**6.56**	0.47	0.50	0.50	0.73
Silhouette	Hierarchical	**0.93**	0.65	0.66	0.33	0.27
	K-means	**0.93**	0.64	0.66	0.33	0.26
	PAM	**0.93**	0.64	0.66	0.26	0.27
Three cluster pattern (18 items)		Number of clusters				
Validation index	Clustering algorithm	2	**3**	4	5	6
Dunn	Hierarchical	0.92	**17.63**	0.55	0.55	0.56
	K-means	0.91	**17.63**	0.45	0.47	0.61
	PAM	0.91	**17.63**	0.39	0.39	0.57
Silhouette	Hierarchical	0.62	**0.97**	0.73	0.55	0.30
	K-means	0.62	**0.97**	0.74	0.57	0.32
	PAM	0.62	**0.97**	0.73	0.55	0.30
Four cluster pattern (24 items)		Number of clusters				
Validation index	Clustering algorithm	2	3	4	5	6
Dunn	Hierarchical	0.74	0.74	**3.26**	0.51	0.58
	K-means	0.74	0.75	**3.26**	0.51	0.58
	PAM	0.03	0.09	**3.26**	0.39	0.26
Silhouette	Hierarchical	0.51	0.65	**0.88**	0.78	0.67
	K-means	0.51	0.65	**0.88**	0.78	0.67
	PAM	0.27	0.57	**0.88**	0.78	0.64
Five cluster pattern (30 items)		Number of clusters				
Validation index	Clustering algorithm	2	3	4	5	6
Dunn	Hierarchical	0.24	0.37	0.43	**0.61**	0.44
	K-means	0.24	0.37	0.43	**0.61**	0.44
	PAM	0.14	0.34	0.16	**0.62**	0.57
Silhouette	Hierarchical	0.39	0.50	0.55	**0.62**	0.56
	K-means	0.39	0.50	0.55	**0.62**	0.56
	PAM	0.37	0.48	0.48	**0.62**	0.57

pattern is identified as the optimal factor structure of these items, regardless of which clustering algorithm is used. The result suggests that two-factor structure can be correctly visualized or mapped in a two dimensional space of MDS analysis.

6.3.2 Three-Factor Structure

Figure 6.2 shows the latent factor map of these 18 items (panel A), which clearly suggests a pattern of three clusters among items. The K function test suggests the clustered pattern in the space, as shown in panel B of Fig. 6.2 where the value of estimated K function is greater than the value of theoretical Poisson process. As shown in panel A of Fig. 6.2, the items in each cluster correspond well with the

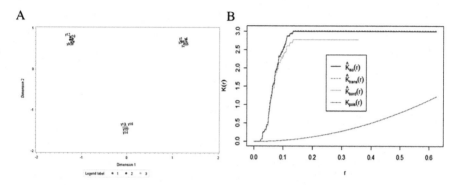

Fig. 6.2 Panel A: Three factor structure of 18 items. Panel B: *K* function of CSR test, which indicates that observed point pattern deviates significantly from the CSR

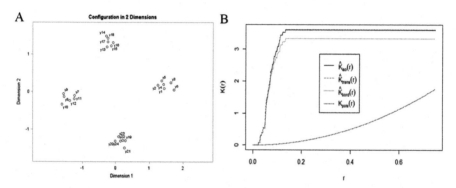

Fig. 6.3 Panel A: Four factor structure of 24 items. Panel B: *K* function of CSR test, which indicates that observed point pattern deviates significantly from the CSR

items that define each factor. Cluster validation measures based on hierarchical, k-means, and PAM clustering algorithm indicated a three-cluster patterns with *DI* and *SW* value being maximized for the three-cluster solution (see Table 6.1). As in the case of the two-factor structure pattern, three-factor structure pattern is identified as the optimal factor structure of these items, regardless of which clustering algorithm is used. The result suggests that three-factor structure can be correctly visualized or mapped in a two dimensional space from MDS analysis.

6.3.3   Four-Factor Structure

Figure 6.3 shows the latent factor map of these 24 items (panel A), which clearly suggests a pattern of four clusters among items. The *K* function test suggests the clustered pattern in the space, as shown in panel B of Fig. 6.3 where the value of estimated *K* function is greater than the value of theoretical Poisson process. As shown in panel A of Fig. 6.3, the items in each cluster correspond well with the items that define each factor. Cluster validation measures based on hierarchical,

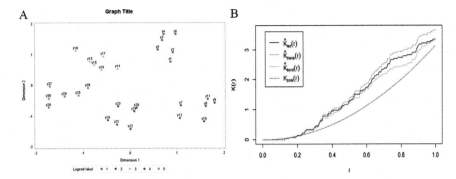

Fig. 6.4 Panel A: Five factor structure of 30 items. Panel B: K function of CSR test, which indicates that observed point pattern deviates significantly from the CSR

k-means, and PAM clustering algorithm indicated a four-cluster patterns with DI and SW value being maximized for the four-cluster solution (see Table 6.1). As in the previous cases, four-factor structure pattern is identified as the optimal factor structure of these items, regardless of which clustering algorithm is used. The result suggests that four-factor structure can be correctly visualized or mapped in a two dimensional space from MDS analysis.

6.3.4   Five-Factor Structure

Figure 6.4 shows the latent factor map of these 30 items (panel A), which clearly suggests a pattern of five clusters among items. The K function test suggests the clustered pattern in the space, as shown in panel B of Fig. 6.4 where the value of estimated K function is greater than the value of theoretical Poisson process. As shown in panel A of Fig. 6.4, the items in each cluster correspond well with the items that define each of the five factors. Cluster validation measures based on hierarchical, k-means, and PAM clustering algorithm indicated a five-cluster patterns with DI and SW value being maximized for the five-cluster solution (see Table 6.1). As in the previous cases, five-factor structure pattern is identified as the optimal factor structure of these items, regardless of which clustering algorithm is used. Thus, a two dimensional space can correctly display multi-factor structure.

6.4   Case Study 1: Identify Latent Structure of the Behavioral Activation for Depression Scale (BADS)

In previous sections, we show that a two-dimensional configuration can depict the complex factor structure pattern if the items have a clear simple structure. However, this will not likely be the case in actual research setting. In this part, we

Table 6.2 Twenty one items of the BADS Instrument developed by Kanter et al. (2006)

1. I stayed in bed for too long even though I had things to do.
2. There were certain things I needed to do that I didn't do.
3. I am content with the amount and types of things I did.
4. I engaged in a wide and diverse array of activities.
5. I made good decisions about what type of activities and/or situations I put myself in.
6. I was active, but did not accomplish any of goals for the day.
7. I was an active person and accomplished the goals I set out to do.
8. Most of what I did was to escape from or avoid something unpleasant.
9. I did things to avoid feeling sadness or other painful emotions.
10. I tried not to think about certain things.
11. I did things even though they were hard because they fit in with my long-term goals for myself.
12. I did something that was hard to do but it was worth it.
13. I spent a long time thinking over and over about my problems.
14. I kept trying to think of ways to solve a problem but never tried any of the solutions.
15. I frequently spent time thinking about my past, people who have hurt me, mistakes I've made, and other bad things in my history.
16. I did not see any of my friends.
17. I was withdrawn and quiet, even around people I know well.
18. I was not social, even though I had opportunities to be.
19. I pushed people away with my negativity.
20. I did things to cut myself off from other people.
21. I took time off work/school because I was too tired or didn't feel like going in.
22. My work/schoolwork/chores/responsibilities suffered because I was not as active as I needed to be.
23. I structured my day's activities.
24. I only engaged in activities that would distract me from feeling bad.
25. I began to feel badly when others around me expressed negative feelings or experiences.

show how an instrument can be examined based on the theoretical expectation of the factor structure (i.e., if the factor structure follows the simple structure pattern) discussed above.

Kanter et al. (2006) developed a 25-item self-report instrument to measure the purported changes in client behavior guided by response-contingent positive reinforcement (RCPR), which may occur directly or through increases in avoidance behavior controlled by aversive stimuli (Dimidjian et al. 2011). The measure is called the Behavior Activation for Depression Scale (BADS, see Table 6.2). Results, based on both exploratory factor analysis (EFA) and confirmatory factor analysis (CFA) from western samples, suggested a four-factor structure of the BADS (Barraca et al. 2011; Kanter et al. 2009; Raes et al. 2010): Activation, Avoidance/Rumination, Work/School Impairment, and Social Impairment. One interesting question about the instrument may be cultural differences regarding depression activation in non-Western population (Lu et al. 2010; Marsella et al. 1958; Zhang et al. 2011).

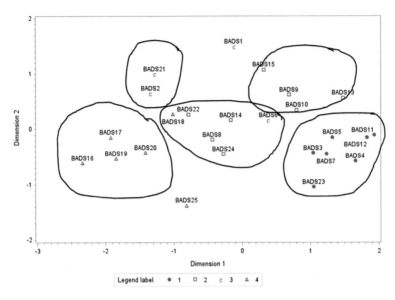

Fig. 6.5 BADS latent factor structure map. Circle indicates items that form original activation factor; triangle indicates items that form original social impairment factor; square indicates items that form avoidance factor; c indicates items that form original school impairment factor

In Western culture, individuals are viewed as independent, self-contained, and autonomous, with depressive symptoms being attributed to internal disturbances (Lewis-Fernandez and Kleinman 1994); In non-Western culture, such as in China, individuals are viewed as interdependent, connected with others, and defined by the social context. Thus, the same symptoms may be attributed to interpersonal disturbances (Markus and Kitayama 1991). In other words, the symptoms are defined by a particular cultural experience, and the meanings and implications of these same symptoms may vary considerably across cultures (Lu et al. 2010; Tsai and Chentsova-Dutton 2010). For example, some avoidance behaviors in a Western cultural context may be reviewed as mal-adaptive and social impairment, which may activate depression; but the same kinds of behaviors may be considered as normal or as coping strategies in a non-Western cultural context. Thus, the relationships among avoidance, rumination, or impairment behaviors may have a somewhat different pattern found in western culture.

With these cultural differences in mind, we performed a two-dimensional MDS analysis to obtain the latent factor map among these 25 items. Fig. 6.5 shows this latent factor map.

It can be seen that there are five possible clusters of items that lie more close to each other, as indicated by the drawn circles. Overall, the items in these five circles (i.e., clusters) match the original factor structure of activation, avoidance, work/school impairment, and social impairment, particularly for activation items, with all seven items clustering tightly together. Social impairment cluster has four original items that lie close together, but items 18 and 25 depart from this cluster. This may

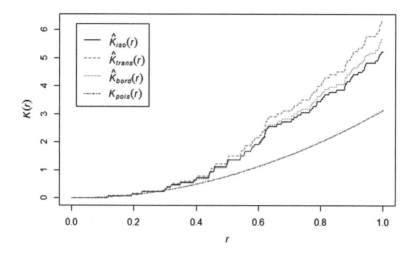

Fig. 6.6 K function plot with estimated function $\hat{K}$ (r) against theoretical function $K_{\text{pois}}(r)$ for BADS items

indicate that the behaviors assessed by these two items somewhat differ from the rest of the items. The most problematic items are those that define the original avoidance and school impairment factor. Specifically, items in original avoidance factor seem to split into two clusters. One cluster includes four original avoidance item and one social impairment item (i.e., item 18, which is more like avoidance item), which seem to assess avoidance. The second cluster includes two original avoidance items and one school impairment item (item 6), which seem to assess negative attempts (i.e., try not to do something). Original avoidance items 13 and 15 lie apart from each other and from the other items, which seems to assess dwelling on thoughts. The original four school impairment items scatter apart, with only two items laying close together (items 2 and 21). Items 1 and 6 lies far apart.

Based on the latent factor map, it seems that these five clusters capture the core patterns of BADS items in this Chinese sample. To further test whether the configuration of these items is CSR, K function test is conducted and the results are shown in Fig. 6.6. Clearly, which suggest that the BADS items have a clustered pattern rather than a random pattern. In addition, cluster validation indexes *DI* and *SW* value are maximized for a five cluster solution.

The five factors for this Chinese sample are: activation, social impairment, school impairment, avoidance, and negative attempts. The main differences between these five core patterns of BADS items and the original four factor structure are that (1) avoidance factor splits into two somewhat distinct clusters (avoidance and negative attempts) and (2) four items (items 1, 13, 15, and 25) that lie apart from the rest of the items do not seem to form the core pattern of these factors. Therefore, these four items can be removed from the item pool for further analysis.

Confirmatory factor analysis on the remaining 21 items with five factors is conducted. Each factor is defined by the items in the same circle as shown in Fig. 6.5. To determine the goodness-of-fit of the model, following fit indices were used: the Comparative Fit Index (CFI; Bentler 1990) and the goodness of fit (GFI; Byrne 1994), with a value of .95 and .90 indicating a excellent and acceptable fit, respectively; the Root Mean Square Error of Approximation (RMSEA; Steiger and Lind 1980, June) and the Standardized Root Mean Squared Residual (SRMR; Hooper et al. 2008), with value of less than 0.05 indicating a good fit and less than .08 demonstrating an acceptable fit.

The results of the five-factor model indicate a good model fit, with RMSEA = 0.059, 90% confidence interval = 0.050–0.064, p = 0.071; SRMR = 0.062, CFI = 0.93; GFI = 0.91. In order to see whether the original factor structure developed by Kanter et al (2006) could also have a good fit in this Chinese sample, we test the original 25-item four-factor model. The fit of the model is not good, with RMSEA = 0.065, 90% confidence interval = 0.060 − 0.071, p = 0.001; SRMR = 0.078, CFI = 0.807; GFI = 0.80. Thus, it seems that these 21 items define the five factor model better than the original items in this sample. Readers who are interested in this instrument can consult Li et al. (2014), who have discussed the cultural differences with respect to the behavioral activation for depression.

6.5   Case Study 2: Identify Latent Structure of DIBLES

Achievement test data from a group of 1169 kindergarteners were used as another example of data structure visualization. During the kindergarten, these children were tested three times (beginning, middle, and end of the kindergarten) using subscales of Dynamic Indicators of Basic Early Literacy Skills (DIBELS) (Good and Kaminski 2002). DIBELS was designed to assess three key early word literacy areas: phonological awareness, alphabetic principles, and fluency with connected text. The measures included for this example were (the more detailed description of these measures can be found at DIBELS official website[1]):

Initial sounds fluency (ISF) A measure of phonological awareness that assesses a child's ability to recognize and produce the initial sound in an orally presented word. For example, the examiner says, "This is sink, cat, gloves, and hat. Which picture begins with /s/?" and the child points to the correct picture.

Letter naming fluency (LNF) A standardized, individually administered test that provides a measure of risk of early literacy. Students are presented with a page of upper- and lower-case letters arranged in a random order and are asked to name as many letters as they can in 1 min.

---

[1] The description of the measures in the present study is based on those from official website of DIBEL measures. DIBELS official website is: https://dibels.uoregon.edu/measures.php.

Phoneme segmentation fluency (PSF) It is a measure that assesses a student's ability to segment three- and four-phoneme words into their individual phonemes fluently. The examiner orally presents words of three to four phonemes. It requires the student to produce verbally the individual phonemes for each word. For example, the examiner says "sat," and the student says "/s/ /a/ /t/" to receive three possible points for the word.

Nonsense word fluency (NWF) A measure of the alphabetic principle – including letter-sound correspondence in which letters represent their most common sounds and of the ability to blend letters into words in which letters represent their most common sounds. For example, if the stimulus word is "vaj", the student could say /v/ /a/ /j/ or say the word /vaj/ to obtain a total of three letter-sounds correct. The child is allowed 1 min to produce as many letter-sounds as he/she can.

Word use fluency (WUF) It is a test of vocabulary and oral language for assessment of at-risk for poor language and reading outcomes.

Depending on the time of assessment during the kindergarten, different subscales were used to assess word literacy progress. For example, at the beginning of the kindergarten, ISF, LNF, and WUF were assessed; at the middle of the kindergarten, ISF, LNF, PSF, NWF, and WUF were assessed; at the end of the kindergarten, LNF, PSF, NWF, and WUF were assessed. Although some of the same measures (e.g., LNF) were administered at a different time, the same measure seemed to assess different aspects or difficulty levels of the word literacy. Some interesting questions are: How are these subscales related to each other or have something in common? Could the same measure administered at a different time point be related closely together? These questions can help us to clarify how the subscales of DIBELS could be used in the analysis to study children's word development.

Basic non-metric MDS model was applied to the data, with 12 measures used as input. Specifically, these 12 measures came from 3 measures at the beginning of the kindergarten, 5 at the middle of the kindergarten, and 4 measures at the end of the kindergarten. The analysis was performed using *PROXSCAL* procedure (Data Theory Scaling System Group n.d.) in *SPSS* version 24. In the analysis, I used random start as initial MDS configuration, and the number of dimensions was specified to be 1–3. The results of fit measures from the analyses indicated that $S_1 = .09$ and Dispersion Accounted For (DAF) was .99 for the two dimensional solution. The three dimensional solutions had smaller S_1 value, but Dispersion Accounted For (DAF) was essentially the same. Thus, it seemed that the two dimensional solution could represent the structure underlying the data. Figure 6.7 shows the two-dimensional structure of the data. Inspection of the configuration indicated that the points along the dimension were distinct without any points collapsed together. Thus, the solution was not likely to be a degenerate solution.

The interesting information obtained from Fig. 6.7 was that the subscales were grouped based on the time dimension rather than content of subscales of DIBELS. That is, the subscales administered at each time formed a distinct cluster

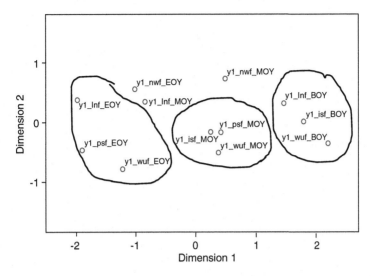

Fig. 6.7 Two dimension structure of 12 subscales of DIBELS during kindergarten. isf *Initial sounds fluency*, lnf *Letter naming fluency*, psf *Phoneme segmentation fluency*, nwf *Nonsense word fluency*, wuf *Word use fluency*. _E is end of year measurement; _M is middle of year measurement; _B is beginning of year measurement

on the basis of when the subscales were administered regardless of the content they assessed. Thus, it seemed reasonable that we could compute an average score of the subscales at each time point as an approximation of the word literacy progress at that time. For example, an average score at different time points can then be used for growth trajectory analysis of children's word literacy development. In addition, there are three subscales (nwf_moy, nwf_eoy, and inf_moy) did not seem to group closely together with the other corresponding subscales, indicating these three sub-scales may have different meaning to students. This difference may warrant further analysis. For the purpose of illustration, we re-analyzed the data without these three subscales. Figure 6.8 shows the configuration of the remaining 9 subscales. As can be seen, these 9 subscales line up well based on the time of assessment rather than the content of the subscales.

The interpretation of the results from the MDS analysis can typically be based on patterns of configuration and the meaning attached to such patterns, such as what we know about the variables and what connotations they may have. Therefore, it is sometimes not possible to interpret the whole of a configuration but rather to focus on part of it. Moreover, the issues of similarity transformations such as rotation, reflection, re-scaling, and translation can directly affect the interpretations of the configuration. Coxon (1982) discusses in great detail about the interpretation of the configuration. Because of these issues, the interpretation of the results from MDS analysis is not as straightforward as that in other methods such as factor analysis or cluster analysis; but all of these methods need more knowledge about the content area rather than just based on analytic results.

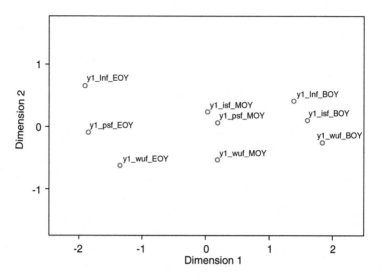

Fig. 6.8 Two dimension structure of nine subscales of DIBELS during kindergarten (without nwf_moy, nwf_eoy, and inf_moy). isf *Initial sounds fluency,* lnf *Letter naming fluency,* psf *Phoneme segmentation fluency,* nwf *Nonsense word fluency,* wuf *Word use fluency.* _E is end of year measurement; _M is middle of year measurement; _B is beginning of year measurement

6.6   Conclusion

The key point addressed in this chapter is that complex factor structures can be visualized and mapped in a two-dimensional space from MDS analysis. Traditionally, MDS model has been used in the similar way to factor analysis with respect to studying factor structure (e.g., Davison and Skay 1991). In such an application, MDS dimensions are considered to have the same meaning as factors from factor analysis. That is, each dimension represents a latent construct as does a factor. Thus, if a three-factor structure is assumed to underlie a set of items, then a three-dimensional solution is sought in MDS analysis to represent the three-construct structures.

However, what we are showing in this chapter is that MDS model can be used as a latent factor map that depicts the relationships among the items in contrast to the more common practices of MDS as a factor analytic tool. Thus, dimensions from MDS analysis do not have to represent latent constructs; that is, each dimension does not need to indicate the underlying construct of a set of items, and the dimensions simply provide a frame of reference. A two-dimensional solution of MDS can adequately capture the multifactor structure among items rather than having more than two dimensions to represent these multiple factor structures, as we have shown here. Simulation-based data are used to show that the latent map can correctly display the pattern of clustered items that define a latent factor if these items form a clear simple structure pattern, as that stated by Thurstone (1947).

A latent factor map from MDS analysis can serve as a start talking point for studying the relationships among items with respect to the latent constructs embedded in these items. One advantage of using latent factor map is that we can visually identify the core items that are lie close together for further analysis. To illustrate this point, we used the real data to demonstrate how we further evaluated the BADS measure in a Chinese sample using latent factor map and further test the measurement model via confirmatory factor analysis. As a tool for the behavioral sciences, the latent factor map from an MDS analysis can be a mid-step between complex theory and models by providing researchers with a way to generate plausible models that represent the cutting edge of how we statistically test our theories. As Aiken and West (1991) did with the scatterplot for graphical representation of regression interaction, latent factor map provides an analog, which is a graphical representation of multifactor structures among questionnaire items. It provides a way to directly translate latent factor map to testable measurement models and back again.

There are also some limitations to this approach. First, although we can identify the core items that may define a construct or a network, there is still an issue of whether the items lay apart should be part of the cluster. Second, it is somewhat subjective with respect to how a cluster is defined, particularly when the items do not lie close together. In the case of BADS items, we can see that items related to avoidance and school impairment may be clustered in a different way. These issues cannot be definitely solved based on latent factor map and only replication or theory can help to clarify the conceptual issues at hand. Despite these limitations, visualization of item structure using a MDS two-dimensional map can be a useful method to conduct research.

References

Aiken, L. S., & West, S. G. (1991). *Multiple regression: Testing and interpreting interactions*. Thousand Oaks: Sage.

Barraca, J., Pérez-Álvarez, M., & Bleda, J. H. L. (2011). Avoidance and activation as keys to depression: Adaptation of the behavioral activation for depression scale in a Spanish sample. *The Spanish Journal of Psychology, 14*(2), 998–1009.

Bentler, P. M. (1990). Comparative fit indices in structural models. *Psychological Bulletin, 107*, 238–246.

Bivand, R. S., Pebesma, E. J., & Gómez-Rubio, V. (2013). *Applied spatial analysis with R* (2nd ed.). New York: Springer.

Brock, G., Pihur, V., Datta, S., & Datta, S. (2008). clValid: An R package for cluster validation. *Journal of Statistical Software, 25*(4), 1–22.

Bühler, J., Keller, F., & Läge, D. (2014). Activation as an overlooked factor in the BDI–II: A factor model based on core symptoms and qualitative aspects of depression. *Psychological Assessment, Advance Online Publication, 26*(3), 970. https://doi.org/10.1037/a0036755.

Butner, J. E., Gagnon, K. T., Geuss, M. N., Lessard, D. A., & Story, T. N. (2014). Utilizing topology to generate and test theories of change. *Psychological Methods, 20*(1), 1–25. Online First. doi: https://doi.org/10.1037/a0037802.

Byrne, B. M. (1994). *Structural equation modeling with EQS and EQS/Windows*. Thousand Oaks: Sage Publications.

Cohen, A. (2008). The underlying structure of the Beck Depression Inventory II: A multidimensional scaling approach. *Journal of Research in Personality, 42*, 779–786. https://doi.org/10.1016/j.jrp.2007.09.007.

Coxon, A. P. M. (1982). *The user's guide to multidimensional scaling*. London: Heinemann Educational Books.

Data Theory Scaling System Group. (n.d.). *PROXSCAL (Version 1.0)*. Leiden university, Netherlands: Faculty of Social and Behavioral Sciences.

Davies, P. M., & Coxon, A. P. M. (Eds.). (1982). *Key texts in multidimensional scaling*. London: Heinemann Educational Books.

Davison, M. L. (1985). Multidimensional scaling versus components analysis of test intercorrelations. *Psychological Bulletin, 97*(1), 94–105.

Davison, M. L., & Skay, C. L. (1991). Multidimensional scaling and factor models of test and item responses. *Psychological Bulletin, 110*, 551–556.

DeSarbo, W. S., Howard, D., & Jedidi, K. (1991). Multiclus: A new method for simultaneously performing multidimensional scaling and cluster analysis. *Psychometrika, 56*, 121–136.

Diggle, P. J. (2003). *Statistical analysis of spatial point patterns*. London: Arnold.

Dimidjian, S., Barrera, M. R., Martell, C., Munoz, R. F., & Lewinsohn, P. M. (2011). The origins and current status of behavioral activation treatments for depression. *Annual Review of Clinical Psychology, 7*, 1–38.

Dopazo, J., & Carazo, J. M. (1997). Phylogenetic reconstruction using a growing neural network that adopts the topology of a phylogenetic tree. *Journal of Molecular Evolution Psychiatrique, 44*(2), 226–233.

Dunn, J. C. (1974). Well separated clusters and fuzzy partitions. *Journal on Cybernetics, 4*, 95–104.

Fraley, R. C., & Raftery, A. (2007). Model-based methods of classification: Using the mclust software in chemometrics. *Journal of Statistical Software, 18*(6), 1–13.

Good, R. H., & Kaminski, R. A. (Eds.). (2002). *Dynamic indicators of basic early literacy skills* (6th ed.). Eugene: Institute for the Development of Educational Achievement.

Handl, J., Knowles, J., & Kell, D. B. (2005). Computational cluster validation in post-genomic data analysis. *Bioinformatics, 21*(15), 3201–3212.

Hartigan, J. A., & Wong, M. A. (1979). A k-means clustering algorithm. *Applied Statistics, 28*, 100–108.

Hooper, D., Coughlan, J., & Mullen, M. R. (2008). Structural equation modelling: Guidelines for determining model fit. *The Electronic Journal of Business Research Methods, 6*(1), 53–60.

Kanter, J. W., Mulick, P. S., Busch, A. M., Berlin, K. S., & Martell, C. R. (2006). The Behavioral Activation for Depression Scale (BADS): Psychometric properties and factor structure. *Journal of Psychopathology and Behavioral Assessment, 29*(3), 191–202.

Kanter, J. W., Rusch, L. C., Busch, A. M., & Sedivy, S. K. (2009). Confirmatory factor analysis of the Behavioral Activation for Depression Scale (BADS) in a community sample with elevated depressive symptoms. *Journal of Psychopathology and Behavioral Assessment, 31*, 36–42. https://doi.org/10.1007/s10862-008-9088-y.

Kaufman, L., & Rousseeuw, P. J. (1990). *Finding groups in data. An introduction to cluster analysis*. New York: Wiley.

Kohonen, T. (1997). *Self-organizing maps* (2nd ed.). New York: Springer-Verlag.

Läge, D., Egli, S., Riedel, M., & Möller, H. J. (2012). Exploring the structure of psychopathological symptoms: A re-analysis of AMDP data by robust nonmetric multidimensional scaling. *European Archives of Psychiatry and Clinical Neurosciences, 262*, 227–238. https://doi.org/10.1007/s00406-011-0271-x.

Lewis-Fernandez, R., & Kleinman, A. (1994). Culture, personality, and psychopathology. *Journal of Abnormal Psychology, 103*(1), 67–71.

Li, M., Ding, C., Kanter, J. W., Zeng, Q., & Yang, D. (2014). Further evaluation of the psychometric properties of the behavioral activation for depression scale. *International Journal of Psychology and Psychological Therapy, 14*(1), 45–57.

Liebovitch, L. S., Peluso, P. R., Norman, M. D., Su, J., & Gottman, J. M. (2011). Mathematical model of the dynamics of psychotherapy. *Cognitive Neurodynamics, 5*, 265–275. https://doi.org/10.1007/s11571-011-9157-x.

Lu, A., Bond, M. H., Friedman, M., & Chan, C. (2010). Understanding cultural influences on depression by analyzing a measure of its constituent symptoms. *International Journal of Psychological Studies, 2*(1), 55–70.

Markus, H. R., & Kitayama, S. (1991). Culture and the self: Implications for cognition, emotion, and motivation. *Psychological Review, 98*(2), 224–253.

Marsella, A. J., Sartorius, N., Jablensky, A., & Fenton, F. (1958). Crosscultural studies of depressive disorders: An overview. In A. Kleinman & B. Good (Eds.), *Culture and depression* (pp. 299–324). Berkeley, CA: Berkeley University of California Press.

Maxwell, A. E. (1972). Difficulties in a dimensional description of symptomatology. *British Journal of Psychiatry, 121*, 19–26.

Molenaar, P. C. M. (1985). A dynamic factor model for the analysis of multivariate time series. *Psychometrika, 50*, 181–202. https://doi.org/10.1007/BF02294246.

Molenaar, P. C. M., & Campbell, C. G. (2009). The new person-specific paradigm in psychology. *Current Directions in Psychological Science, 18*, 112–117. https://doi.org/10.1111/j.1467-8721.2009.01619.x.

Raes, F., Hoes, D., Van Gucht, D., Kanter, J. W., & Hermans, D. (2010). The Dutch version of the Behavioral Activation for Depression Scale (BADS): Psychometric properties and factor structure. *Journal of Behavioral Therapy and Exprimental Psychiatry, 41*(3), 246–250.

Rousseeuw, P. J. (1987). Silhouettes: A graphical aid to the interpretation and validation of cluster analysis. *Journal of Computational and Applied Mathematics, 20*, 53–65.

Schlessinger, I. M., & Guttman, L. (1969). Smaller space analysis of intelligence and achievement tests. *Psychological Bulletin, 71*, 95–100.

Schwartz, S. H. (2006). Basic human values: Theory, measurement, and applications. *Revue française de sociologie, 42*, 249–288.

Steiger, J. H., & Lind, J. M. (1980). *Statistically based tests for the number of common factors.* Iowa City: Paper presented at the Psychometric Society.

Steinmeyer, E. M., & Möller, H. J. (1992). Facet theoretic analysis of the Hamilton–D Scale. *Journal of Affective Disorders, 25*, 53–61. https://doi.org/10.1016/0165-0327(92)90093-L.

Thurstone, L. L. (1947). *Multiple factor analysis.* Chicago: University of Chicago Press.

Tsai, J. L., & Chentsova-Dutton, Y. (2010). Understanding Depression across cultures. In I. H. Gotlib & C. L. Hammen (Eds.), *Handbook of depression.* New York: The guilford press.

Tukey, J. W. (1980). We need both exporatory and confirmatory. *The American Statistician, 34*, 23–25.

Wright, S. (1921). Correlation and causation. *Journal of Agricultural Research, 20*, 557–585.

Zhang, B., Fokkema, M., Cuijpers, P., Li, J., Smits, N., & Beekman, A. (2011). Measurement invariance of the Center for Epidemiological Studies Depression Scale (CES-D) among Chinese and Dutch elderly. *BMC Medical Research Methodology, 11*, 74.

Chapter 7
Individual Differences MDS Model

Abstract Discuss the fundamental concepts of individual differences MDS analysis. An example of real data is provided to illustrate interpretation of the results. Estimation of the model is presented but readers can skip this part. Potential use of the model is discussed.

Keyword Individual differences MDS model · INDISCAL · Group space · Individual dimensional weight

In this chapter, we discuss how individual differences can be modeled in MDS analysis. The technical aspects of individual differences MDS model (INDSCAL) was discussed in Chap. 3. As we discussed in Chap. 3, individual differences MDS model (Carroll and Chang 1970) is also known as weighted Euclidean model and it is more used in practice. Thus, in this chapter we mainly focus on the ideas of INDSCAL and how it can be used in educational and psychological research. In addition, we discuss the use of INDSCAL in longitudinal analysis, which is not traditionally discussed in MDS literature.

7.1 Ideas of INDSCAL

Individual differences MDS model is typically used when we have participants make ratings on a set of variables and want to examine how individuals differ among themselves in the way they perceive the characteristics of the construct as measured by this set of variables. This is why it is called individual differences MDS model. As indicated by Horan (1969) and Caroll and Chang (1970), we can presume that each individual or a group of individuals may use various attributes of the construct (e.g., effective teaching) when making ratings on the items with respect to the construct; that is, we may view or define effective teaching in different ways. Then we have a latent or group space (i.e., latent common space) that consists of all the attributes all the individuals happen to use. Each individual's space can now be thought

© Springer International Publishing AG, part of Springer Nature 2018   97
C. S. Ding, *Fundamentals of Applied Multidimensional Scaling for Educational and Psychological Research*, https://doi.org/10.1007/978-3-319-78172-3_7

as a special case or sub-case of the group space because the individual is using some or part of the total available information. Each individual's space can be termed as his or her private space. For example, we may often have correlation or distance matrices computed from a set of items of self-efficacy on mathematic ability for different groups of students such as male vs. female or disability status. Then we want to know how these subgroups differ. As another example, we can test the students' self-efficacy on mathematic ability four times over a year. Then we have one correlation or distance matrix for each time, resulting in four correlation or distance matrices for each student or averaged across all students. We want to see whether the students differ in perceived self-efficacy on mathematic ability over time. That is, we want to see how each group's private space differs from each other.

In these examples, we have two ways to handle the distance matrix. The first way is to compute distance matrix for each individual. The second way is to compute distance matrix for a subgroup across all individuals in that subgroup (e.g., female group) or for a particular time across all individuals. The first case is more suitable to analysis of single-subject design in which we can compare how each individual differ with respect to behavioral phenomenon under inquiry. The second case is more common in psychological and educational research setting.

To operationalize this idea of individual differences with respect to the group (i.e., latent space) into MDS analysis, we assume that each individual attaches a different weight or preference to each dimension which represents his or her degree of salience, attention, typicality, or importance of that dimension when he or she makes rating. Thus, each individual has his or her unique set of weights, and these weights represent the way in which the individuals differ with respect to the importance or salience attached to each of the dimensions. For example, an individual who attaches equal salience to each of the dimensions will have a set of weight of the equal or very similar value. It happens that the group or latent space represents such an individual. In contrast, individuals who attach different weight to each dimension systematically deviate from this group space into his or her own private space. Accordingly, INDSCAL is a method of modeling both group space and private space, showing how individuals vary in terms of differing weights being associated with the same dimensions. Although INDSCAL has a dimensional interpretation in that we attach some meaning to each dimension (i.e., interpretation is made according to what each of the dimensions may indicate), we could also use clustered pattern in the configuration and their relationships to individual weights for interpretation.

In order to be more concrete on these ideas, Fig. 7.1 shows an example of group space and individual space.

The example in Fig. 7.1 was a self-assessment survey of professional development outcomes completed by teachers who participated in a 5-day training workshop on common core state standards as well as teaching pedagogy. Table 7.1 shows the content of each survey question.

As can be seen in Fig. 7.1, there were clearly three clusters of items in a two-dimensional space. Items 3, 4, 5, 7, and 11 seemed to assess learning on teaching practices in general; items 6 and 8 on teaching related to ELL; items 2, 9, 10 on

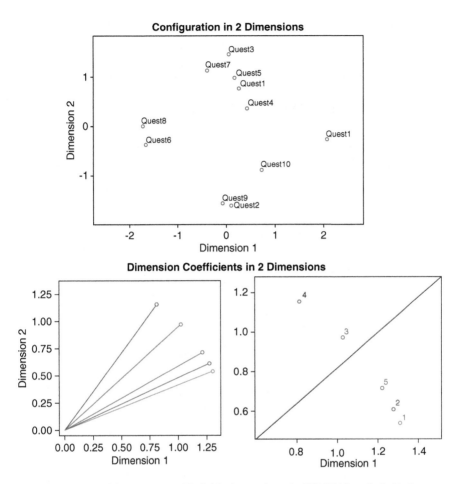

Fig. 7.1 Examples of Group space and individual space from the INDSCAL analysis. Each vector represents each day rather than individual, suggesting the salience or perceived focus of training for that day. The dash line indicates that the subjects are equally represented by the two-dimensions. The great departure from this theoretically equal presentation indicates the individual differences

learning new teaching skills related to IIMP. Item 1 seemed to assess the knowledge level of common core state standards in the mathematical content area. This item was alone by itself since it was not related to any teaching skills or practices.

The individual space at the bottom of Fig. 7.1 shows the individual's weight vector. First, the length of these five vectors was equal, indicating they fit the data equally well. Second, the direction of vectors for days 1, 2, and 5 seemed to point more toward Dimension 1, while that vector 4 toward Dimension 2. This result indicated that at Days 1, 2, and 5 teachers reported to learn more on learning new teaching skills related to IIMP and common core state standards. At Day 4 teachers reported to learn more on new teaching skills or practices. At Day 3 they reported to

Table 7.1 Survey items assessing outcomes of professional development on teaching pedagogy

Quest1. I have adequate knowledge of the common Core state standards (CCSS) in the mathematical content area.
Quest2. I have learned new strategies to help students solidify their understanding of mathematical concepts and practice new skills.
Quest3 . I have learned new pedagogical mathematic teaching activities that I can apply to my classroom instruction.
Quest4. I have learned critical thinking practices to provide differentiated instructional strategies to apply to my classroom instruction.
Quest5. I have learned how to develop effective cooperative teaching strategies to form a sense of community.
Quest6. I have learned effective and appropriate teaching strategies to address the needs of ELL learners I (will) have in my classes
Quest7. I have learned collaborative tools to develop and maintain a professional learning community to support student learning.
Quest8. I am more aware of the needs of ELL learners when I (will) prepare mathematic instruction.
Quest9. I have learned a variety of teaching tools from today's IIMP.
Quest10. I can develop an IIMPed math lesson based on what I have learned from this IIMP session.
Quest11. I have learned how intentional and guided IIMPs can move me to an advanced level of preparing and implementing durable teaching practices.

Table 7.2 Simulated distance matrix among three items for two individuals

Individual 1			Individual 2		
Item 1	Item 2	Item 3	Item 1	Item 2	Item 3
0	2	2	0	1	2
2	0	2	1	0	2
2	2	0	2	2	0

learn equally about everything since its dimensional weights were about the same along each of the two dimensions.

Thus, the individual differences MDS model provides us with a clear picture of how individual perceived a phenomenon or behave in different ways. In this example, we examine intra-individual differences longitudinally. Of course, we can also study inter-individual differences if we had five different groups of teachers rather than one group of teachers who were assessed five times over time. This is the first time that INDSCAL is applied to education setting in this fashion.

Table 7.3 Scalar product matrix among three items for two individuals

Individual 1				Individual 2		
	Item 1	Item 2	Item 3	Item 1	Item 2	Item 3
Item 1	1.33	−0.67	−0.67	0.67	0.17	−0.83
Item 2	−0.67	1.33	−0.67	0.17	0.67	−0.83
Item 3	−0.67	−0.67	1.33	−0.83	−0.83	1.67

Table 7.4 Initial configuration

Dim 1	Dim 2
−0.41	0.71
−0.41	−0.71
0.82	0.00

7.2   Estimation of Group Configuration and Individual Dimensional Weights

To understand how the INDSCAL analysis works, it is useful to have some ideas of how the group configuration and individual weights are estimated. The estimation goes through the iterative process, which is outlined below based on the discussion by Davison (1983). In order to be concrete, we use simulated data to illustrate the process. The data consist of two distance matrices among three items or variables, one for each of the two individuals. The distance matrix for each individual is shown below (Table 7.2).

Step 1 Convert each individual's distance into scalar product matrix (i.e., double-centered matrix), as shown in Table 7.3.

Step 2 Specify a starting or initial configuration. This can be done using different methods such as metric initial configuration or random start, as discussed in Chap. 5. The initial configuration can be obtained by (1) computing average scalar product matrix and (2) do eigenvalue decomposition or principal component analysis. Table 7.4 shows the initial scale value by principal component analysis of the averaged scalar product matrix.

Step 3 Start iterations.

Phase 1: Estimate Individual Weight First, the scalar product matrix for each individual is converted into matrix A, each row of which is for each individual and each column is for a pair of items. That is, rows of matrix A represent individuals

Table 7.5 Matrices A and B

		(1,1)	(1,2)	(1,3)	(2,1)	(2,2)	(2,3)	(3,1)	(3,2)	(3,3)
A=	P1	1.33	−0.67	−0.67	−0.67	1.33	−0.67	−0.67	−0.67	1.33
	P2	0.67	0.17	−0.83	0.17	0.67	−0.83	−0.83	−0.83	1.67
B=	Dim 1	0.17	0.17	−0.33	0.17	0.17	−0.33	−0.33	−0.33	0.67
	Dim 2	0.50	−0.50	0.00	−0.50	0.50	0.00	0.00	0.00	0.00

Note. (n, m) indicates position of the value in the scalar product matrix, with the first number indicates column and the second number indicates row. For example, (1, 2) in row one indicates the value at the first column and the second row, which is −0.67.

Table 7.6 Estimated individual weights along with dimension

Dimension	Individual 1	Individual 2
1	1.19	1.26
2	1.19	0.84

Table 7.7 New matrix A of augmented individual scalar product matrix

Individual 1				Individual 2		
	Item 1	Item 2	Item 3	Item 1	Item 2	Item 3
Item 1	1.33	−0.67	−0.67	0.67	0.17	−0.83
Item 2	−0.67	1.33	−0.67	0.17	0.67	−0.83
Item 3	−0.67	−0.67	1.33	−0.83	−0.83	1.67

Table 7.8 New matrix B

	(1,1)	(1,2)	(1,3)	(2,1)	(2,2)	(2,3)
Dim 1	−0.58	−0.58	1.15	−0.65	−0.65	1.29
Dim 2	1.00	−1.00	0.00	0.50	−0.50	0.00

Note. For each pair of (w, v), w indicates individual weight and v indicates item or variable. For example, pair (2, 1) indicates the value for the second individual with the first variable.

and columns represent distance between each pair of items. Second, initial starting configuration is converted into matrix B, where each row represents dimension and each column indicates each pair of items computed by $b_{k(i,j)} = x_{ik}x_{jk}$. Table 7.5 shows the matrices A and B.

After constructing matrices A and B, the individual weights can be estimated as

$$W = \sqrt{\left(BB^T\right)^{-1} BA^T}$$

Table 7.6 shows the estimated individual weight matrix.

This completes the phase 1 of the first iteration and starts Phase 2 of the first iteration.

Table 7.9 Current scale value estimates

	Dim 1	Dim 2
Item 1	−0.61	0.90
Item 2	−0.61	−0.90
Item 3	1.23	0.00

Phase 2: Estimate the Scale Value of the New Configuration To estimate the new configuration, new matrices A and B need to be reconstructed. The new matrix A consists of an augmented individual scalar product matrix, which is shown in Table 7.7.

Matrix B consists of k row, with each row representing a dimension, and wx columns (i.e., item and individual or subject weight pair). The entries of matrix B is $b_{k(sj)} = w^2_{ks}x_{jk}$, where w^2_{ks} and x_{jk} are the recent or previous estimates of individual weights and scale values (e.g., from the initial configuration and the first estimated individual weights). Table 7.8 shows this new matrix B.

After the new matrix A and B are constructed, the matrix of new coordinates of the configuration can be estimated as follows:

$$X = AB^T \left(BB^T\right)^{-1}$$

This matrix X becomes the current coordinate or scale value estimates, which is shown in Table 7.9.

After the estimation of the current scale values, the first iteration is finished and the second iteration starts. The iteration process stops when the sum of squared differences between predicted and observed scalar products are minimized:

$$F = \Sigma\left(d_{ijs} - d^*_{ijs}\right)$$

where d_{ijs} is the actual scalar product matrix and d^*_{ijs} is model estimated or predicted scalar product matrix. The iteration stops when value in F from one iteration to the next does not improve according to the pre-specified value such as 0.001.

After the completion of iterations, the scale values of each dimension is standardized so that the variance of the scale values along each dimension equals to 1.00. The individual weights are estimated one last time.

7.3 Dimensionality and Interpretation

Determining dimensionality in INDSCAL analysis is somewhat different from the basic MDS analysis in that we usually rely on individual's percentage of variance accounted for by the model rather than on the stress value of the model. Sometimes an additional dimension may be needed because some individuals have high weights on this dimension, although it does not improve the overall fit of the model. In this case, we can keep this additional dimension because these individuals use of it are quite similar to each other but different from the rest.

The interpretation of the results from the INDSCAL model (or weighted Euclidean model) follows the same principles as discussed previously with one exception: rotation. That is, the solution cannot be rotated since the group configuration is tied into the participants' configuration and the solution is unique to these individuals. The configuration is unique because the stretching and shrinking is permitted only along the coordinate axes. Thus, rotation problem disappears in weighted Euclidean model.

However, it is first necessary to understand clearly the features of the group space, individual or subject space, and their interrelationships. The group space, X, is a latent configuration of a set of variables in a particular number of dimensions. In fact, the group space from the INDSCAL analysis is always similar to the solution or configuration from the basic MDS analysis as discussed in Chap. 5 except for a difference in orientation and stretching of axes. It acts as the reference configuration from which the individuals' space may be derived. This group configuration is unique in the sense that it cannot be rotated as in other MDS models because it is tied to the individual space. Strictly speaking, the group space represents an individual case who equally weights the dimension, and if an individual's subject weight departs markedly from equality (i.e., from the diagonal line), then we may tell where the individual differences lie. In the above example of teaching training data, we can see that day 3 was not greatly away from the diagonal line, while the rest of days were far away from the diagonal line. Thus, the MDS solution from the basic MDS analysis is based on the averaged data from all subjects or individuals, and this averaged space may misrepresent the perceptual structure of some individuals. The INDSCAL model provides a way to "disaggregate" the information by modeling each individual's perceptual structure with respect to the group or averaged space.

On the other hand, individual space is indicated by a set of weights and it has the same dimensions as the group space. Individual weights in individual space are represented by a vector located by the value of the weights on each of the dimensions, as shown in Fig. 7.1. The important information in the subject weight to consider is (1) the direction in which a point is located from the origin, which indicates the individual's perceptual tendency and (2) the distance from the origin, which indicates how well the individual's data are explained by the model. In order to assess the degree of individual differences, it is better to focus on the angular separation between subject vectors. The smaller the angle of separation, the more similar is the pattern of weights. In a lower dimensional space such as two or even three dimensional space, we can visualize the sheaves of vectors in the subject space.

Thus, the squared individual's weight on a dimension is approximately equal to the proportion of variance in the individual's data that can be accounted for by that dimension, and the squared distance from the origin of the subject space to the subject's point in that space is approximately equal to the proportion of variance in the individual's data that can be accounted for by the model. Moreover, if the subject weights are a very small negative value, it may be considered as approximation to a zero weight. If the value of negative subject weights is large, it may indicate that the model does not hold well for the individuals.

When we find the individual differences with respect to the group space, we can perform subsequent analysis by relating individual's weights to a set of covariates to examine the association between such individual differences and potential predictors. For example, if demographical, attitudinal, or personality information is available, we can examine whether individuals who have high weights on a dimension differ from those with low weights on these variables by conducting regression or discriminant analysis.

7.4 Useful Applications of INDSCAL Analysis

There are several useful applications of MDS INDSCAL model in educational and psychological research. In the first application, we may have the latent configuration from prior investigations and are only interested in determining the individual differences. In this case, the expected or hypothesized group space (i.e., latent configuration) that is obtained from either theory or previous analysis with respect to how the variables under inquiry should be related to each other is used as a starting configuration. The analysis with zero iterations is performed, which keeps the expected configuration fixed while solving for the individual space weights. One of such an analysis focuses on studying individual differences (e.g., female vs. male group) with respect to the known theoretical configuration.

In the application of longitudinal analysis, data from different time period can be compared with respect to a common frame of reference, as we have done in the example of professional development. In such a case, we are interested in knowing how individual's behavior changes over time. Also in trend analysis, we can also compare new data with the old data to see how individuals of the similar characteristics such as gender, the same cohort, or the same income level with respect the configuration (for both group and individual spaces) changes over time.

In the third application, we can use the INDSCAL model to examine value or behavioral feature transmission across generations such as from parents to children with respect to view of the world. In this situation, we can compare weights of parents and children with respect to a common frame of reference of world view. Or we can conduct regression analysis by using parental measures to predict children's preference as assessed by the subject weights.

The fourth application of the INDSCAL model is the instrument development or test construction. In such an application, we can use the model to select items that have a particular set of characteristics with respect to a behavior under inquiry. For example, for a given item that assesses anxiety, INDSCAL model can be used to see to what degree this item assesses frequency, intensity, or harmfulness in comparison to other items in the instrument. In addition, we can also employ INDSCAL to study construct validity in which group differences can be examine based on hypothesized group difference with respect to the instrument. For instance, items

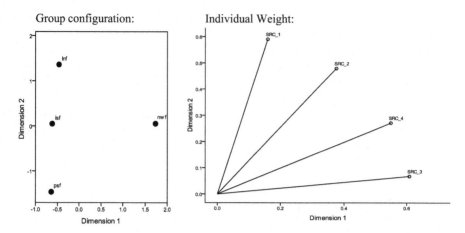

Fig. 7.2 Latent group configuration of subscales of DIBELS for the assessment at the middle of kindergarten and their weight space. (isf *initial sound fluency*, lnf *letter naming fluency*, psf *phoneme segmentation fluency*, nwf *nonsense word fluency*)

that assess anxiety should be weighted more by individuals with a high level of anxiety than those with a low level of the same trait. INDSCAL can provide a visualization of such group differences with respect to a set of items.

7.5　INDSCAL Analysis of DIBELS

In this example, we use the same DIBELS data as in Chap. 6, where we visualized the data structure of DIBELS subscales within a grade level. The research question concerns with how the subscales of DIBELS is structured within a grade level. It is found that these measures are organized according to the time of measurement rather than the content they assess.

In this example of DIBEELS, the question is conceptualized differently, and we are interested in the question of how each child scored differently on a set of word literacy measures at a particular time point. That is, do children reach the same proficiency level on all the subscales at a given time?

For the purpose of illustration, we used the four subscales that were administered in the middle of the kindergarten: initial sound fluency (ISF), letter naming fluency (LNF), phonemic sound fluency (PSF), and nonsense word fluency (NWF). In order to simplify the analysis for didactic purposes, we randomly selected four children and examined their differences with respect to their standing on each of these four subscales. A high scale value between two subscales indicated that children scored them differently. Thus, a distance matrix for each child could be considered as a measure of discrepancy between subscales.

Weighted Euclidean model was conducted on the data from these four children. A two- dimensional solution was estimated, with fit measures indicating a good

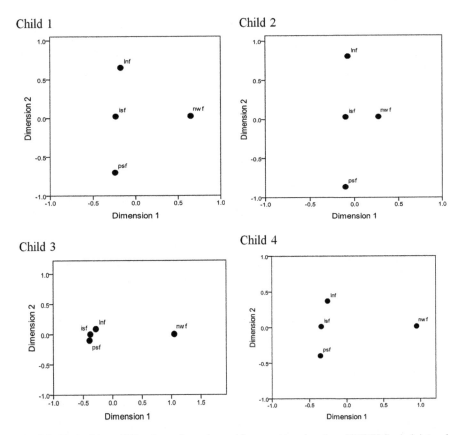

Fig. 7.3 Each of four children's configurations with respect to subscales of DIBELS administered at the middle of kindergarten. (isf *initial sound fluency*, lnf *letter naming fluency*, psf *phoneme segmentation fluency*, nwf *nonsense word fluency*)

model fit. Figure 7.2 shows the group configuration and individual dimensional weight. Dimension 1 seemed to indicate that, on average, children scored NWF differently from the other three subscales. Dimension 2 seemed to indicate that LNF and PSF scored differently from ISF and NWF.

Group configuration: Individual Weight:

Individual weight plot indicated how these children scored differently on the four subscales, and these individual configurations were shown in Fig. 7.3. As can be seen in Fig. 7.3, Child 1's scores on these four subscales were more like that in Dimension 2, scoring similar on ISF and NWF but differently on LNF and PSF. On the other hand, Child 3 scored similar on LNF, ISF, and PSF but differently on NWF. Children 2 and 4 scored more like the group configuration.

These individual configurations may have implications for education intervention. For example, we could examine the cognitive functions that underlie the differences in how children learn the materials as assessed by the DIBELS. By looking into what these differences are, we could also examine children's personal characteristics that may be related to word literacy progress. In addition, the weighted Euclidean model could serve as an analytical technique for single (or multiple) case(s) study in which the purpose is to analyze how people frame and solve problems. The results could produce empirical generalizations regarding intervention rationality, treatment, and normative reasoning.

7.6 Conclusion

In this chapter, we discussed the basic concepts of individual differences MDS model and illustrate how the configuration for both group and individual in INDSCAL model can be estimated and interpreted. A real-life example is used to provide a concrete demonstration. Many applications of INDSCAL model can be useful in educational and psychological research, which needs to be explored more in future research. As it stands now, little educational and psychological research utilizes the model due to its unfamiliarity to researchers. Using INDSCAL model for hypothesis testing and test construction are particularly interesting and it is uncharted territory.

References

Carroll, J. D., & Chang, J. J. (1970). Analysis of individual differences in multidimensional scaling via an N-way generalization of "Eckart-young" decomposition. *Psychometrika, 35*, 238–319.
Davison, M. L. (1983). *Multidimensional scaling*. New York: Wiley.
Horan, C. B. (1969). Multidimensional scaling: Combining observations when individuals have different perceptual structure. *Psychometrika, 34*, 139–165.

Chapter 8
MDS Preference Analysis

Abstract Discuss the fundamental concepts of MDS preference analysis. An example of real data is provided to illustrate interpretation of the results. Single-ideal point MDS analysis is also explained.

Keywords Preference model · Vector representation · Ideal-point · Single-ideal point

Using MDS model for analysis of individual preference is probably one of the most interesting aspects of MDS, but it is also a confusing part in that the concept of individual preference can be defined in various ways. For example, in individual differences MDS analysis discussed in Chap. 7, individual weight can be thought as preferences, although the dimension weight of individuals typically indicates the dimensional saliency. Sometimes even the mean score computed from a set of items can be thought of as an indicator of an individual's preference, with a higher score indicating higher preference. However, the preference MDS analysis has its theoretical roots back in 1950s when Coombs (1950, 1964) first introduced the unfolding MDS with J scale and I scale and proposed a distance model for preference data, often known as the unfolding model. It is the only method that has explicit methodologically theoretical foundation for assessment of individual preferences. In this chapter, we discuss the basic ideas of preference MDS analysis and its potential applications in educational and psychological research.

8.1 Basic Ideas of Preference MDS

The ideas of MDS preference analysis can be described in terms of vector model or distance model (i.e., ideal point model). A vector preference model is the one in which an individual's preference is represented by a vector (i.e., a straight line) in a latent configuration of variables, where the angular separation of the vectors corresponds to the data dissimilarities. On the other hand, in distance model both

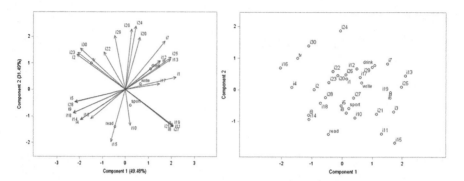

Fig. 8.1 Vector model and distance (ideal point) model of individual preferences with respect to reading, writing, drinking, TV watching, and playing sports

individual preference and behaviors are represented as points in the configuration, where the distance between points in a space represents the data dissimilarities. Figure 8.1 shows a result of MDS preference analysis using both types of models based on a hypothetical data that are preference ratings by 30 individuals with regard to five behaviors (reading, writing, drinking, TV watching, and playing sport) on a scale of 1–5, with 5 being most preferred. As can be seen in Fig. 8.1, some individuals prefer playing sports (vectors that point toward 5 and 6 o'clock), one prefers reading (7 o'clock vectors), some prefer TV watching and drinking (vectors point toward 10 o'clock). Six people prefer anything but playing sports and reading (vectors toward between 11 and 1 o'clock), while seven people prefer anything but writing and drinking (vectors toward 8 o'clock). The same preference is represented by distance model on the right of Fig. 8.1.

In vector model, the direction of the vectors indicates the individual's preference; that is, the direction of the vector indicates the direction that is most preferred by the individuals, with preference increasing as the vector moves from the origin. On the other hand, the relative lengths of the vectors indicate fit of individuals, with the squared lengths being proportion of variance in preference that can be accounted for by the model. As can be seen in Fig. 8.1, some vectors (e.g., individuals 10, 17, and 22) have a shorter length, indicating that the model does not account well for these individuals' preferences. For example, only 18% of preference for individual 10 is accounted for by the model. Thus, to interpret the biplot (plot of row and column) of preference, look for directions through the plot that show a continuous change in some attribute of the behaviors, or look for regions in the plot that contain clusters of behavior points and determine what attributes the behaviors have in common. Behavior points that are tightly clustered in a region of the plot represent behaviors that have the same preference patterns across the individuals. Vectors that point in roughly the same direction represent individuals who have similar preference patterns.

In distance model, the solution consists of a configuration of *n* variables or items points that assess behaviors and *i* individual points where each individual is represented as being at a 'maximal' or 'ideal' point, located in such a way that the distances from this point to the behavior points are in maximum agreement with the individual's preference ratings or rankings. The position of the 'ideal point' is interpreted as the one point in the space where the individual's preferences are at a maximum, and her preference decreases in every direction. This is often termed a 'single peaked preference function' since it assumes that there is only *one* point of maximum preference and that preference decreases from this point.

Normally the behavior points corresponding to the most popular or consensual rankings will lie at the center of the space, and the least popular ones at the periphery. That is, highly popular behaviors will tend to be projected into the center of the individual points so that behaviors can be close to most individual's ideal points and highly unpopular behaviors will be located at the outside of a configuration. Thus, if a behavior is sufficiently unpopular it can be located virtually anywhere on the periphery as long as it is at a maximum distance from the ideal points. But each behavior must be preferred by at least one individual.

An important distinction between the vector and distance models is that distance model can accommodate more I-scales, as long as the number of behavior points is large compared to the number of dimensions, the size of the isotonic regions is small, especially towards the center of the configuration, and they become increasingly well-represented by a point. For this reason, behavior or item points in the central part of a configuration are normally the most stable, while those at the periphery can usually be moved around fairly freely without affecting the goodness of fit. As seen in Fig. 8.1, playing sport and writing are the most preferred behaviors since they located close to the center of the configuration.

In addition to vector and distance MDS preference models, the MDS preference analysis can also be discussed in terms of internal vs. external analysis. Internal preference analysis simultaneously provides estimates of the coordinates for behaviors or items, individual preference or ideal points, and a fit measure. In external preference analysis, coordinates of behaviors or item is assumed to be known, either from theory or previous analysis, and the analysis provides the estimates of individual ideal points based on the known configuration of behaviors. This type of analysis can be used as confirmatory MDS preference analysis. In the current literature, there are very few studies using this kind of analysis.

8.2 Preference Analysis Using PREFSCAL

In the previous sections, we mainly focus on the discussion of basic ideas of MDS preference modeling, using SAS proc prinqual (vector model) and proc transreg (ideal point model) to analyze the hypothetical data for illustration. Another program that can perform MDS preference analysis (traditional ideal point model) is *PREFSCAL* in SPSS (Busing et al. 2005b). Readers interested in technical aspects of the program can consult Busing et al. (2005a). In this chapter, we focus on an application of the *PREFSCAL* program in studying adolescents' general outlook.

The goal is to provide readers a sense of MDS preference analysis in real world situation.

The data used here (n = 15) were a sub-sample of 486 students in grade 7. A battery of various measures that assessed psychosocial adjustments was administered to the participants in the regular classroom setting. For the purpose of this example, we used a 12-item instrument of the Life Orientation Test (LOT) (Scheier et al. 1994) that was developed to assess generalized optimism versus pessimism. The responses were coded along a 5-point Likert-type scale, ranging from "strongly disagree" to "strongly agree." The items were scored so that high values indicate optimism (i.e., a large distance from pessimism). Examples of items include "In uncertain times, I usually expect the best." "If something can go wrong for me, it will." or "I'm always optimistic about my future." In a sense, these items assessed adolescents' attitudinal preferences towards life.

One of the questions can be asked is: What kinds of life orientation preferences do these 15 adolescents in grade 7 show as measured by these 12-items? Given this question, an MDS preference model is a better choice. In addition, it is reasonable to assume that a rating of '2' on a 5-point Likert-type scale by one individual may not be compared with the same rating by another individual since they may have a different reference point. Thus, the '2's as rated by different individuals only indicate that a participant provides a rating of '2' on a particular item, and the same '2's do not indicate the same degree of similarity or dissimilarity. Based on these two considerations, the MDS preference model with row-conditional data type may be a better analytical technique.

A two-dimensional MDS model was specified and the *PREFSCAL* procedure using *SPSS* version 25 yielded the following fit indices:

Iterations final function value		130.716
Badness of fit	Normalized stress	0.088
	Kruskal's stress-I	0.296
	Kruskal's stress-II	0.817
	Young's S-stress-I	0.390
	Young's S-stress-II	0.643
Goodness of fit	Dispersion accounted for	0.912
	Variance accounted for	0.622
	Recovered preference orders	0.927
	Spearman's rho	0.741
	Kendall's tau-b	0.618
Variation coefficients	Variation proximities	0.453
	Variation transformed proximities	0.568
	Variation distances	0.467
Degeneracy indices	Sum-of-squares of DeSarbo's Intermixedness indices	0.058
	Shepard's rough nondegeneracy index	0.729

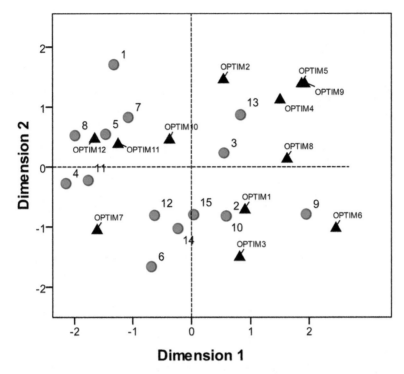

Fig. 8.2 Fifteen participants' ideal points (red circle) with respect to their optimism as assessed by Life Orientation Test. OPTIM = optimism item (triangle)

The results of the MDS preference analysis are shown in Fig. 8.2. First, the algorithm converges to a solution after 130 iterations, with a penalized stress (marked final function value) of 0.72. The variation proximities are close to coefficient of variation for the transformed proximities, indicating the solution provides discrimination between 12 optimism items. The sum-of-squares of DeSarbo's intermixedness indices (DeSarbo et al. 1997) are a measure of how well the points of the different set are intermixed. The closer to 0, the more intermixed the solution. In here the intermixedness is 0.059, indicating that the solution is well intermixed. Shepard's rough nondegeneracy index (Shepard 1974), which assesses the percentage of distinct distances, is 0.729, indicating 73% of distinct distances. Taken together, the results indicate the solution was not degenerate; that is, the points along the dimensions were distinctly separated.

Second, for the Goodness-of-fit indices (how well the model-based distance fit the observed distances), it is advisable to consider several measures together. Kruskal's Stress-II is scale independent; variance accounted for (VAF) is equal to the square of correlation coefficient (i.e., r^2) and is calculated over all values regardless of the conditionality of the analysis. In this example, Kruskal's Stress-II and VAF, and recovered preference orders (RFO) are acceptable.

Third, some relationships among indices with different names should be noted. Dispersion Accounted For (DAF) is also referred to as the sum-of-squares accounted for (SSAF), which is equal to Tucker's congruence coefficient. The square of Kruskal's Stress-I is equal to normalized raw Stress. As Busing et al. (2005a) indicated, the function values of normalized raw Stress, SSAF or DAF, and Kruskal's Stress-I are insensitive to differences in scale and sample size, and these values are suitable for comparing models with different dimensional solutions.

Based on biplot in Fig. 8.2, the following conclusion could be drawn. First, these 12 items form four somewhat distinct clusters, one in each quadrant, and in some way, these items are quite spread out. It should be noted that none of these items is located close to the center of the configuration, indicating these 15 adolescents do not have a particular set of preferences with respect to these attitudes. Six items (2, 3, 5, 6, 7, and 9) seemed to be on the periphery of the biplot, indicating these attitudes are less preferred. Second, nine participants' attitudinal preferences did not seem to match those assessed by the items. Participants 5, 7, and 8 preferred items 11 (*every cloud has a silver lining*) and 12 (*count on good things happening to me*); participants 2 and 10 preferred items 1 (*usually expect the best*) and 3 (*something will not go wrong from me*); participant 9 preferred item 6 (*enjoy friends*). Third, if we were to make inferences about the instrument based on these 15 people, the data might suggest that the instrument was not very sensitive to Chinese adolescents' attitudinal preferences since 9 out of 15 (60%) adolescents were not responsive to the items. On the other hand, if we were to make inferences about what these adolescents' attitudinal preferences were, five of them (33%) seemed to have attitude of adolescent fable--invulnerability, and the rest of these 7th graders did not seem to show any optimistic attitude. Such result might be indicative of less cognitive development with respect to outlook for this group of 15 Chinese students. Of course, we would not make such inferences for the adolescent population with a sample of 15 students. It was done here for didactic purposes.

8.3   MDS Single-Ideal Point Model

In addition to the traditional vector and ideal point (i.e., distance) model, MacKay (2001) proposed a probabilistic MDS single-ideal point model. The idea of MDS single-ideal point model is the same as the other MDS preference models, which can be traced to Thurstone (Thurstone 1928) and Coombs (1950). Essentially, a probabilistic MDS single-ideal point model requires a single-ideal point solution across all individuals to be estimated rather than a number of ideal points, one for each person. A single-ideal solution represents both individuals and behaviors as a point in Euclidean space. The distance relation between individuals and behaviors as indicated by the behaviors or items provides information about the preference structure of the individuals in such a way that individuals are closer to the behaviors they prefer. The model is initially used to represent a rectangular matrix of preferences by i individuals for v objects or variables as distances between i ideal points and v actual objects or variables by estimating the coordinates of individuals and behaviors in the same latent space. Thus, a MDS single-ideal point model is a spatial model in which i individuals and v items or behaviors are represented as points in multidimensional space. The coordinates x_i of an individual or a group of individuals is generally referred to as his or her (or that group's) ideal point and, hence, it is called the single ideal-point model.

The preference of an individual or a group of individuals for a behavior or object is an inverse function of the distance between the point that represents the actual objects and the ideal point that represents the individuals. A large distance between an object and an ideal point indicate that the object has high disutility (i.e., less liked or preferred). In other words, an individual responds negatively to an actual object (a variable or item) when the attitude or behavior represented by the object or item does not closely reflect the attitude or behavior of the individual. In the MDS single-ideal point model, such disagreement occurs when the individual is located too far away from the object. On the other hand, individuals respond positively to actual items or objects that have locations similar to their own.

In the probabilistic MDS single-ideal point model, the ideal point and actual items are represented not by points but by distributions. Based on the probabilistic MDS single-ideal point model of Hefner (1958) as proposed by Mackay and his associates (MacKay 2007; MacKay and Zinnes 1986; Zinnes and MacKay 1983), the coordinates x_{ik} of a behavior or object have the Euclidean properties:

$$d_{ij} = \sqrt{\sum_{k-1} \left(x_{ik} - x_{jk} \right)^2} \qquad (8.1)$$

where d_{ij} is the distance random variable between item i and j, and x_{ik} or x_{jk} are coordinates that are assumed to be normally and independently distributed with mean μ_{ik} and variance σ_{ik}^2. The variance σ_{ik}^2 can be assumed equal (i.e., isotropic) or unequal (i.e., anisotropic) for each item i on each dimension k in a Euclidean space. The goal of the analysis is to estimate the mean location μ_{ik} of coordinates x_{ik} or x_{jk} and variance σ_{ik}^2, including location and variance of the ideal point. In order to obtain the parameter estimates μ_{ik} and σ_{ik}^2, one needs to specify the probability function of the distance random variable d_{ij}, which depends on the variance structure and sampling properties. The detailed discussion of how a probability MDS single-ideal point model is derived may be found in MacKay and his associates (MacKay 1989, 2007; MacKay and Zinnes 1986; Zinnes and MacKay 1983, 1992).

MacKay et al. (1995) indicated one primary reason why probabilistic MDS models are of particular interest in modeling preferences characterized by a single-ideal point. The probabilistic MDS is able to estimate mean (i.e., centroid) location and variance of preferred behaviors. When variability in preferred behavior exists, or when there are measurement errors inherited in single-items of an instrument, it is desirable to take such variability or measurement errors into consideration. Technically, for each ideal point or actual behavior or item, i, there is a corresponding k-dimensional random vector X_j that has an x variate normal distribution with

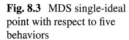

Fig. 8.3 MDS single-ideal point with respect to five behaviors

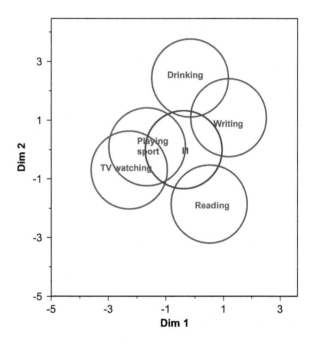

Table 8.1 Distance between ideal point and each of the five behaviors

	Ideal point	I scale
Reading	2.06	3.03
Writing	1.91	2.93
TV watching	2.00	2.97
Drinking	2.45	3.27
Sport	1.27	2.70

mean vector u_j and covariance matrix Σ_j. Individuals' choices are assumed to be based on values sampled from the X_j distributions. If an individual has a consistently preferred behavior, be it actual or ideal, then we expect the diagonal elements of the covariance matrix Σ_j to be small. However, if the individual does not have a consistently preferred behavior or there are more measurement errors, the diagonal elements of the Σ_j are expected to be large.

The model fit can be tested using information criterion statistics, such as CAIC (Bozdogan 1987), BIC (Schwarz 1978), or log-likelihood ratio tests. Thus, we can test various models with respect to kinds of variances assumed, latent groups in the data, or the number of ideal-points that may need to reflect individuals' typical behavior. The ability to test hypotheses about the structure of the variance can also be just as interesting to researchers as the ability to test hypotheses about the location of actual objects and ideal points. For example, a psychologist might have an interest in knowing if the variability in a client's anxiety behaviors about a positive event and a negative event were the same as a result of interventions or a part of developmental processes.

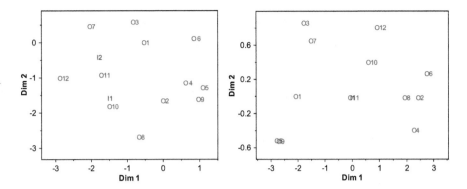

Fig. 8.4 The left figure shows a two-ideal solution, as indicated by I1 and I2. The bottom figure shows a single-ideal solution, as indicated by I1. Circle with a number indicates optimism item

The hypothetical data used in previous example is used again to illustrate what MDS single-ideal point model can inform us. Figure 8.3 shows the results of the analysis using *PROSCAL* (MacKay and Zinnes 2014). The circle indicates the variance around the points, which is 1.76, assuming equal variance across all behaviors. It seems that playing sport and writing are fairly close to the ideal point. Table 8.1 shows the distance between the ideal point and each of the five behaviors. As shown in Table 8.1, the distance between ideal point and playing sport and writing is the smallest, which corresponds to the I scale. The result from MDS single-ideal point analysis is fairly consistent with that from traditional distance model as shown in Fig. 8.1 in which playing sport and writing are close to the center of the configuration.

If we assume that there will two groups of individuals (e.g., males vs. females), we can also use MDS single-ideal point model to conduct group-based single-ideal point analysis, with each group having its own single-ideal point. If no group information is known a priori, mixture MDS single-ideal point analysis can be conducted, where each individual is assigned to be a group based on the estimated probability of group membership. In type of analysis has not been performed in psychological and educational research, but it has potentially interesting applications.

To show how MDS single-ideal point model can be used to test multiple vs. single ideal points in the preference data, the data of the same 15 adolescents in the preference modeling via *PREFSCAL* shown in previous section are used for a such purpose. Based on Fig. 8.2, it seemed that there may be two groups of adolescents with different life orientation preferences. In other words, a model of two-ideal points seemed to underlie the data. However, it is also possible that a single-ideal point may be adequate to account for the differences in these adolescents' preference. Thus, we used maximum likelihood MDS single ideal-point analysis to test a single-ideal point vs. a two-ideal point preference model. Of course, there were other possible models such as a two-dimensional vs. a one-dimensional model or a different combination of dimensionality and ideal points can also be tested.

The single-ideal vs. the two-ideal two-dimensional solutions estimated by *PROSCAL* are shown in Fig. 8.4. The hypotheses were tested using information criterion statistics, such as CAIC (Bozdogan 1987) or BIC (Schwarz 1978). The CAIC value for the single-ideal solution was 1882.67, whereas the two-ideal solution was 1880.66. The CAIC difference between the two models was less than 10, indicating that the single-ideal model was adequate to account for individual differences in life orientation preference (Burnham and Anderson 2002). This finding was consistent with what was found in traditional ideal point analysis conducted in *PREFSCAL*, in which a group of nine adolescents was not responsive to the items, and six adolescents indicated life orientation preference.

8.4 Conclusion

In this chapter, we discussed the fundamentals of MDS preference analysis using both simulated and real data. We used data that are more likely to be seen in educational and psychological setting rather than data that are less commonly seen such as car rating. Our discussion is more of practitioner-oriented; that is, only focused on the practical aspects of MDS preference analysis, omitting many technical components of the models. Also, we do not discuss external preference analysis in this chapter because we want to discuss it in a later chapter where issues related to measurement and hypothesis testing are presented. We want to make external preference analysis be more useful in today's research situations by relating it to what we are commonly seen in current research.

MDS preference analysis can have many applications such as in longitudinal data analysis. In here we only attempt to pique researchers and practitioners interests to use this method. One research problem can be addressed from a different angle using various methods, which can either shed more lights or provide some unique information, at least possibly providing a validity triangulation on some research questions. MDS preference analysis will not replace more popular methods of preference analysis but it can be another method for addressing the same research issues from a different perspective.

References

Bozdogan, H. (1987). Model selection and Akaike's information criterion (AIC): The general theory and its analytical extensions. *Psychometrika, 52*(3), 345–370.
Burnham, K. P., & Anderson, D. R. (2002). *Model selection and multimodel inference: A practical information-theoretic approach* (2nd ed.). New York: Springer.
Busing, F. M. T. A., Groenen, P. J. K., & Heiser, W. J. (2005a). Avoiding degeneracy in multidimensional unfolding by penalizing on the coefficient of variation. *Psychometrika, 70*(1), 71–98.

Busing, F. M. T. A., Heiser, W. J., Neufeglise, P., & Meulman, J. J. (2005b). *PREFSCAL: Program for metric and nonmetric multidimensional unfolding, including individual differences modeling and fixed coordinates (version 14)*. Chicago, IL: SPSS Inc.. Retrieved from http://publib. boulder.ibm.com/infocenter/spssstat/v20r0m0/index.jsp?topic=%2Fcom.ibm.spss.statistics. help%2Fsyn_prefscal.htm.

Coombs, C. H. (1950). Psychological scaling without a unit of measurement. *Psychological Review, 57*(3), 145–158.

Coombs, C. H. (1964). *A theory of data*. New York: Wiley.

DeSarbo, W. S., Young, M. R., & Rangaswamy, A. (1997). A parametric multidimensional unfolding procedure for incomplete nonmetric preference/choice set data. *Marketing Research, 34*(4), 499–516.

Hefner, R. (1958). *Extensions to the law of comparative judgment to discriminable and multidimensional stimuli*. Unpublished Ph.D. dissertation, University of Michigan.

MacKay, D. B. (1989). Probabilistic multidimensional scaling: An anisotropic model for distance judgments. *Journal of Mathematical Psychology, 33*, 187–205.

MacKay, D. B. (2001). Probabilistic unfolding models for sensory data. *Journal of Food and Preference, 12*, 427–436.

MacKay, D. B. (2007). Internal multidimensional unfolding about a single ideal: A probabilistic solution. *Journal of Mathematical Psychology, 51*, 305–318.

MacKay, D. B., & Zinnes, J. L. (1986). A probabilistic model for the multidimensional scaling of proximity and preference data. *Marketing Science, 5*, 325–344.

MacKay, D. B., & Zinnes, J. (2014). *PROSCAL professional: A program for probabilistic scaling*: www.proscal.com

MacKay, D. B., Easley, R. F., & Zinnes, J. L. (1995). *A single ideal point model for market structure analysis* (pp. 433–443). XXXII: Journal of Marketing Research.

Scheier, M. F., Carver, C. S., & Bridges, M. W. (1994). Distinguishing optimism from neuroticism (and trait anxiety, self-mastery, and self-esteem): A re-evaluation of the life orientation test. *Journal of Personality and Social Psychology, 67*, 1063–1078.

Schwarz, G. (1978). Estimating the dimension of a model. *Annals of Statistics, 6*(2), 461–464.

Shepard, R. N. (1974). Representation of structure in similarity data: Problems and prospects. *Psychometrika, 39*, 373–421.

Thurstone, L. L. (1928). Attitudes can be measured. *American Journal of Sociology, 33*, 529–554.

Zinnes, J. L., & MacKay, D. B. (1983). Probabilistic multidimensional scaling: Complete and incomplete data. *Psychometrika, 48*, 24–48.

Zinnes, J. L., & MacKay, D. B. (1992). A probabilistic multidimensional scaling approach: Properties and procedures. In F. G. Ashby (Ed.), *Multidimensional models of perception and cognition* (pp. 35–60). Hillsdale: Lawrence Erlbaum Associates.

Chapter 9
Configuration Similarities

Abstract Comparing and testing similarities among a set of configurations are explained. Ideas of comparing configuration similarities can be extended for hypothesis testing. An example of real data is provided to illustrate how to evaluate configuration similarities using Procrustes analysis, including PINDIS model. Hypothesis testing using the PINDIS model is also presented.

Keywords Configuration similarity · Procrustes analysis · The PINDIS analysis

MDS models are spatial configuration in which the relationships among items or variables and among individuals are represented as a map so that the data structure can be visualized. As a spatial model, the MDS configuration is invariant to distance. Two seemingly different looking configurations may be the same in nature. For example, if a study is to replicate a previous MDS solution, then it is important to know the ways, and the extent, to which the current MDS solution resembles that of the original study. As another example, if we have employed more than one variant of MDS analysis on the same data, or more commonly, have scaled the data of different subgroups of individuals such as males and females or different age groups, the issue of configural similarity between the resulting configurations needs to be addressed.

Taking this idea of configural similarity one step further, we can also conduct hypothesis testing (i.e., confirmatory) MDS analysis in which hypothesized configural pattern is treated as target or previously-known one. The goal of the analysis is to see the ways and the extent to which the data support or confirm the expected solution (i.e., model data fit). In this chapter, we discuss the ways in which the configural or spatial similarities (sometimes called common space analysis), including hypothesis testing, can be examined and investigated.

© Springer International Publishing AG, part of Springer Nature 2018   121
C. S. Ding, *Fundamentals of Applied Multidimensional Scaling for Educational
and Psychological Research*, https://doi.org/10.1007/978-3-319-78172-3_9

9.1 Basic Ideas of Configural Similarity

Before testing configuration or configural similarity, we should be sufficiently persuaded that the fit of the MDS solution to the data is good enough in terms of either fit indexes or interpretation to warrant any further analysis. The question 'How similar are two configurations?' depends on two things: (1) what aspects of the configuration are considered *relevant*, and (2) what properties of the configuration are *unique*. For example, if one configuration were simply twice the size of the other but in every other way identical, it is unlikely that most of us would consider this are relevant difference, and we would normally compare *relative* rather than absolute distances. Other irrelevant aspects include: the orientation of the configuration in a Euclidean distance model since any rotation leaves distances unchanged; the origin of the space since it would normally be treated as arbitrary, unless the model were a vector model (since change of origin alters scalar products and hence alters the angles separating the vectors) or the point chosen as the origin was substantively meaningful. Thus, differences which are irrelevant can often make identical configurations look to be very different. Appearances are not a reliable guide as to how two configurations are alike due to orientation, origin transformation, reflection (also known as flipping), or absolute distance (also known as stretch, shrink, or scale). How, then, does one go about comparing them?

The configural similarity can be considered from the following perspectives. We must consider what aspects of configuration count as important and what are irrelevant. Two configuration patterns are assumed to be identical if they only involve differences of orientation, origin, and absolute distance. Any index of similarity should remain unchanged when the origin of configurations are translated into any other point in the space and configurations are rescaled (stretched, shrunk), moved, or rotated through any angle. The differences due to these three operations are termed similarity transformation since they preserve Euclidean distances. When the similarity transformation does not change the relative distances (i.e., leave original relative distance intact), it is admissible or permissible transformation. One the other hand, when the similarity transformation changes the original relative distances in some way in order to get a better fit, it is inadmissible transformation.

Thus, an index of how similar two configurations are can be thought of as being a function of the distances between the points in the two configurations. Gower (1979, September) has provided an excellent review of such indices by examining the form of the function relating the distances in the two configurations. A common index is product moment correlation r, which involves the correlations between two distances. A related goodness of fit measure is the r^2 between coordinates of the two configurations, which have been brought into maximum or optimal conformity by similarity transformation. This r^2 index has the properties of its value depending neither upon the number of points, nor upon the number of dimensions, nor on the scale of the configuration. It can be used to answer the question, "Does configuration X match Y better than X matches Z", when we come to compare several configurations.

Several analytical procedures can be used to test configural similarity, including hypothesis testing. In the following sections, we discuss these methods by example.

9.2 Procrustes Analysis

Procrustes analysis involves rotating or moving two or more configuration matrices X and Y into closest conformity with each other, allowing rotation, reflection, rescaling, and translation of origin. It is also termed generalized Procrustes analysis (Gower 1975). The basic idea of Procrustes analysis is simple. First, given a set of configurations, we begin by moving or rotating them into closest similarity and creating a new average or centroid configuration. Each point in this centroid configuration is a least-square fit to the corresponding point of the original configuration; that is, this centroid configuration, denoted as G, is the best fitting configuration via the iterative algorithm (Gower 1975).

In case of hypothesis testing, a theoretical or hypothesized configuration pattern will serve as the centroid configuration throughout the analysis. We test how closely the configuration(s) estimated from the data fit this centroid (i.e., hypothesized) configuration.

Second, we assess how closely each original configuration fits the centroid configuration using r^2 between the coordinates of each original configuration and those of the centroid configuration. The sum of squares of the residuals, that is, $\Sigma(x_i - g_i)$, assesses the difference between each configuration and the centroid configuration.

Procrustes analysis provides the basic general similarity model in which only admissible transformation is carried out. This model can be denoted as P_0 model (Coxon et al. 2005) and it provides a reference point for other models in which inadmissible transformation is carried out.

9.2.1 Example

Age effects in adolescent coping behaviors have been repeatedly reported. Coping behaviors change throughout the course of adolescence due to altered cognitive, social, and behavioral abilities as well as a shift in the severity and importance of different stressors (Frydenberg and Lewis 1991). Age differences in coping include:

1. An increase in active and internal coping was documented between early and late adolescence, both cross-sectionally and longitudinally (Seiffge-Krenke 1995; Seiffge-Krenke and Beyers 2005).
2. A greater tendency in older adolescents to show emotion-oriented coping behavior was found (Compas et al. 1988).

3. It has been shown that the total number of available coping strategies increases with age (Frydenberg et al. 2003), thus indicating a more differentiated coping pattern in dealing with specific stressors.
4. Tension-reducing strategies (such as letting out aggressions, drinking alcohol, or taking drugs) increase with age as well as the ability to beneficially use self-reflective strategies.
5. Older adolescents discuss problems less with their parents, but turn more towards peers or institutions (Frydenberg and Lewis 1993; Seiffge-Krenke 1995).

Similarly, in studying adolescent coping strategies among seven nations, Gelhaar et al. (2007) found that active coping was most prominent among early adolescents; internal coping was highest among late adolescents, while withdrawal peaked in mid adolescence. Specifically,

1. Early adolescents compared with the other two age groups: discussing the problem with parents, talking straight about the problem without worrying much, did not worry, not to think about the problem, expecting the worst, withdrawing,
2. Mid adolescents: trying to get help from institutions, made compromises.
3. Late adolescence: accepting one's limits, thought about problems when they appeared, consuming alcohol or drugs.

The purpose here is to examine structure aspect of differences in coping strategies across three age groups (early, mid, and late adolescents). Specifically, the question is whether all age groups have an identical coping dimensional structure or more realistically there are some systematic changes in dimensional structure by age. This question is the first and fundamental step in studying subsequent issues regarding age differences in coping since only when we know that structural aspect of coping behaviors is the same across age group we can examine how age group differs in their preference of coping choices.

The data used in this example were 744 Chinese students in Grade 7 (n = 258), Grade 10 (n = 215), and in university (n = 271). The average age of the participants in Grade 7, 10, and in university was 13.6 (SD = 1.27), 17.1 (SD = 1.12), and 22.3 (SD = 1.08) years old, respectively. The average education level of the parents among these participants was high school.

The instrument used was an 18-item coping behavior survey adapted from a questionnaire developed by Seiffge-Krenke and Shulman (1990). Students were asked how likely they used each of the 18 coping behaviors when they had a problem, e.g., "*I discuss the problem with my parents/other adults,*" or "*I behave as if everything is alright.*" Each item was rated on a 5-point Likert-type scale from 1 (*most likely to use*) to 5 (*least likely to use*).

The coping data were first scaled separately for each age group using SAS MDS procedure. The goal is to determine the number of dimensions that best approximate the data structure underlying each age group. The goodness of fit measures based on two dimensional solution revealed a good model-data fit for each age group (early, mid, and late), Stress = 0.09 (R^2 = 0.96), Stress = 0.07 (R^2 = 0.99), Stress = 0.12 (R^2 = 0.93), respectively. For three dimensional solution, the fit was: Stress = 0.06

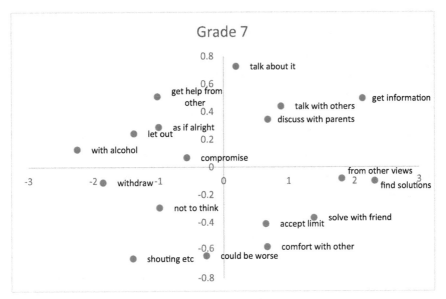

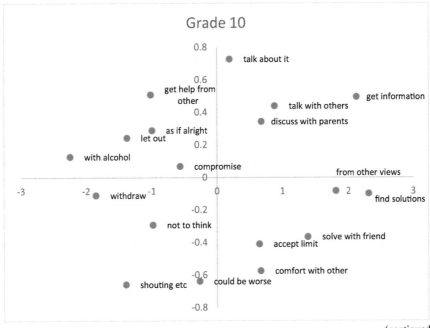

(continued)

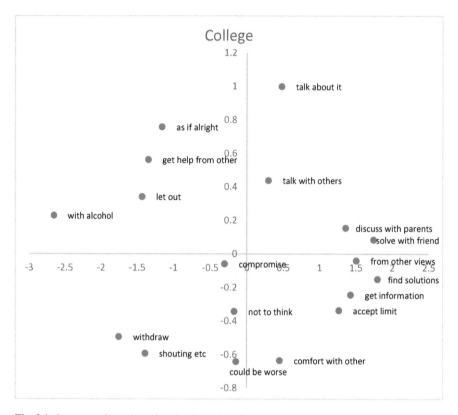

Fig. 9.1 Latent configuration of coping behaviors for each grade/age level

(R² = 0.97), Stress = 0.07 (R² = 0.99), Stress = 0.07 (R² = 0.97), respectively. The difference in fit was small, with $\Delta R^2 < 0.05$, which suggests that increasing number of dimension does not improve model fit substantively. The two-dimensional solution for each age group is shown in Fig. 9.1. As can be seen in Fig. 9.1, there is a great similarity among three configurations of coping behaviors.

Using three estimated configurations of each grade as data input, we run MSD Procrustes analysis by NEW MDS(X) program (Coxon et al. 2005). The centroid configuration is Fig. 9.2. The fit of each configuration to centroid as assessed via P_0 model is 0.96, 0.96, and 0.92, respectively, indicating there is a nearly perfect match for each of the three comparisons.

9.3   The PINDIS Models

Procrustes analysis via P_0 model provides a baseline or reference model for assessing configuration similarity. Based on this basic Procrustes analysis, Lingoes (1977) developed a series of increasing complex models for assessing configuration

CENTROID CONFIGURATION : dimensions 1 and 2

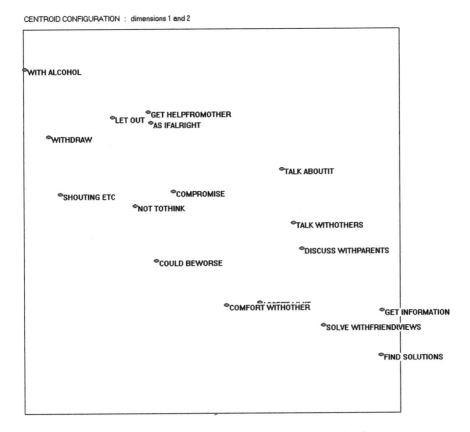

Fig. 9.2 Centroid configuration of coping behaviors of three grades/age levels

similarity. This set of models is known as PINDIS (Procrustes Individual Differences Scaling). The analysis by PINDIS involves a set of configurations obtained from any MDS analysis, with the purpose of examining similarity among them using series of transformation models of increasing complexity. The complexity entails two operations: (1) what is done to the centroid in order for each original configuration to be moved into optimal fit to the centroid configuration and (2) what individual differences parameters (i.e., dimensional weights or vector weights) are estimated or applied in the model to move the centroid into greater similarity to each original configuration. These increasing complex transformations bring better fit. Now we describe these models as discussed by Davies and Coxon (1982).

As mentioned previously, the basic general similarity model is P_0, which only carries out admissible transformation. In this model, no operation is performed on centroid configuration G, nor are any individual differences parameters estimated. In a sense, this is the most conservative model for assessing configuration similarity. If P_0 model suggests a great similarity between configurations, the other models also will. Thus, P_0 model provides a lower bound value of configuration similarity. The fit of the model is given by $r(G, X)$.

Both P_1 model and P_2 are distance models, which carry out inadmissible similarity transformation and is analogs to INDSCAL or IDIOSCAL, in which the centroid configuration is rotated in both P_1 and P_2. P_1 rotates G to a single new orientation and P_2 rotates G and W to different orientation for each individual configuration so the conformity will be increased. More specifically, in P_1 model (G^r, W_i), the centroid configuration is first rotated to be an optimal fit for dimensional weighting (G^r, one rotation) and then a set of individual dimension weights are estimated for each original configuration (W_i). This model is the same as INDSCAL (except that the negative weights indicate the reflection of the corresponding dimension) and is the simple dimensional model. The fit of model P_1 is given by $r(G^r W_i, X)$. In P_2 model (G^r_i, W_i), however, the centroid configuration is rotated to each individual configuration (G^r_i, i rotations) and then individual dimension weights are differentially estimated for each configuration (W_i). The fit of model P_2 is given by $r(G^r_i W_i, X)$. This is similar to IDIOSCAL model (Carroll and Wish 1973).

Both P_3 and P_4 model are vector models and carry out inadmissible similarity transformation. They are similar to P_1 and P_2 models in terms of model complexity. In P_3 model (G^t, V_i), the origin of the centroid configuration is first translated to an optimal fit or position (G^t) and then individual vector weights are estimated from the origin to each of the item points (V_i). This is simple vector or perspective model. The negative vector weight indicates the flipping of the vector in the opposite direction. The fit of model P_3 is given by $r(G^t V_i, X)$.

In P_3 model, within an individual set of weights, interest of inquiry can focus on which item vector weights are largest and/or which have negative sign. This is because these vector weights imply the greatest relocation or reposition compared to the centroid, indicating that the significant differences are concentrated in these item points, but that the remaining structure of the configuration closely resembles the centroid.

In addition, the vector weights are comparable across individual configurations (not true for P_4 model). The item points where vector weights vary most from configuration to configuration are the ones which are least stable in the configuration and could be removed from analysis (a nice feature for instrument development). If the variation in weights for a given item vector is higher in some individual configuration than in others, it suggests that variation is concentrated in a particular area of substructure of the configuration.

On the other hand, in P_4 model (G^t_i, V^t_i), each individual configuration is first translated in its own origin (G^t_i) and vector weights are differentially estimated (V^t_i).The fit of model P_4 is given by $r(G^t_i V^t_i, X)$. Thus, P_4 model allows each individual configuration to have its own 'point of view' (origin), thus having a different origin and a different set of weights. For this reason, P_4 model is often called 'points of view' model, as Coxon et al. (2005) indicated.

Finally, P_5 model is the combination of both distance and vector model.

When we have a hypothesized configuration rather than calculating centroid, PINDIS model can be used for hypothesis testing where known structure underlie

Table 9.1 Fit value for each of the three grade/age comparison

	<P0> Z,X[i]	<P1> ZW[i],X[i]	<P2> Z[i] W[i],X[i]	<P3> V[i] Z,X[i]	<P4> V[i] Z[i],X[i]	<P5> V[i] ZW[i],X[i]
Grade 7	0.96	0.99	0.99	0.83	0.00	1.00
Grade 10	0.96	0.99	0.99	0.83	0.00	1.00
College	0.92	0.94	0.95	0.94	0.00	0.98
Mean	0.00	0.97	0.97	0.87	0.00	0.99

Note: 0.0 in the table means that particular PINDIS transformation is not reported

Table 9.2 Vector weights across three configurations of coping behaviors

Item name	Grade 7	Grade 10	College
Discuss with parents	0.000	0.000	0.000
Talk about it	0.178	0.178	2.231
Get help from other	−0.684	−0.684	1.331
Accept limit	0.973	0.973	−0.688
Talk with others	1.490	1.490	5.256
As if alright	−0.738	−0.738	1.352
Let out	−0.805	−0.805	1.175
Could be worse	−0.136	−0.136	0.779
Find solutions	−1.128	−1.128	0.094
Compromise	−0.749	−0.749	1.059
Shouting etc.	−0.646	−0.646	0.985
From other views	−1.068	−1.068	−0.280
Get information	−1.624	−1.624	0.085
Not to think	−0.769	−0.769	0.732
With alcohol	−0.827	−0.827	1.149
Comfort with other	0.842	0.842	0.359
Solve with friend	−0.196	−0.196	−0.597
Withdraw	−0.832	−0.832	1.001

the data. In this case, the target configuration is fixed or as input data without any rotations or translation of origin. Thus, PINDIS can be used in an exploratory or a confirmatory way or in combination of both.

9.3.1 Example

Let's continue our examination of grade/age difference in structural aspect of coping behaviors. In previous section, we saw that the fit of the P_0 model for each configuration of coping behaviors was quite good. We conducted the PINDIS analysis on the same data using NEW MDS(X) program. The results of the analysis are shown in Table 9.1.

As can be seen from Table 9.1, all the fit values indicate the perfect match among three coping configurations, particularly with models with inadmissible transformation such P_1 or P_2.

It is interesting to see that the fit value of P_3 model was not good for grades 7 and 10. To learn more about what may go on with P_3 model, we examined vector weights across three grade level since these vector weights indicate (1) which items are repositioned, as assessed by the largest or negative vector weight value, to optimal fit the centroid configuration and (2) which items are less stable when its corresponding vector weight are compared across all the configurations. Table 9.2 shows the vector weight across three configurations. As can be seen in Table 9.2, there are quite a few items with negative vector weights for Grades 7 and 10, indicating that the point of these items had a significant difference with centroid configuration. This may be the reason of low fit value for Grades 7 and 10, but not for college level. In addition, the vector weights of these items varied across configurations, particularly with respect to those of college level, indicating that these items were stable up to Grade 10. This finding may suggest that the coping preferences may change at college level, given the same coping structure. Further preference analysis using vector model can be used to examine how preference in coping shifts over time.

9.3.2 Example of Hypothesis Testing

In previous section, we discuss how to examine the spatial structure similarity using Procrustes and or PINDIS analysis. Using the same analytical procedure, we can easily perform hypothesis testing about pre-specified latent structure and see if this hypothesized configuration is consistent with the data. The way to perform the confirmatory MDS analysis is to enter hypothesized configuration(s) and enter configuration estimated from the data as the individual configuration(s). That is, we have hypothesized configuration (i.e., target configuration) and we have configuration estimated from the current data. Then we can examine how similar they are. Intuitively, the more similar they are, the better the chances are that the hypothesized configuration is supported by the data. We also can use vector weights from P_3 model to examine what the discrepancies may be. Another way of performing confirmatory MDS is to use *Proscal* program (MacKay and Zinnes 2014), which provides maximum likelihood estimation of the configuration. We can use hypothesized configuration as a target and see how closely this target is consistent with the data. The fit measure will be correlation coefficient. One advantage of using *Proscal* is that we can also test variance structure of the coordinates.

The following example uses data from a coping study that investigates coping structure of high school students. Based on findings from previous studies, coping behaviors can be conceptualized as three somewhat distinct aspects: withdrawal, emotion-focused, and problem-solving focused. A short coping survey of 10 items was administered to a group of 316 high school students. The interest of the inquiry

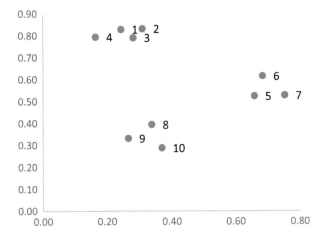

Fig. 9.3 Hypothesized structure of coping behaviors. Items 1–4 indicate problem-focused coping, Items 5–7 indicate withdrawal coping, and Items 8–10 indicate emotion-focused coping

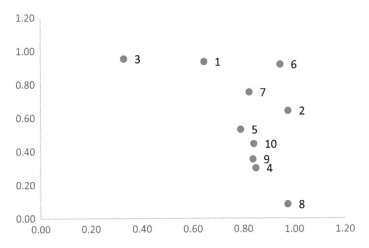

Fig. 9.4 Estimated structure of coping behaviors among 316 high school students

was whether the coping behaviors had hypothesized structure as suggested previously. Figure 9.3 shows the hypothesized configuration of coping.

This target or hypothesized configuration was compared with that estimated coping configuration from the data. Figure 9.4 shows this estimated configuration from the data.

It seemed that the hypothesized configuration was not supported by the data. Indeed, the value of P_0 model indicates that two configurations was only 0.27. It seemed that for this group of students, there was no particularly distinct structure of coping, that is, they were likely to use these behaviors as one group or one factor.

9.4   Conclusion

In this chapter, we discuss how different latent data structures can be compared using MDS Procrustes and PINDIS analysis procedure. The hypothesis testing analysis, that is, confirmatory MDS analysis, can be conducted with this analytic method. We used examples to illustrate the utilities of Procrustes and PINDIS analysis. It should be noted that the not many empirical studies have used this method for studying similarity of data structures or testing hypothesis about a particular structure. There are some potential applications of this method to examine group differences in data structure, such as factor structures between males and females in the context of measurement invariance. We can also use the procedure for studying change in behavior patterns over time in longitudinal studies. The method provides a different angle or perspective for examining behaviors.

References

Carroll, J. D., & Wish, M. (1973). Models and methods for three-way multidimensional scaling. In R. C. Atkinson, D. H. Krantz, R. D. Luce, & P. Suppes (Eds.), *Contemporary developments in mathematical psychology*. San Francisco, CA: W. H. Freeman.

Compas, B. E., Malcarne, V. L., & Fondacaro, R. M. (1988). Coping with stressful events in children and young adolescents. *Journal of Consulting and Clinical Psychology, 56*, 405–411.

Coxon, A. P. M., Brier, A. P., & Hawkins, P. K. (2005). *The New MDSX program series, version 5*. Edinburgh: New MDSX Project.

Davies, P. M., & Coxon, A. P. M. (Eds.). (1982). *Key texts in multidimensional scaling*. London: Heinemann Educational Books.

Frydenberg, E., & Lewis, R. (1991). Adolescent coping: The different ways in which boys and girls cope. *Journal of Adolescence, 14*(2), 119–133. https://doi.org/10.1016/0140-1971(91)90025-m.

Frydenberg, E., & Lewis, R. (1993). Boys play sport and girls turn to others: Age, gender and ethnicity as determinants of coping. *Journal of Adolescence, 16*, 253–266.

Frydenberg, E., Lewis, R., Kennedy, G., Ardila, R., Frindte, W., & Hannoun, R. (2003). Coping with concerns: An explanatory comparison of Australian, Colombian, German, and Palestinian adolescents. *Journal of Youth & Adolescence, 32*, 59–66.

Gelhaar, T., Seiffge-Krenke, I., Borge, A., Cicognani, E., Cunha, M., Loncaric, D., Macek, P., Steinhausen, H.-C., & Metzke, C. W. (2007). Adolescent coping with everyday stressors: A seven-nation study of youth from central, eastern, southern, and northern Europe. *European Journal of Developmental Psychology, 4*(2), 129–156.

Gower, J. C. (1975). Generalised procrustes analysis. *Psychometrika, 40*, 33–51.

Gower, J. C. (1979, September). *Comparing multidimensional scaling configurations*. Paper presented at the Working papers in multidimensional scaling, Proceeding of MDS(X) Seminar, University of Cambridge, mimeo, Cardiff: MDS(X) project.

Lingoes, J. C. (1977). Progressively complex linear transformations for finding geometric similarities among data structures. Mimeo.

MacKay, D. B., & Zinnes, J. (2014). *PROSCAL professional: A program for probabilistic scaling*: www.proscal.com

Seiffge-Krenke, I. (1995). *Stress, coping, and relationships in adolescence*. Hillsdale: Erlbaum.

Seiffge-Krenke, I., & Beyers, W. (2005). Coping trajectories from adolescence to young adulthood: Links to attachment state of mind. *Journal of Research on Adolescence, 15*(4), 561–582.

Seiffge-Krenke, I., & Shulman, S. (1990). Coping style in adolescence: A cross-cultural study. *Journal of Cross-Cultural Psychology, 21*, 351–377.

Part III
New Applications of MDS Analysis

In this section, we discuss some new applications of MDS in educational and psychological research.

Chapter 10
Latent Profile Analysis

Abstract The MDS is discussed as a profile analysis approach of re-parameterizing the linear latent variable model in such a way that the latent variables can be interpreted in terms of profile patterns rather than factors. It is used to identify major patterns among psychological variables and can serve as the basis for further study of correlates and/or predictors of profiles and other background and external variables. I outline the procedure of MDS profile analysis and discuss the issues that are related to parameter estimation and interpretation of the results.

Keyword Profile analysis

In this chapter, we discuss a relatively new application of the multidimensional scaling model for latent profile analysis, with latent variables being coordinates of MDS configuration. This approach requires thinking of the MDS dimensions as profiles rather than as factors so that the latent variables (i.e., coordinates of each observed variable) can be interpreted in terms of profile patterns. It is an exploratory profile analysis method to identify major patterns in behavioral variables and can serve as the basis for further study of correlates and/or predictors of profiles and other background/external variables.

10.1 Profile Analysis in Education and Psychology

A great many investigations, either in psychology or in education, deal with profiles of test scores or behaviors (e.g., Cronbach and Gleser 1953; Davison 1994; Pfeiffer et al. 2000). For example, approximately 74% of school psychology training programs put some focus on the use of profiles of subtest scores in their cognitive assessment courses (Affnso et al. 2000). Pfeiffer et al. (2000) indicated that the majority of school psychologists employ profile analysis in dealing with the WISC-III subtests. Moreover, with relatively more attention being devoted to the use of person-oriented analyses, the methodologies that focuses on profile analysis, such as latent profile analysis, latent class analysis, or latent mixture analysis (Bergman and Magnusson 1997; Collins and Lanza 2010; Muthen and Muthen 2000), have been increasingly popular in psychological research. In education, students' academic progress is typically reported in terms of profiles. For example, Speece and Cooper (1990) examined 1st grade students to identify profiles/groups associated with academic development and uncovered profile patterns that suggested normal development, learning disabilities, mild retardation, and language problems.

Given the importance of a profile or type in the education or social sciences, many methods have been designed to discover types from multivariate data. The search for the best methods to address types has been a persistent theme in psychology and education, especially when population is heterogeneous (Magnusson 1998). The development of new analytical techniques has changed how researchers study classification of individuals. One such new technique is latent finite mixture modeling that is appropriate for identifying latent profiles of behaviors associated with subgroups of population. In this chapter we discussed the use of the MDS model to investigate types or profiles of people. It should be noted that use of the MDS approach to latent profile analysis is not because of inadequacy of techniques for finite mixture modeling; instead, the MDS model provides another promising alternative for the assessment of latent profiles as well as typologies of people indicated via these profiles. Thus, rather than comparing different methods (readers may consult Davison and Sireci (2000) for an excellent comparison of MDS and other methods), this chapter highlights the potential of the MDS model to assist in person-oriented study, that is, idiothetic investigations. Idiothetic investigations can be understood as a way of combining aspects of normative and idiographic methodologies in psychological research (Allport 1937; Lamiell 1981). MDS profile analysis is such a methodology. However, this method currently is underutilized in education and psychology because of its unfamiliarity within the research communities.

10.2   MDS Model in Studying Latent Profiles

Traditionally, common applications of MDS models were employed for two purposes. The first was called dimensional application (Davison 1983), the focus of which was to understand the psychological stimulus dimensions to which people attend (e.g., Davison and Jones 1976). Examples include individual differences MDS in which individual differences with respect to dimension salience are studies. The second was data reduction, in which the researcher sought to reduce the complex interrelationships between stimuli to a simpler and more understandable form. This later use is quite similar to that of factor analysis, and both techniques can be used to study similar issues. For this reason, MDS may be considered or employed as a form of factor analysis, which is an application most familiar to researchers.

Thus, multidimensional scaling is not a new technique. The profile analysis and interpretation of dimensions, however, is relatively new (Davison et al. 1996). Many studies have involved multidimensional scaling of psychological scales (e.g., Paddock and Nowicki 1986), but the data were not interpreted in terms of profiles.

10.2.1   MDS Profile Model Specification

In classical vector MDS representations of structure, each data point in the profile is represented in a Euclidean space of continuous dimensions, that is:

$$m_{sv} = \sum_k w_{sk} x_{kv} + c_s + e_{sv} \qquad (10.1)$$

where m_{sv} is an observed score of person s on variable v, w_{sk} is profile match indices for person s on dimension k, that is, w_{sk} is a participant by dimension matrix, with the order of s participants by k dimensions; x_{kv} is a variable location parameter (i.e., scale value or coordinate) along dimension k, c_s is a level parameter, and e_{sv} is an error term. For the model in Eq. 10.1, the following *ad hoc* constraints are imposed on the MDS profile analysis:

$$\sum_v x_{kv} = 0 \qquad \text{for all k} \qquad (10.2a)$$

$$(1/s)\sum w^2_{sk} = 1.0 \quad \text{for all k} \qquad (10.2b)$$

$$\sum w_{sk} w_{sk'} = 0 \qquad \text{for all k} \qquad (10.2c)$$

Constraint 10.2a states that each profile is ipsative; that is, the mean of the scores in each profile is zero. Thus, profiles will produce profile patterns (scatter plus shape), but not the mean (i.e., level) of the profiles, which is reproduced by level parameter c_s. Constraint 10.2b specifies that the mean squared profile match index along each profile equals one, and constraint 10.2c states that profile match indices are orthogonal for every pair of profiles. In addition, all the variables in the profiles need to be on a common metric.

In the MDS profile model represented in Eq. 10.1, dimensions are represented as profiles, and the fundamental variables x_{kv} are scores for variables (called scale values in MDS). One of the major goals of MDS profile analysis is to explore and capture normative profiles expressed in scale value x_{kv} along profile k. By normative profile we mean it is an average profile across all individuals in the sample. The scale values indicate a particular arrangement of variables in the profiles. It should be noted that multiple variables are used to identify profiles, but not necessarily considered manifestations of a single, homogeneous trait or ability. That is, the multiple variables do not need to be internally consistent: profiles represent types of people in a population.

The idiographic aspect of the model is associated with the individual profile match indices, w_{sk}. Each individual has the number of profile match indices that are equal to the number of profiles identified in the data. If two profiles were identified, then each individual would have two profile match indices, one for each identified profile. The profile match indices quantify the sensitivity of the participant's responses to a variable's location along the profile. Thus, for a given participant who fits the model, a positive profile match index indicates that the individual's observed data tend to manifest the expected profile, while a negative profile match index indicates that the individual's data tend to exhibit a pattern opposite to the profile. The magnitude of the profile match indices reflects the degree to which a participants' observed data tend to match the identified normative profile, k. Although there are no criteria to evaluate what constitutes a large w_{sk} index or a small w_{sk} index, the key issue is the degree to which an individual in general shows the identified profile of data. In MDS profile analysis, thus, the emphasis is on nomothetic investigation as well as on idiographic study.

Although MDS profile analysis has not been used widely, the model discussed here is not new. Bechtel, Tucker, and Chang (1971), Davison (1994), Davison and Skay (1991), and Tucker (1960) call it the "vector" model. Benzecri (1969), Weller and Romney (1990), and Greenacre (1984) call it the "correspondence analysis" model. Cattell (1967) called it the "Q-factor" model, a special case of Eq. 10.1 in which the observed data are standardized by row and the level parameter c_s drops from the equation.

10.2.2   Model Estimation

Readers who are not interested in technical aspects of MDS profile analysis can skip this section. In essence, the model estimation of scale value in MDS profile analysis is the same as that in basic MDS analysis. After obtaining the scale value, regression analysis is performed in which the scale values are treated as predictors and observed variables as dependent variable. The analysis will then produce regression weights and a constant for each individual, which corresponds to profile match index and the level parameter. This is the gist of the model estimation process. The detailed description is as follows.

In a MDS analysis based on the model of Eq. 10.1, the goal is to estimate (1) the profile parameters (scale values) x_{kv}, which are the estimates of scores for variables in a profile, and (2) the individual fit statistics and the profile match indices w_{sk}, which is indicative of each individual's resemblance to the profile. MDS profile analysis starts with algorithms for estimating the profile parameters in the model. The best-known procedure is the classical nonmetric model. In this model, the proximity data are assumed to have the form:

$$\delta_{vv'} = f\left(d_{vv'}\right) \tag{10.3}$$

and

$$d_{vv'} = \left[\sum_{k}\left(x_{kv} - x_{kv'}\right)\right]^{1/2} \tag{10.4}$$

where f is a monotone function of $d_{vv'}$. x_{kv} and $x_{kv'}$ are the profile parameters which locate stimuli or variable v and v' respectively along profile k. The squared Euclidean distances, $\delta_{vv'}^2$, can be computed from observed responses to variable pairs:

$$\delta_{vv'}^2 = \sum_s \left(m_{sv} - m_{sv'} \right)^2 \tag{10.5}$$

The level parameter c_s, which is the mean score of the variables in that profile (i.e., a row), is estimated by

$$c_s = (1/v) \sum m_{sv} \tag{10.6}$$

After we obtain the latent profile estimates x_{kv} in Eq. 10.1, we can get least squares estimates of the individual profile match indices w_{sk} by

$$W = MX \left(X'X \right)^{-1} \tag{10.7}$$

where X is a matrix of x_{kv} and M is a matrix of m_{sv} in Eq. 10.1. This leads to an s by k matrix W of w_{sk}, with each participant having k number of profile match indices, one for each profile. These continuous profile match indices reflect (1) the extent of inter-individual variability along a profile and (2) intra-individual variability across profiles. As mentioned previously, the profile match indices w_{sk} indicate how well a person manifests a normative profile. That is, the normative profiles do not always apply to all individuals. In addition, an individual fit statistic is also computed, which is equal to the squared multiple correlation R^2 in the multiple regression, indicating the proportion of variance in the subject's data that can be accounted for by the model-derived profiles.

10.2.3 Characteristics of MDS Profile Analysis

One of the strengths of using MDS for profile analysis is its simultaneous representation of what typical configurations or profiles of variables actually exist in the population (called latent, average, or expected profiles) and how each individual differs with respect to these latent profiles. That is, this approach provides a global model of membership in subgroups (i.e., distinct profiles) of the population inferred from the data, and of the degree to which each participant manifests each expected profile. In MDS profile analysis, parameters of dimension capture differences between variables. The individual differences in profiles are quantified by profile match indices and individual fit statistics. The fit statistic indicates the proportion of variance in the individual's observed profile data that can be accounted for by the latent or expected profiles. If the variance in an individual's data can be accounted for by an expected profile, the value of the fit statistic will be large (for example, fit ≥0.8 on a 0–1 scale range). If, on the other hand, the variance in an individual's data cannot be accounted for by the expected profiles, the fit statistic will be small (for example, fit ≤ 0.3). Thus, this approach makes it possible to identify individuals who develop in an idiographic manner, indicating that the overall (i.e., nomothetic) model typical of most people does not apply to a particular person. If an individual, for example, responded randomly to the questions or along very different behavioral characteristics, this would result in poorer fit statistics for that individual.

In addition, MDS profile analysis gets at discrete classes but maintains a dimensional framework; that is, it provides information on type of individuals based on the degree of more or less rather than either present or absent. In the profile model, we attempt to profile types of people (i.e., subgroups) by means of normative profiles, but each individual fits these profiles to different degrees. Thus, researchers can conduct separate analyses of individual subjects to see whether a very different profile of relationships between stimuli can be identified for the individual, or whether no clear profile of relationships can be found. It is precisely this type of idiographic profile of development that MDS profile analysis attempts to identify.

The MDS profile analysis described here is an exploratory technique. The profile model is most suitable for the situations in which normative profiles are to be derived from the data, rather than specified by theory, although we can also conduct MDS confirmatory profile analysis if we would like to test a theory or confirm findings from previous studies. It provides estimates of normative profiles as well as estimates of idiographic parameters in the model (that is, profile estimates for each individual), not simply summary statistics such as means, variances, and covariances. If one wishes to conduct idiographic studies, one may take the parameter estimates for individuals and study the association with other variables (e.g., demographic variables) in subsequent analysis.

Technically, the statistical assumptions of MDS profile analysis are minimal. The MDS profile model allows for simultaneous estimation of intra- and inter-individual profiles without the requirement of multivariate normality. Moreover, MDS profile analysis is based on a distance model (Borg and Groenen 2005; Davison 1983) rather than the standard linear model. Thus, it can be used to model nonlinear relationships among variables.

10.3 Example: Organization of Psychosocial Adjustment Among Adolescents

The data used for this example were from the study on adolescent psychosocial development project, which included 208 college students (90 males and 118 females), with the average age of the participants being 21 years. The participants completed a battery of questionnaires. The instrument used here was six measures from the Self-image of Questionnaire for Young Adolescents (SIQYA)(Petersen, et al. 1984): Body Image (BI), Peer Relationships (PR), Family Relationships (FR), Mastering & Coping (MC), Vocational-Educational Goals (VE), and Superior

Adjustment (SA). All six variables were scaled on a common 6-point Likert scale and were positively coded so that a high score indicated positive adjustment. For example, a high score on the Family Relationships scale was indicative of a positive perception of family relationships by the participants, and a high score on the Superior Adjustment scale suggested perceived positive well-being by the participants. Readers may want to consult Petersen, et al. (1984) for detailed descriptions of these scales.

In addition, three mental health well-being measures were included as outcome covariates: (1) the Kandel Depression Scale (Kandel and Davies 1982), a scale for assessing depressive affect; (2) the UCLA Loneliness Scale (Russell et al. 1980), which assesses subjective feelings of loneliness or social isolation; and (3) the Life Satisfaction Scale (Pavot and Diener 1993), an index that assesses subjects' global evaluation of the quality of his or her life.

According to Petersen, et al. (1984), these six scales measure self-image or self-concept: i.e., a phenomenological organization of individuals' experiences and ideas about themselves in all aspects of their lives. Self-image is manifested through functioning in various social domains, such as school, family, and peer group, as well as through psychological functioning, such as impulse control and ease in new situations. Thus, self-image is multidimensional and should be measured and analyzed as such. In the framework of the person-oriented approach, theoretical expectations about individuals are evaluated with respect to at least three aspects of psychosocial adjustment: (a) nomothetic investigation of psychosocial adjustment in a population; in other words, any latent profiles indicative of subgroups in the sample; (b) idiographic study of individual characteristics with respect to the adjustment profiles; and (c) association between the profiles and other variables, such as mental health. We will illustrate the use of the MDS profile method to address research questions relevant to each of these three questions.

Using the data described above, an analysis using the MDS profile model in Eq. 10.1 was performed. Consider the sample data in Table 10.1 for 14 individuals out of 208 participants. These participants were selected only for illustrative purposes.

To address these three research questions, the focus of analysis becomes: what typical profiles of psychosocial adjustment of this kind actually exist in adolescents? To what degree does an individual follow his/her own development with respect to these "normative" profiles, that is, the fit of the model to an individual's data, and how are these profiles associated with adjustment outcomes? The MDS profile analysis was performed using the MDS analysis procedure found in commonly used statistical packages, such as that in SAS or SPSS.

In the current example, the squared Euclidean distances among these adjustment scales were computed based on Eq. 10.5. The distance matrix is shown in Table 10.2. Except for measurement and sampling error, the rank order of the model-based distance between pairs of points, $d_{vv'}$, is the same as the rank order of the data $\delta_{vv'}$. This implies that the distance will be related to the model parameters, x_{vk}; hence the scale values from the MDS solution represent estimates of the profile parameters.

Table 10.1 Scored data for MDS profile analysis

ID	Gender	BI	PR	FR	MC	VE	SA	PMI-1	PMI-2	FIT	Level	LS	Dep	PL
1	Female	2.82	5.10	5.00	4.60	5.70	4.30	−0.73	0.29	0.94	4.59	25.00	1.67	1.67
2	Male	3.82	5.00	4.71	4.90	5.40	4.90	−0.38	0.23	0.99	4.79	42.00	2.00	2.00
3	Female	4.09	5.80	5.77	4.90	5.50	5.10	−0.39	0.18	0.65	5.19	23.00	2.17	1.33
4	Male	5.09	5.30	4.69	6.00	6.00	5.50	−0.16	0.24	0.32	5.43	38.00	2.33	2.00
5	Male	5.55	5.70	3.88	5.50	5.40	4.50	0.19	0.54	0.55	5.09	34.00	2.33	1.50
6	Female	5.55	5.80	5.12	6.00	6.00	5.90	−0.06	0.25	0.46	5.73	42.00	1.17	1.17
7	Female	3.91	4.50	5.77	4.90	5.70	4.90	−0.52	−0.29	0.98	4.95	28.00	3.00	1.17
8	Male	4.73	5.00	5.12	5.40	5.50	5.50	−0.20	0.02	0.64	5.21	39.00	1.83	1.67
9	Male	4.73	4.20	5.77	5.60	5.70	5.10	−0.32	−0.48	0.87	5.18	33.00	2.50	2.17
10	Male	4.27	4.70	3.94	5.00	5.50	4.80	−0.21	0.30	0.48	4.70	34.00	3.00	2.17
11	Female	4.64	4.80	5.41	5.30	5.60	5.20	−0.27	−0.14	0.96	5.16	30.00	1.83	2.00
12	Female	4.91	4.70	5.41	5.00	5.80	4.60	−0.21	−0.23	0.57	5.07	38.00	1.83	1.17
13	Female	3.82	5.90	4.77	5.60	5.90	5.50	−0.48	0.59	0.97	5.25	43.00	3.00	1.00
14	Male	4.82	3.50	5.47	6.00	5.50	6.00	−0.27	−0.63	0.48	5.21	41.00	1.33	2.83

Note. BI body image, *PR* peer relations, *FR* family relations, *MC* mastery & coping, *VE* vocational & educational goal, *SA* superior adjustment, *PMI-1* profile match index for profile 1, *PMI-2* profile match index for profile 2

Table 10.2 Proximity matrix of six psychosocial adjustment variables

	BI	PR	FR	MC	VE	SA
BI	0.00					
PR	16.68	0.00				
FR	18.43	14.94	0.00			
MC	13.78	10.69	9.20	0.00		
VE	26.63	11.66	9.91	3.81	0.00	
SA	12.41	10.44	6.22	1.87	6.94	0.00

Note. BI body image, *PR* peer relations, *FR* family relations, *MC* mastery & coping, *VE* vocational & educational goal, *SA* superior adjustment

Thus, under the constraints stipulated in Eqs. 10.2a, 10.2b, and 10.2c, the MDS profile analysis uses the proximity matrix in Table 10.2 as data input and estimates the scale values x_{kv} through an iterative estimation algorithm, yielding one dimension for each profile. A nonmetric MDS analysis procedure was used because the distance data were assumed to be monotonically related to model-based distances in an underlying space. A profile is composed of the scale values x_{kv}, with large scales being salient marker variables of the profile. Table 10.3 shows the scale values for the data in Table 10.2. These scale values were derived from a two-profile model and the resulting solution was retained based on (1) interpretability and (2) model fit index, STRESS formula 1 value (S_1) (Kruskal 1964). The STRESS value was 0.00, indicating a good fit between data and the model; that is, the rank order in the data could be well reproduced by the model.

Table 10.3 Scale values of two MDS profiles for psychosocial adjustment

	Profile 1	Profile 2
Body image (BI)	2.28	−0.50
Peer relations (PR)	0.23	1.49
Family relations (FR)	−0.70	−1.20
Mastery & Coping (MC)	−0.25	0.14
Voc-Ed goals (VE)	−1.49	0.00
Superior adjust. (SA)	−0.08	0.08

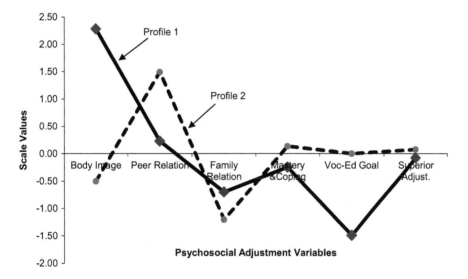

Fig. 10.1 Normative profiles of psychosocial adjustments for young adults

Figure 10.1 shows the two psychosocial adjustment profiles. The scale values along the profile represent a particular arrangement of scores for that prototype, which will reproduce observed score profiles (i.e., scatter and shape) but not the level of observed data. In a way, one can think of each MDS profile as representing a prototypical individual (i.e., type). That is, x_{kv} is the score of prototypical person s on variable v and the set of scale values x_{kv} ($v = 1,2,3...V$) is the profile of prototypical person s on the v measures with the level component removed. Each MDS profile represents a profile indicative of a subgroup. In our data, Profile 1 represents a prototypical individual with high scores on Body Image and low scores on the Vocational-Educational (Voc-Ed) Goal scale. Thus, for individuals who fit the model, those whose adjustment profile resembles the Body Image versus Voc-Ed Goals shape tend to report either a higher score on body image than on Voc-Ed goals or a higher score on Voc-Ed goals than on body image.

Profile 2 represents a prototypical individual with high scores on the Peer Relationships scale and low scores on the Family Relationships scale. Subjects whose psychosocial adjustment profile resembles this shape tend to report either higher on peer relationships than on family relationships or higher on family relationships than on peer relationships.

Thus, in MDS profile analysis, a vector of scale values is a particular arrangement of scores along the profile patterns. It represents each person's responses, m_{sv}, as a linear combination of the k prototypes x_{vk}, which indicates the profile patterns.

Columns 9–11 in Table 10.1 show the profile match indices for profiles 1 and 2 and fit statistics for each of the 14 participants. The sign of the profile match indices indicates that the subject's observed data exhibit either the profile or the opposite of the profile. For instance, the profile index on profile 1 for subject 1 was −0.73, suggesting that this participant tended to manifest the profile pattern opposite to the profile, that is, she tended to report a higher score on vocational-educational goals than on body image. Furthermore, variance in her observed data was mainly accounted for by profile 1 (fit = 0.94) since the profile match index on profile 2 was quite small (PMI-2 = 0.29 in comparison to PMI-1 = −0.73).

A word of caution is warranted. In MDS profile analysis the actual appearance of a particular profile depends on the way variables are listed. Since it is arbitrary which variable is listed in which position, the physical appearance of the profile can be arbitrarily changed without impacting level, dispersion, or shape of the profile. Because of this, some researchers call high points in a profile a "profile" and low points in the profile a "mirror image of the profile" (Davison 1994). What is a "mirror image profile?" Consider Profile 1 with high scores on the Body Image scale and low scores on the Voc-Ed Goal scale. Scale values along Profile 1 would reflect a prototype individual with high scores on Body Image measures and low scores on Voc-Ed measures. A large positive profile match index w_{sk} on the Profile 1 would characterize people with a high score on Body Image profile. The mirror image of Profile 1 is the Voc-Ed goal profile, characterized by high scores on Voc-Ed Goal measures and low scores on Body Image measures. A large negative profile match index would characterize subjects' mirror image. Although there are no available criteria to evaluate the effect size of profile match indices, the key point is the degree to which a subject in general tends to manifest the expected profiles of data.

The importance and utility of these profile match indices for individuals are that (1) by correlating these indices of individual differences in profile with other variables--such as age, education, gender, or psychological variables--one is in a position to study, for example, whether there is a gender difference with respect to the profiles (e.g., males are more likely to resemble profile 2 and females) and (2) one can examine how individuals think about themselves. This can be considered as a within-person pattern in that a participant may be more likely to manifest one expected profile than the other; that is, one could evaluate how individuals perceive themselves with respect to these profiles. For example, in the case of subject 1, she tended to be more education-achievement oriented than focused on her body appearance.

A fundamental premise of psychology is that psychosocial adjustment organization influences the operation of other psychological variables. Thus, adjustment profiles alone do not explain behavior, but rather, constitute only the first step. One

Table 10.4 Regression analysis of predicting psychological well-beings from the model derived profiles

	Depression	Psychological loneliness	Life satisfaction
Profile 1	−0.36**	−0.08	0.27**
Profile 2	−0.08	−0.27**	0.16
Level	−0.31**	−0.59**	0.45**

Note. Numbers are standardized regression coefficients
** $p < 0.01$

of the primary goals of psychologists has been the development of behavioral patterns that affect psychological well-being. In our current example, we investigated how model-derived profiles were associated with three mental health well-being measures: (1) the Kandel Depression Scale; (2) the UCLA Loneliness; and (3) the Life Satisfaction Scale. For such an analysis, we fit the regression model with profile match indices and level estimate as independent variables and three well-being measures as outcome variables. The analysis was performed just to provide a complete illustration of the MDS profile analysis.

The results are shown in Table 10.4. As can be seen in the table, level parameter estimates, which represented average scores of individuals' psychosocial adjustment, had significant standardized regression weights for all three measures. It would seem that participants who had overall positive psychosocial adjustment scores reported less depression or psychological loneliness and reported a higher degree of life satisfaction.

In addition to the association between the level and well-being measures, Profile 1 also had a significant standardized regression coefficient for the depression measure and the life satisfaction measure. It would seem that participants who had high scores on body image reported a higher degree of life satisfaction but those who reported high scores on vocational-educational goal reported a higher degree of depression. Profile 2 also was found to have significant standardized regression coefficients for psychological loneliness. Specifically, participants who had higher scores on the family relationships profile reported a higher degree of psychological loneliness.

Of course, we need to further discuss the meaning or implication of these findings with respect to some theories. The findings of these analyses were just used to illustrate that MDS profile analysis can be used for studying: (1) psychosocial adjustment patterns existing in a population, (2) the normative profiles that do not apply to all participants, who could follow entirely different profile patterns, and (3) the model-derived profiles that could provide additional information beyond that of the average scores. At a most general level, an MDS profile can help us determine whether a single model of psychological behaviors, which allows both individual- and group-specific parameter estimates, can provide a sufficient account of both normal and non-normal processes.

10.4   Conclusion

In this chapter we discussed an MDS-based profile analysis in an attempt to enhance our understanding of psychological mechanisms underlying or covarying with human behaviors. An important preliminary step in this effort entailed augmentation of the analytical strategies used in psychological research to allow simultaneous estimation of group- and individual-specific parameters. The MDS profile analysis discussed here allows this possibility by estimating group-specific profiles while simultaneously estimating individual-specific profile match indices. The potential utility of this approach lies in the fact that it separates level parameters (i.e., means) from profile patterns; it thus focuses on individual differences in profile patterns. It provides an exploratory method to classify persons on a continuum scale rather than on a dichotomous scale. It can provide an opportunity for studying correlates and predictors of group and/or individual behavior patterns.

This idiothetic research approach (hybridization of nomothetic and idiographic) should serve as a useful tool to link to more idiographic, but nomothetically informed, applications. We have argued that MDS techniques provide a promising method of characterizing relevant individual differences in psychological profiles. In addition, we have suggested that general linear models can be used in conjunction with MDS-derived profiles of psychological organization to illuminate the role of psychosocial adjustment in the operation of mental well-being. Admittedly, however, such applications are tentative because we simply do not yet know enough about the role of psychosocial processes in mental health to capitalize on these opportunities. We hope, nonetheless, to pique the reader's interest in the potential applications of the MDS profile analysis methods for individualized psychological assessment.

There are some caveats, on the other hand, that need to be noted regarding MDS profile analysis. First, the determination of the number of dimensions or profiles can be subjective. The major criteria are based on interpretability and reproducibility of the profile patterns, along with the model fit statistic. Second, the interpretation of the statistical significance of the scale values (i.e., variable parameter estimates) is somewhat arbitrary. There are no objective criteria for decision-making regarding which scale values are salient. Some researchers (e.g., Davison and Sireci 2000; Ding 2005) suggested a bootstrapping method to estimate the standard error of scale values and statistical significance of these scale values. Third, it is not well known to what degree the profiles recovered by an MDS profile analysis approach can be generalized across populations. Based on the research so far, it seems that different profiles may be recovered in two different populations, such as in a female population and a male population. On the other hand, it is also possible that the same profile solutions may emerge from different populations. Fourth, this approach is based on deterministic MDS techniques that may misconstrue large proximity measures as indicators of large inter-stimulus distances due to large rating variability on a stimulus. In this aspect, probabilistic MDS models offer definite advantages, for it takes into consideration of such variability in the estimation of scale values.

References

Affnso, V. C., Oakland, T. D., Larocca, R., & Spanakos, A. (2000). The course on individual cognitive assessment. *School Psychology Review, 29*(1), 52–64.

Allport, G. W. (1937). *Personality: A psychological interpretation*. Oxford: Holt.

Bechtel, G. G., Tucker, L. R., & Chang, W. C. (1971). A scalar product model for the multidimensional scaling of choice. *Psychometrika, 36*, 369–388.

Benzecri, J. P. (1969). Statistical analysis as a tool to make patterns emerge from data. In S. Watanabe (Ed.), *Methodologies of pattern recognition* (pp. 35–74). New York: Academic Press.

Bergman, L. R., & Magnusson, D. (1997). A person-oriented approach in research on developmental psychopathology. *Development and Psychopathology, 9*(2), 291–319.

Borg, I., & Groenen, P. J. F. (2005). *Modern multidimensional scaling: Theory and applications* (2nd ed.). New York, NY: Springer.

Cattell, R. B. (1967). The three basic factor analytic research designs: Their interrelations and derivatives. In D. N. Jackson & S. Messick (Eds.), *Problems in human assessment* (pp. 288–299). New York: McGraw-Hill.

Collins, L. M., & Lanza, S. T. (2010). *Latent class and latent transition analysis: With applications in the social, behavioral, and health sciences*. New York: Wiley.

Cronbach, L. J., & Gleser, G. C. (1953). Assessing similarity between profiles. *Psychological Bulletin, 50*, 456–473.

Davison, M., & Jones, L. E. (1976). A similarity-attraction model for predicting sociometric choice from perceived group structure. *Journal of Personality and Social Psychology, 33*, 601–612.

Davison, M. L. (1983). *Multidimensional scaling*. New York: Wiley.

Davison, M. L. (1994). Multidimensional scaling models of personality responding. In S. Strack & M. Lorr (Eds.), *Differentiating normal and abnormal personality* (pp. 196–215). New York: Springer.

Davison, M. L., Gasser, M., & Ding, S. (1996). Identifying major profile patterns in a population: An exploratory study of WAIS and GATB patterns. *Psychological Assessment, 8*, 26–31.

Davison, M. L., & Sireci, S. G. (2000). Multidimensional scaling. In H. E. A. Tinsley & S. D. Brown (Eds.), *Handbook of applied multivariate statistics and mathematical modeling* (pp. 323–352). San Diego: Academic Press.

Davison, M. L., & Skay, C. L. (1991). Multidimensional scaling and factor models of test and item responses. *Psychological Bulletin, 110*, 551–556.

Ding, C. (2005). Determining the significance of scale values from multidimensional scaling profile analysis using a resampling method. *Behavioral Research Methods, 37*(1), 37–47.

Greenacre, M. J. (1984). *Theory and applications of correspondence analysis*. Orlando: Academic Press.

Kandel, D. B., & Davies, M. (1982). Epidemiology of depressive mood in adolescents. *Archives of General Psychiatry, 39*, 1205–1212.

Kruskal, J. B. (1964). Nonmetric scaling: A numerical method. *Psychometrika, 29*, 28–42.

Lamiell, J. T. (1981). Toward an idiothetic psychology of personality. *American Psychologist, 36*, 276–289.

Magnusson, D. (1998). The logic and implications of a person-oriented approach. In R. B. Cairns, L. R. Bergman, & J. Kagan (Eds.), *Methods and models for studying the individual* (pp. 33–64). Thousand Oaks: Sage.

Muthen, B. O., & Muthen, L. K. (2000). Integrating person-centered and variable-centered analyses: Growth mixture modeling with latent trajectory classes. *Alcoholism: Clinical and Experimental Research, 24*, 882–891.

Paddock, J. R., & Nowicki, S. J. (1986). The circumplexity of Leary's interpersonal circle: A multidimensional scaling perspective. *Journal of Personality Assessment, 50*, 279–289.

Pavot, W., & Diener, E. (1993). Review of the satisfaction with life scale. *Psychological Assessment, 5*, 164–172.

Petersen, A. C., Schulenberg, J., Abramowitz, R. H., Offer, D., & Jarcho, H. D. (1984). A self-image questionnaire for young adolescents (SIQYA): Reliability and validity studies. *Journal of Youth and Adolescence, 13*, 93–111.

Pfeiffer, S. I., Reddy, L. A., Kletzel, J. E., Schmelzer, E. R., & Boyer, L. M. (2000). The practitioners's view of IQ testing and profile analysis. *School Psychology Quarterly, 15*, 376–385.

Russell, D., Peplau, L. A., & Cutrona, C. E. (1980). The revised UCLA loneliness scale: Concurrent and discriminant validity evidence. *Journal of Personality and Social Psychology, 39*, 472–480.

Speece, D. L., & Cooper, D. H. (1990). Ontogeny of school failure: Classification of first-grade children. *American Educational Research Journal, 27*, 119–140.

Tucker, L. R. (1960). Intra-individual and inter-individual multidimensionality. In H. Gulliksen & S. Messick (Eds.), *Psychological scaling: Theory and applications* (pp. 155–167). New York: Wiley.

Weller, S. C., & Romney, A. K. (1990). *Metric scaling: Correspondence analysis.* Newbury Park: Sage.

Chapter 11
Longitudinal Analysis Using MDS

Abstract Discuss how to extend the MDS model for longitudinal data analysis in the context of growth mixture modeling. Scale values can be interpreted in terms of growth or change parameters. Posteriori profile probability is introduced to classify individuals into different growth/change profile types. An example of real data is provided to illustrate the idea.

Keyword Growth profile analysis · Posteriori profile probability · Person fit index

In this chapter, we discuss how to use multidimensional scaling to explore and analyze longitudinal data. In order to provide a context of such an analysis, we first describe an example often encountered in the literature that calls for longitudinal analysis. Then we move onto how to use multidimensional scaling analysis in such a situation.

11.1 A Numerical Example

Tracking and monitoring student progress in mathematic achievement has been an important issue. Concerned that students did not possess the basic mathematical knowledge needed to function in complex society, legislators focused on mandates to increase both performance and accountability in schools. Since 2001, all schools across the nation are required to ensure students make adequate yearly progress in math and reading. As a result, many schools are required to mandate tests in math for all students in grades three through eight. For example, a local school district assessed student mathematical achievement repeatedly at 3rd, 4th, 5th, and 6th grades (i.e., in year 97, 98, 99, and 2000). At each assessment time, students completed the Stanford Math Test-Ninth edition that was used by the school district to measure students' math progress over the years. The scores were reported as scaled scores for each student across these four waves of data collection. Table 11.1 shows correlations and descriptive statistics for the dataset. The mean score indicates a linear growth. Figure 11.1 shows the growth patterns of 15 students randomly selected from the data.

© Springer International Publishing AG, part of Springer Nature 2018   149
C. S. Ding, *Fundamentals of Applied Multidimensional Scaling for Educational and Psychological Research*, https://doi.org/10.1007/978-3-319-78172-3_11

Table 11.1 Correlations, Means, and Standard Deviations for the Math Achievement Data of 15 Students across Four Occasions

	97	98	99	00
Math 97	1.00			
Math 98	0.72	1.00		
Math 99	0.68	0.76	1.00	
Math 00	0.66	0.77	0.83	1.00
M	593.17	629.36	646.85	664.15
SD	38.96	34.41	36.00	33.99

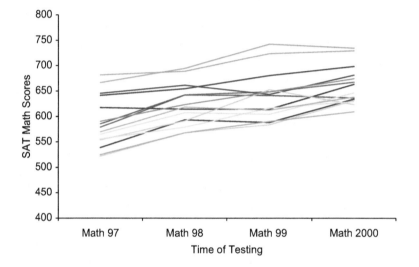

Fig. 11.1 Individual Students Growth Pattern of Math Achievement Over Four Measurement Occasions ($N = 15$)

This example is a typical research context in which individuals are measured at multiple time points on a particular variable (and it could also be on multiple variables) (Bock, 1975), and the key purpose of the analysis is to detect differences in patterns of individual growth. Given this situation, one question is how we go about analyzing such data; that is, what should be the model for change, as McArdle suggested (McArdle, 2009). A common methodology framework for longitudinal data analysis is latent growth curve modeling from the perspective of structural equation modeling (McArdle, 2009), which provides a powerful and flexible tool for researchers to study individual differences in growth as well as the correlates and predictors of the development. McArdle (2009) provided an extensive review of different longitudinal modeling approaches using structural equation models. It is beyond the scope of this chapter to discuss the details of these approaches. The discussion about the similarity and differences between multidimensional scaling approach and these other approaches can be found in Ding and his colleagues (Ding, 2005, 2007; Ding & Davison, 2005; Ding, Davison, & Petersen, 2005). It is now suffice to point out that recent developments in estimation and hypothesis testing of longitudinal data analysis are largely based on confirmatory structural equation approach. As Raykov (2000) pointed out, a major advantage of using covariance structure analysis is that this method explicitly takes account of measurement error and estimates error structures to incorporate individual differences.

However, if the nature of the data is concerned with change but not in the sense of growth, some latent growth models using structural equation approaches may not efficiently provide statistical estimates of change patterns (i.e., not growth pattern). In here, we particularly differentiate growth from change. Growth has conventionally been defined as systematic or directional changes, with the change considered as linear or monotonic (Willett, Ayoub, & Robinson, 1991). In contrast, change may be defined as being multidimensional in that it includes complex patterns such as oscillation between ups and downs. The multidimensional scaling approach described here is an alternative exploratory technique most suitable for the situation in which the growth or change patterns are to be derived from the data, rather than pre-specified by theory. Of course, we could also conduct confirmatory MDS growth profile analysis based on some theory or previous findings.

Based on the example described above, we discuss in the following sections how multidimensional scaling can be used in analyzing such longitudinal data.

11.1.1 Basic Ideas of Multidimensional Scaling (MDS) for Longitudinal Data Analysis

In Chap. 10, we discussed the multidimensional scaling model for profile analysis of cross-sectional data (Davison, Gasser, & Ding, 1996; Davison, Kuang, & Kim, 1999; Ding, 2006). Such a model can also be suitable for either growth curve analysis or change analysis, which involves (1) estimation of growth rates in form of scale values and re-scaling them to facilitate interpretation in the context of both growth curve analysis and change pattern analysis, (2) estimating the individual differences parameters and classification of individuals based on posterior probability, and (3) then predict growth or change using covariates. In the following sections, we discuss each of these points in more detail.

In the longitudinal analysis via multidimensional scaling model, the variables are defined as t measurements over time with the following equation:

$$m_{p(t)} = \sum_k w_{pk} x_{k(t)} + c_p + e_{p(t)} \tag{11.1}$$

where $m_{p(t)}$ is the score of person p at time t; w_{pk} is, a weight characterizing the pth individual with respect to the kth growth or change pattern. In other words, w_{pk} maps the observed data onto the several growth trajectories or change profiles represented by dimensions. $x_{k(t)}$, the scale value, is the location at time t along trajectory or profile (i.e., dimension) k. Essentially, what Eq. 11.1 says is that the observed change

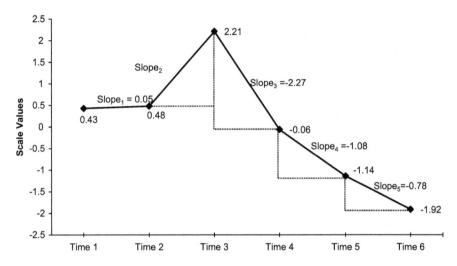

Fig. 11.2 Distance between each time interval as representation of growth rate for a set of variables

or growth patterns can be accounted for by some latent change or growth patterns and error (i.e., uniqueness due to individual differences).

Since MDS is a distance model, Fig. 11.2 illustrates the concept of distance as measured by scale value to represent growth rates. In Fig. 11.2, a set of variables over a six- time points is plotted along one dimension.[1] The differences between scale values of adjacent time points indicate the change (i.e., slope) for a given time interval. As can be seen in the figure, little or no growth occurs from time 1 to time 2 (slope$_1$ = 0.05), but a large change is observed from time 3 to time 4 (slope$_3$ = −2.27). It should be noted that although the interval must be the same for each individual, time intervals do not need to be equally spaced because growth rate is the slope for each particular interval. If the time unit between time 1 and time 2 is 3 months but the time unit between time 3 and time 4 is 1 year, then slope$_1$ indicates growth for the 3 months and slope$_2$ is the growth for 1 year.

To interpret the scale value properly, the origin of the scale values needs to be "centered" accordingly. Because Euclidean distances are invariant with respect to the choice of an origin, in MDS analyses, the fit of the model to the distance data is invariant with respect to a translation of origin. Therefore, once an MDS solution is obtained, the zero point on each dimension can be re-set in one of several ways, depending on the desired interpretation of the level parameter. The particular way of

---

[1] In MDS, dimensions are defined as a set of m directed axes that are orthogonal to each other in a geometric space. In the applied context, dimensions may be viewed as underlying representations of how the points may form certain groupings, which would meaningfully explain the data. This concept is similar to latent classes or factors in mixture modeling. Distance is defined as distribution of points along k dimension among pairs of objects (e.g., time points) in a plane that shows changes.

"centering" the origin of scale values along each dimension determines whether the model is a growth model or a change model.

If growth along the time dimension is to be studied, the MDS growth profile model can be created by centering the dimension zero point in a way that is meaningful for growth curve analysis. Given the importance of the initial level in the literature on growth, the zero point can be set to correspond to the scale value at the first time period (i.e., $x_{k(1)} = 0$ for all $\underline{k}$), then scale values will indicate growth rates for different time intervals. The intercept, c_p, becomes the expected or estimated score under the model for person p at the initial time t = 1; that is, the intercept corresponds to the initial level.[2]

On the other hand, if the data involve change, not growth, the above-mentioned method of centering would be inappropriate since a change pattern does not follow a monotonic (at least implicitly) trajectory as does a growth curve, especially when change patterns are cyclical or multidimensional. In this case, the zero point of scale values on each dimension is set equal to the mean scale value along that dimension; that is, mean of scale values = 0 for all k. If the zero point on each dimension is so defined, then scale values will indicate change patterns over time, and the intercept, c_p, becomes the average score of person $\underline{p}$ over several time periods. In most MDS algorithms, the origin of the scale values is set in this way by program default. Thus, the scale values do not need to be re-centered.

Estimates of $x_{k(t)}$, c_p and w_{pk} in MDS

Fundamentally, the estimation of $x_{k(t)}$, c_p and w_{pk} in MDS growth profile analysis is the same as that described in Chap. 10. For the purpose of convenience, we repeat the idea again below.

In an MDS analysis, the analysis begins with a matrix containing a distance measure defined over all possible pairs of variables. The distance module in many standard statistical packages (e.g. SAS, SPSS, R) includes an option for the computation of squared distance or distance measures defined over all possible pairs of variables over time.

When the computed distance matrix is submitted to a multidimensional scaling algorithm, either metric or nonmetric, the analysis will yield one dimension for each latent growth curve. A metric MDS algorithm is appropriate if it assumes that, except for the error, the distance data are linearly related to squared Euclidean distances. A nonmetric MDS algorithm is appropriate if it is based on the assumption that, except for the error, the distance data are monotonically related to squared Euclidean distances. The set of scale values $x_{k(t)}$ over time t along dimension k is an

---

[2] The issue of setting the origin for each dimension in the PAMS model corresponds to the "centering" issue in multiple regression. That is, just as the interpretation of the intercept parameter in multiple regression changes depending on how the predictor variables are centered, the interpretation of the intercept parameter in latent growth curve models changes depending on placement of the zero point along each growth dimension.

estimate of growth or change parameter. After we obtain the scale value, we can then estimate the person parameters, c_p and w_{pk}, through regression by treating scale values as independent variables and c_p and w_{pk} as the dependent variable.

Using the data from our example, the distance matrix based on the data was shown in Table 11.2.

This distance matrix was then used as input for nonmetric MDS analysis. As suggested by Borg and Groenen (2005), the choice between nonmetric and metric MDS is not consequential since the results tend to be the same. The analysis was done using *Proc MDS* in SAS. The results of the MDS analysis shows that two-dimension solution is appropriate, as assessed by MDS fit index, Stress formula 1 (Kruskal, 1964). The Stress formula 1 value was close to zero ($S_1 = 0.001$), indicating that the rank ordering of the six distance data points could be perfectly reproduced by the model estimated one-dimensional solution. More importantly, the person fit index R^2, which indicates the percentage of variance in the observed profiles that can be accounted for by the two-dimensional model, suggests that two latent growth profile patterns describe most of the observed individual growth pattern well, with median R^2 being 0.96 in comparison to median R^2 being 0.88 for one-dimensional model. Figure 11.3 shows the distribution of individuals' fit for one- and two-dimensional models, which clearly indicates that most of the observed individual growth pattern are well accounted for by the two-dimensional model.

The estimated MDS scale values over four data points are presented in Table 11.3. These scale values are re-centered by re-scaling the initial estimates so that the zero point corresponds to the scale value of time 1. Fig. 11.4 shows the latent growth pattern based on the re-centered scale values in Table 11.3.

Table 11.2 Distance matrix of math score over 4 years

YEAR	97	98	99	00
97	0			
98	25.74	0		
99	37.28	24.87	0	
2000	48.90	32.66	24.18	0

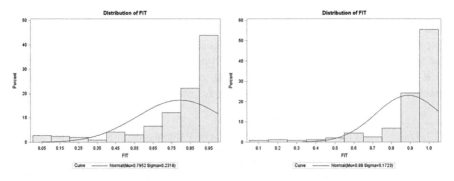

Fig. 11.3 Distribution of individuals' fit measure for one- and two-dimensional model

Table 11.3 Scale Values for the Growth Pattern of Math Achievement Over 4 Years

	Scale Value	
	Growth profile 1	Growth profile 2
Math 97	0.00 --	0.00 --
Math 98	1.59 (45%)	0.59 (16%)
Math 99	2.44 (24%)	−0.85 (−40%)
Math 00	3.57 (32%)	0.38 (35%)
Average growth rate	33%	4%

Note. Percentage in parenthesis is growth rate.

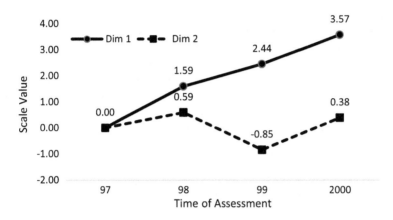

Fig. 11.4 Estimated Growth Pattern of Math Achievement

After we re-center the scale values, least squares estimate of the person parameters, c_p and w_{pk}, can be obtained through regression. Because the origin of the scale values was re-set to correspond to the scale value at time 1, the intercept can be interpreted as the predicted estimate of the initial level; that is, the estimated average score at time 1, which is 595.26 in our current example. The average of the profile weights was 20.07 for growth profile 1, with a standard deviation of 8.50, and 1.61 for growth profile 2, with a standard deviation of 14.75, which indicated that there were quite amount of individual variation in growth profile 2 in comparison to growth profile 1. The correlation between the intercept c_p (i.e., initial status) and the profile weight w_{pk} was −0.50 for growth profile 1 and 0.04 for growth profile 2. These correlations indicated that for students who resembled growth profile 1, having high initial math scores tended to make less gain in achievement over the four-year period, but for students who resembled growth profile 2, there was no relation between their initial achievement and later growth pattern.

Interpreting Scale Values

In MDS analysis, MDS is based on distance models, and the distance between any pair of adjacent time points (t_j and $t_j + 1$) represents a growth rate for that time interval, as shown in Fig. 11.4. Also, for a given time interval, and the time intervals do not need to be evenly spaced; the growth rate is the slope for each particular interval. Put another way, a scale value of, say, 1.59 at time 2 has the same meaning for a scale value of, say, 2.44 at time 3, which indicate an equivalent distance between two time points, as shown in Fig. 11.4, regardless of whether the time interval is equal or unequal. Thus, a particular set of scale values in MDS growth analysis indicates the changes over time in a specific behavior during a particular time frame.

However, MDS scale values are difficult to interpret because they have no upper or lower bound and can range from zero to $\pm\infty$. In our example, the interpretation of scale values of 1.59 at time two and of 2.44 at time three for growth profile 1, is not quite intuitive and it is hard to evaluate the magnitude of change. All we know is that the change is positive (i.e., growth), with a difference of 0.85 in scale value units between these two time points. Therefore, it would be good if we have a familiar metric that can be used to evaluate the magnitude of growth based on scale values.

Since the scale values in the spatial distance model are of Euclidean space, indicating the distance between two points, they satisfy the following three axioms (Davison, 1983):

$$d(a,b) \geq 0,$$

$$d(a,a) = 0,$$

$$d(a,b) = d(b,a)$$

where d represents the distance between points a and b. Thus, we can assume that when the scale values between any pair of time points are equal, they indicate no change. In contrast, when there is a difference in scale values between any pair of time points, it indicates that there may be a change in the behavior under inquiry.

Thus, we can calculate the percentage of growth in scale values between any pair of time points in the following fashion:

1. Calculate the difference in scale values between time t and time $t + 1$ for each time interval.
2. Calculate the total change in scale values over the entire time period under study using the absolute difference in scale values since the sign only indicates the direction of change. This is a total change score for each profile. For the current example, that total change score is 3.57 for growth profile 1 and 3.26 for growth profile 2.

3. Calculate the percentage of growth for each time interval by dividing the difference in scale values by the total change score. The resulting number indicates the percentage of growth with respect to the total amount of change.

In our example, the last column of Table 11.3 shows the growth rate in percentage for each of the three time intervals. The growth scale values depict the growth pattern in terms of three line segments. Each segment covers one time interval: 3rd grade to 4th grade, 4th grade to 5th grade, and 5th grade to 6th grade. Differences in growth rate over the several time intervals are represented by the slopes of the line segments for those intervals. For a given person who fits the model, growth is more rapid over intervals with steep line segments than over intervals with shallow line segments. As can be seen in Table 11.3, the growth rate for students who resembled growth profile 1 were largest (45%) from 97 to 98. In contrast, the growth rate for students who resembled growth profile 2 was 16% from 97 to 98 but negative (−40%) from 98 to 99. Thus, the average growth rate was 33% over 4 years for students resembling growth profile 1 but only 4% for growth profile 2.

Estimating Profile Type of Individuals

Based on the least squares estimate of the person parameter w_{pk}, individuals can be classified into each growth dimension or growth profile by using posteriori profile probability (Ding, 2007). For each individual p, the probability, p, of profile membership in profile k can be calculated as follows:

$$P_p\left(k|w_{pk}\right) = \frac{p_p\left(w_{pk}|k\right)\pi_p}{\sum p_p\left(w_{pk}|k\right)\pi_p} \tag{11.2}$$

where $P_p(k|w_{pk})$ is the estimated probability of observed individual p belonging to profile k, given the individual's profile match index or weight w_{pk}, and π_p is the estimated proportion of profile variance among the total variance in the observed profiles for a given individual. The quantity $p_p(w_{pk}|k)$ is the probability of observing w_{pk} for a given profile k. In a sense, the probability $p_p(k|w_{pk})$ can be viewed as an approximation of the posterior probability of profile type membership. The posteriori profile probability is calculated after estimation of the growth or change pattern. The

Table 11.4 Estimated Growth Pattern Weights of Math Achievement for Six Students

Case	Intercept (c_p)	Profile Weight (w_{pk})	R^2	Profile Type
1	604.34	16.42	0.99	1
2	657.43	8.13	0.58	1
3	651.76	4.78	0.18	1
4	613.53	12.10	0.09	2
5	605.07	8.08	0.53	2
6	614.75	−23.73	0.99	2

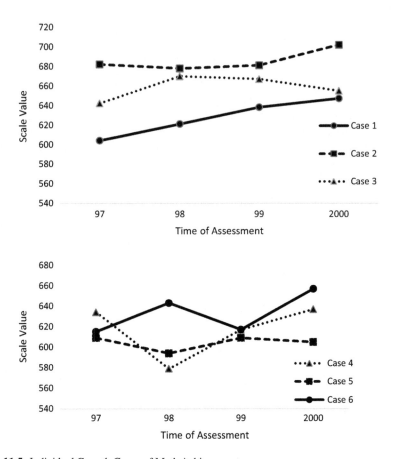

Fig. 11.5 Individual Growth Curve of Math Achievement

resulting profile type can then be used in subsequent analyses with covariates. For example, we could investigate the relationships between growth profile type and the covariate of sex or motivation level.

In our example, 307 students were classified as growth profile 1 type, and 30 students were classified as growth profile 2 type. To illustrate observed individual's growth profile types, Table 11.4 shows the estimated intercept, profile weights, and R^2 for six selected students. Fig. 11.5 shows their observed growth profiles by profile type. As can be seen in Fig. 11.5, students 1 and 6 closely resembled their latent profile type (with high fit index). In contrast, students 3 and 4 did not resemble their latent profile type (with low fit index). Students 2 and 5 were somewhere between with respect to their latent profile type (with moderate fit index).

To summarize, MDS analysis of longitudinal data proceeds in the following steps. First, distance measures are computed over all possible pairs of variables over time. These distance measures are analyzed via MDS to yield estimates of the parameters $x_{k(t)}$ in our model. In the second step, if the data are growth in nature, the zero point along each dimension is re-set so that the estimates of the intercept parameters will represent the initial level. In contrast, if the data are change in nature, the zero point along each dimension is set equal to the mean scale value of that dimension so that the estimates of the intercept represent the average score over time, and the scale values indicate change patterns along that dimension or profile over time. Third, we calculate the percentage growth from the estimated scale values. Fourth, the person parameters c_p and w_{pk} are estimated by regressing each person's raw data onto the MDS scale values. Fifth, posteriori profile probability is estimated for each individual to classify him or her into a growth or change profile type.

11.2 An Example of Change Profile Analysis

In the above sections, we discussed how to use MDS for growth analysis. In this example, we show how MDS works with change data, which identify underlying cyclical patterns such as mood change. The major difference between these two examples is concerning the centering of scale value. For growth data, scale value is typically centered so that the level parameter (i.e., average score) corresponds to the initial score (i.e., time 1 score), while for change data, scale value is typically centered so that the level parameter is the average score over time. The other aspects of analysis remain the same.

To illustrate an application of change data, data on adolescent (n = 30) reported mood status was used (Petersen, 1989). Specifically, we demonstrate one mood change variable---drowsy-alert --- over the period of 1 week, collected by the procedures of the Experiential Sampling Method (ESM) (Csikszentmihalyi & Larson, 1987). Specifically, over a period of 1 week the students were beeped 7 times per day at the following time intervals: between 7:30 am and 9:30 am, 9:30 am and 11:30 am, 11:30 am and 1:30 pm, 1:30 pm and 3:30 pm, 3:30 pm and 5:30 pm, 5:30 pm and 7:30 pm, and 7:30 pm and 9:30 pm. In addition, the students were asked to report their mood status on a 7-point semantic differential scale (Osgood, Suci, & Tannenbaum, 1957) before they went to bed and right after they got up in the morning. The exception was on Monday morning due to logistical reasons, where the students started to report their mood status from 9:30 am on. Thus, there were 61 data points collected on the mood variable. The variable was scaled so that a high score indicated a high degree of drowsiness and a low score indicated a high degree of alertness.

To facilitate the analysis, the data on drowsy-alert variable was grouped into three-time data points per day by averaging the data points of the morning, afternoon, and evening/night, leading to one data point for the morning, one data point for the afternoon, and one for the evening and night. Thus, for a given student, there were 21 data points (3 times a day for 7 days) used in the example.

As in the case of MDS growth profile analysis, the model presented in Eq. 11.1 was used to model drowsy-alert change patterns. The scale values were estimated using the nonmetric MDS procedure in SAS. As discussed above, the zero point of scale values along each dimension in change profile analysis is set equal to the mean scale value along that dimension. Thus, the level parameter estimate c_p indicates the average score over 21 data points for each person; the scale values indicate the change patterns rather than the growth in the data.

Because of lack of theoretical articulation with respect to mood swing in the normal adolescent population, it was difficult to determine how many dimensions were needed to describe the drowsy-alert change patterns based on theories adequately. The MDS fit index, Stress formula 1 value, was 0.32 for a one-dimensional solution, 0.14 for a two-dimensional solution, 0.08 for a three-dimensional solution, and 0.06 for a four-dimensional solution. The person fit index R^2 were about the same for three- and four-dimensional solution. The median R^2 was 0.56 for the three-dimensional solution. Judging from these results, it seemed that the 3-dimensional solution might be better in approximating the data without overfitting the model. The moderate size of R^2 might indicate that there might be more individual variations or more measurement errors in the data that could not be accounted for by the model.

Table 11.5 shows the change scale values for the 3-dimensional solution. Figs. 11.6, 11.7 and 11.8 show the plot of each change profile (i.e., dimension). As shown in these figures,

Table 11.5 Scale Values for Drowsy-Alert Change Profile Patterns

		Dim1	Dim2	Dim3
Monday	a.m	1.749	2.375	−1.703
	p.m	1.459	0.717	0.277
	Eve./night	−2.551	1.225	−0.798
Tuesday	a.m	−1.063	2.832	1.190
	p.m	0.574	0.284	1.202
	Eve./night	−1.495	0.544	−0.125
Wednesday	a.m	0.048	0.387	0.661
	p.m	1.381	−0.594	−0.586
	Eve./night	−0.722	−0.876	−0.177
Thursday	a.m	0.216	0.443	0.679
	p.m	0.943	−0.772	−0.002
	Eve./night	−1.760	−1.584	0.631
Friday	a.m	0.204	−0.373	0.588
	p.m	0.675	−0.304	0.736
	Eve./night	−0.894	0.240	0.055
Saturday	a.m	1.772	−0.449	0.081
	p.m	1.204	−0.591	−1.225
	Eve./night	−0.880	−0.781	−2.221
Sunday	a.m	0.532	−0.640	0.106
	p.m	0.386	−1.134	1.117
	Eve./night	−1.777	−0.949	−0.486

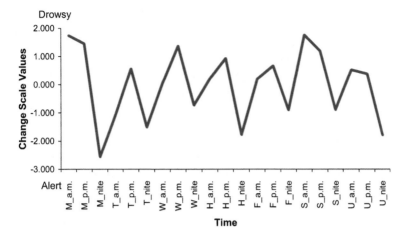

Fig. 11.6 Dimension 1: A daily cycle of mood change of daytime drowsiness versus evening/night alertness

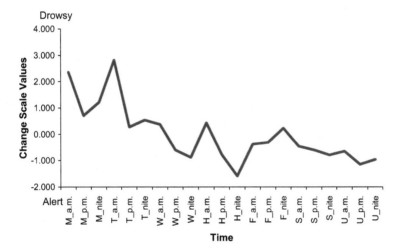

Fig. 11.7 Dimension 2: A weekly change pattern that gradually passes from highest drowsiness on Monday to lowest drowsiness (or highest alertness) on Sunday

Dimension 1 seemed to indicate a daily cycle of mood change: daytime drowsiness versus evening/night alertness. Students who resembled this profile would be drowsier during the daytime and more alert at evening/night time. Whereas Dimension 1 seems to represent a daily cycle of change, Dimensions 2–4 seem to represent weekly cycles. Dimension 2 shows a weekly change pattern that gradually passes from highest drowsiness on Monday to lowest drowsiness (or highest alertness) on Sunday. Respondents who resemble this profile pattern would manifest their highest degree of drowsiness early in the week and their highest degree of

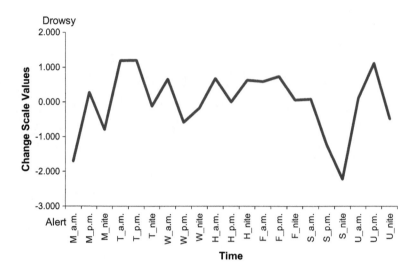

Fig. 11.8 Dimension 3: A weekly mood cycle with highest drowsiness on Tuesday and Sunday and lowest drowsiness on Monday and Saturday

alertness late in the week. Dimension 3 seems to represent a different weekly mood cycle with the highest drowsiness on Tuesday and Sunday and lowest drowsiness on Monday and Saturday. Such respondents are most alert on the first day of the week and the first day of the weekend.

These drowsiness findings demonstrated a MDS analysis of change, as opposed to growth. All three dimensions were interpreted in terms of change cycles. One interesting feature of the analysis is the detection of cycles with different periodicities. That is, Dimension 1 seems to reflect a cycle with a period of 1 day. The remaining dimensions appear to cycle with a period of 1 week. Their cyclical form differs sharply from the monotonically increasing (decreasing) form of growth (or decline) patterns.

11.3 Conclusion

In recent years, latent growth curve modeling has been widely used in longitudinal research. In this chapter, we discussed how to use MDS for analysis of longitudinal data with respect to growth or/and change. It was shown that if data were not growth in nature, latent growth modeling might not effectively handle the cyclical patterns in the data, as shown in the second example. In contrast, MDS is an exploratory analysis and can accommodate both growth and change in the data by appropriately setting the origin of the scale values. Thus, MDS analysis can be adapted to either model growth curve or model change but not growth, depending on the nature of the data.

The MDS growth/change analytical approach offers several advantages. First, the nature of the underlying growth or change patterns is determined by the data not researchers, although hypothesis testing approach can be performed via the method. While a priori specification of a unidimensional growth pattern model is often feasible, the difficulty of specifying the growth or change patterns a priori increases as the number of dimensions increases, as illustrated in the adolescent mood example above. Second, by appropriately setting the origin of the MDS solution, the approach can accommodate any of several desired interpretations for the intercept parameter estimate. Third, the assumptions are minimal. It assumes that the observed data are related to growth or change patterns by the model in Eq. 11.1 and it assumes homogeneity of error variances over time. Fourth, the approach can accommodate raw scores just as easily as deviation scores or Z-scores. Finally, the approach can provide level and growth pattern parameter estimates for each individual, thereby facilitating the study of the parameters themselves and their relationship to covariate. The approach provides estimates of model fit for each individual.

References

Bock, R. D. (1975). *Multivariate statistical methods in behavioral research.* New York, NY: McGraw-Hill.

Borg, I., & Groenen, P. J. F. (2005). *Modern multidimensional scaling: Theory and applications* (2nd ed.). New York, NY: Springer.

Csikszentmihalyi, M., & Larson, R. (1987). Validity and reliability of the experience-sampling method. *Journal of Nervous and Mental Disease, 175*, 526–536.

Davison, M. L. (1983). *Multidimensional scaling.* New York: Wiley.

Davison, M. L., Gasser, M., & Ding, S. (1996). Identifying major profile patterns in a population: An exploratory study of WAIS and GATB patterns. *Psychological Assessment, 8*, 26–31.

Davison, M. L., Kuang, H., & Kim, S. (1999). The structure of ability profile patterns: A multidimensional scaling perspective on the structure of intellect. In P. L. Ackerman, P. C. Kyllonen, & R. D. Roberts (Eds.), *Learning and individual differences: Process, trait, and content determinants* (pp. 187–204). Washington, D. C: APA Books.

Ding, C. S. (2005). Applications of multidimensional scaling profile analysis in developmental research: An example using adolescent irritability patterns. *International Journal of Behavioral Development, 29*(3), 185–196.

Ding, C. S. (2006). Multidimensional scaling modeling approach to latent profile analysis in psychological research. *International Journal of Psychology, 41*, 226–238.

Ding, C. S. (2007). Studying growth heterogeneity with multidimensional scaling profile analysis. *International Journal of Behavioral Development, 31*(4), 347–356.

Ding, C. S., & Davison, M. L. (2005). A longitudinal study of math achievement gains for initially low achieving students. *Contemporary Educational Psychology, 30*, 81–95.

Ding, C. S., Davison, M. L., & Petersen, A. C. (2005). Multidimensional scaling analysis of growth and change. *Journal of Educational Measurement, 42*, 171–191.

Kruskal, J. B. (1964). Multidimensional scaling by optimizing goodness of fit to a nonmetric hypothesis. *Psychometrika, 29*, 1–27.

McArdle, J. J. (2009). Latent variable modeling of differences and changes with longitudinal data. *Annual Reivew of. Psychology, 60*, 577–605. https://doi.org/10.1146/annurev.psych.60.110707.163612.

Osgood, E. C., Suci, G. J., & Tannenbaum, P. H. (1957). *The measurement of meaning*. Urbana, IL: University of Illinois Press.

Petersen, A. C. (1989). Coping with early adolescent challenge: Gender-related mental health outcomes (Grant No. 89127289). William T. Grant Foundation.

Raykov, T. (2000). Modeling simultaneously individual and group patterns of ability growth and decline. In T. D. Little, K. U. Schnabel, & J. Baumert (Eds.), *Modeling longitudinal and multilevel data: Practical issues, applied approaches and specific examples*. Mahwah, NJ: Lawrence Erlbaum Associates.

Willett, J. B., Ayoub, C. C., & Robinson, D. (1991). Using growth modeling to examine systematic differences in growth: An example of change in the functioning of families at risk of maladaptive parenting, child abuse, or neglect. *Journal of Consulting and Clinical Psychology, 59*(1), 38–47.

Chapter 12
Testing Pattern Hypotheses with MDS

Abstract Discuss how to conduct confirmatory MDS analysis of profile similarities in the context of configuration comparison. Model fit between hypothesized and observed profiles can be assessed with respect to local fit index rather than global fit index. Local fit can be assessed using correlation r, t-test or ANOVA, and F-test. An example is provided to demonstrate the idea.

Keywords Profile similarity · Local fit · Global fit

Traditionally, multidimensional scaling (MDS) is used in an exploratory method to detect and depict the patterns in the data. Much of the earlier efforts were devoted to discussion of the technical aspects of MDS estimation; that is, how to better recover the latent configuration based on the data such as avoiding degenerative solution or obtaining 'true' configuration. There are also discussions on studying configuration similarities and external MDS analysis that uses external information to study or interpret the properties of the MDS solutions. Few studies have discussed this aspect of the MDS analysis with respect to testing hypothesis (i.e., confirmatory analysis). However, the concept of configuration similarities and external MDS analysis can be extended to hypothesis testing since the idea of confirmatory analysis is to compare your hypothesis with the data and to examine the degree of similarities or fit between the two (i.e., hypothesized vs. observed). This is the same as what structural equation modeling tries to accomplish. In Chap. 9, we have discussed the process and procedures of comparing similarities and differences among a set of configurations. In this chapter, we specifically illustrate how to test growth or change profile patterns using MDS analysis and discuss the hypothesis testing of growth profiles rather than comparison among configuration.

© Springer International Publishing AG, part of Springer Nature 2018   165
C. S. Ding, *Fundamentals of Applied Multidimensional Scaling for Educational and Psychological Research*, https://doi.org/10.1007/978-3-319-78172-3_12

12.1   Basic Ideas of Pattern Hypothesis Testing in MDS

The idea of hypothesis testing is and should be straightforward. We have a hypothesis about a particular behavioral phenomenon and we want to see if our hypothesis can be supported by the data. In other words, if our hypothesis is consistent with data, our hypothesis is confirmed, at least by the data at hand. If not, more evidence is needed. The operationalization of confirmatory analysis is done by comparing two or more sets of profiles via correlation estimated from the model or our hypothesis with those computed from the data. Ideally, these two sets of configurations should match, indicating that data support our hypothesis.

Borg et al. (2013) classify confirmatory MDS into two types: regular confirmatory MDS and weak confirmatory MDS. A weak confirmatory MDS is the one in which the hypothesized configuration pattern is used as initial starting value for estimating the latent configuration. Since the goodness-of-fit of the final estimated configuration is partially based on the initial starting value, a quick convergence and goodness of fit may suggest the hypothesized configuration is consistent with the data. In my view, however, this is not really confirmatory since the extent to which observed data match the configuration expected by theory is unknown or inconclusive. Thus, when I speak of confirmatory MDS, it refers to regular confirmatory MDS in which we directly compare configurations or certain aspects of configurations expected by theory or previous findings with observed data.

Some complexity may arise in conducting confirmatory MDS. One issue is how to pre-specify a configuration in a two-dimensional space since we do not often define a set of behaviors as spatial configuration in most studies of social sciences. Thus, to translate theories into a configuration may not be so easy. One way to do so is to use clustering approach, in which we could pre-specify the configuration by clustering certain behaviors together in a two-dimensional space. Then we can compare the configurations from the data and generated by theory, as we discussed in Chap. 9.

However, in profile analysis, either cross-sectional or longitudinal profile analysis, it can relatively be easier to pre-specify a behavioral profile based on theory or previous findings. For example, in longitudinal profile analysis we can pre-specify a growth trend or change pattern of student learning achievement since we often expect certain achievement patterns based on previous findings. Thus, I think that the utility of confirmatory MDS is mainly in profile analysis.

Another issue of confirmatory MDS is what to compare or test. We can certainly compare observed distance matrix with estimated distance matrix from the model. This may be the most straightforward approach and very similar to comparing covariance matrix in confirmatory factor analysis.

Literature also discusses comparing or testing similarities of profiles, which becomes more complicated. This complexity arises with respect to level, shape, and scatter of the profiles and statistical indexes need to take into consideration of all of these aspects. Here are some examples of profiles:

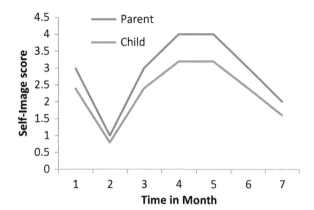

Fig. 12.1 Child self-report and parent's rating of child's self-image trait over a period of 7 months

- How similar are an individual's self-report of their own self-image traits, compared to ratings on the same traits made by another?
- How close is a student to an empirically established "risk profile" consisting of specific values for drug use, parent relations, and psychological distress such as anxiety or loneliness?
- How similar is an individual with respect to a set of behaviors such as math scores at several time points (e.g. 5 times)?

Consider two sets of scores on self-image trait over a period of 7 months in Fig. 12.1; one set is self-reported, and the second set is parent's report about the child.

The first thing we notice is that both raters agree on the rank ordering of the trait for the children. We call this the **shape** of the profile. However, child and parent disagree on the average **level** of the trait in the target over time. We call the mean level of each profile its **elevation**, which is just the mean of the elements in the vector (i.e., the average of a set of scores). Apparently, parents report a higher level of self-image of the child over time. A third element to profiles is called **scatter**, which is the standard deviation of elements in each vector about the vector's mean. Thus, in comparing these two profiles, we need to consider shape, level, and possibly scatter. A measure of profile similarity or equivalence should take these three elements into consideration, as often described in the literature.

In confirmatory MDS analysis, we often have a known profile pattern (i.e., expected profile), and we want to test whether the observed profile is the same as the one expected by theory. In this case, we need to test both shape and level. Please note that as we mentioned previously, we can test two distance matrices, but the distance matrix is determined by the shape of the profile, not by level. Therefore, in confirmatory MDS, we need to be careful as to what we want to accomplish. I will discuss these specific issues involved when we discuss the methods of testing the hypothesis about profiles.

12.2 Methods for Hypothesis Testing of Profiles

There are several ways we can use to conduct confirmatory MDS. Each method may focus on different aspects of testing two or more latent profiles. One way to do so is by using Procrustes analysis as we discussed in Chap. 9. For purpose of convenience, we repeat some of these materials again to remind us about the fact that comparing configurations can be used to hypothesis testing. Briefly, Procrustes analysis (Gower 1975) involves moving hypothesized configuration(s) X or observed configuration matrices into closest conformity and form a new configuration matrix Z, called "centroid configuration," allowing only rotation, reflection, rescaling, and translation of origin. The centroid configuration is best-fitting configuration since each of its points is a least-square fit to the corresponding points of the original configurations. Various names are also used for this centroid matrix, such as average configuration, group configuration, compromise, or consensus configuration. Interested readers can find the iterative procedure for producing the centroid configuration described by Gower (1975).

The goodness-of-fit of a set of models (i.e., hypothesized vs observed) can be examined in is terms of model similarity index P_0 (basic model), P_1, P_2, P_3, and P_4 models. P_0 model involves "admissible transformation" in which the relative distances are unchanged. The other models involve "inadmissible transformation" in that the original relative distances are changed. P_1 and P_2 are distance model in which dimensional weighting are applied to either centroid configuration or each configuration in order to move centroid configuration into maximum conformity with the original configuration. Similarly, P_3 and P_4 are vector or perspective model in which vector weighting are applied to either centroid configuration or each configuration in order to reach such conformity.

Briefly, P_1 model (the weighted distance model with fixed dimensional orientation) rotates the centroid configuration in such a way so that dimension weights in each configuration are estimated accordingly. This is equivalent to INDSCAL analysis. P_2 model (the idiosyncratically rotated and weighted distance model) differentially rotates and estimates the dimension weight of centroid configuration to fit each configuration idiosyncratically. This is equivalent to IDIOSCAL analysis (Carroll and Wish 1973).

P_3 model (the weighted vector model with fixed origin) is weighted vector model in which a set of vector weights consistently transform the centroid configuration into as close as possible to each individual configuration. For any configuration, the closer the weights are close to +1, the more that each configuration resembles the centroid. The large size or sign of the weights may indicate where the differences are located, and the vector weights are comparable across each configuration. When vector weight of a variable point varies across configurations, it indicates that this variable is least stable in the configuration and should be further studied. This is very useful to identify where the mis-fits are when testing configuration hypothesis; that is, it may provide insight into the detail about the source of variation in configuration.

Table 12.1 Rating by parents and child self on his/her self-image trait over time

Time in month	Parent	Child
1	3	2.4
2	1	0.8
3	3	2.4
4	4	3.2
5	4	3.2
6	3	2.4
7	2	1.6

P_4 model (the idiosyncratically translated and weighted vector model) is to differentially translate and weight each individual vector to fit each configuration, which is termed as the "point of view" model in that the idiosyncratic origins can be directly compared. We can compare whether two groups of individuals differ significantly in their perspectives.

These models can be used for different purposes. But for hypothesis testing of configuration or profile equivalence, I would suggest using only basic model P_0 index because P_0 does not distort the relative distance of points. We may use the other models when we want to investigate why or how there are some differences in the profiles.

12.2.1   Testing the Hypothesis of Profile Equivalence

Let us repeat the example shown in Fig. 12.1 and Table 12.1 shows the corresponding rating by parents and child self on his/her self-image trait.

As we mentioned previously, the profile equivalence involves the profile's shape, level, and scatter. In this example, the shape of these two profiles seems to be the same, but the level of the self-image trait seems different, with parents reporting a higher level of the child self-image. In the literature, it was said that a measure of profile equivalence should take into consideration of both shape and level (i.e., the average score of each vector of ratings).

Various measures of profile equivalence have been proposed. Among them includes correlation, intra-class correlation, Cronbach and Gleser's D or D^2 (1953), or McCrae's r_{pa} for "r profile agreement (McCrae 1993). Each of these indices has advantages and disadvantages. For example, correlation is perfect for assessing similarity of shape, but not level or scatter. Cronbach and Gleser's D or D^2 is a measure of geometric distance between vectors, which has no significance test and is impacted by extreme scores. McCrae's r_{pa} is developed to deal with this problem specifically in personality profiles by weighting disagreement at extreme levels of a variable less, and crediting agreement in these extreme values more. However, because of this weighting, scores that are in quite close agreement but near the middle of the distribution will have low r_{pa}. In addition, it is difficult to evaluate "good agreement".

My view on the measure of profile equivalence is this: why do we have to find a global index, which may not be useful? For instance, if the global index is high, it indicates that two profiles are equivalent with respect to shape, level, and scatter. But if the global index is in the middle or low range, what does it indicate? It is possible the shape is the same but not the level or scatter. It could also be any combination of these. Thus, a global fit index is not very helpful in identifying where the misfit locates even if we can develop such a measure by taking into consideration of shape, level, and scatter.

I think that the solution is simply--focusing on local fit index. If all local indices show a good fit, then the profile equivalence is supported. If some local fit index is not acceptable, we will know what the problem may be. Thus, I suggest that we use correlation r_p as a measure of profile shape equivalence, t-test or analysis of variance (if more than two profiles involved) for level difference, and F-test for scatter difference. These tests are well developed and measure each aspect of profile equivalence. A global measure may look fancy and impressive, but these local fit indices may just do a very good job.

Using the data from our example in Table 12.1, we get the follow local fit indices: $[r_p = 1, t_l = 1.10, p = 0.029, F_s(6,6) = 1.56, p = 0.30]$. These results indicate that the two profiles are equivalent with respect to shape, level, and scatter, indicating parent and child have the same assessment of self-image trait. Thus, the hypothesis of profile equivalence is supported.

It should be noted that testing profile equivalence with respect to level and scatter is impacted by the scale of the profile involved. Thus, the scale metric of the profiles should be the same (e.g., scale is from 0 to 5 for both profiles). If the profile scale is different, the shape may be the same but the level and scatter will be different, although there may not be any real differences between two levels or scatters.

12.2.2   Testing a Hypothesis of Specific Patterns

In above sections, we discussed hypothesis testing of configuration or profile equivalence based on observed data. We did not use hypothesized configuration or profile because it is sometimes difficult to pre-specify configuration. Whether the configuration or profile is pre-specified or not, the testing procedure we discussed above is the same. But we need to be cautious about the scale of the profiles and make sure that they are on the same scale before testing level and scatter equivalence of the profiles involved.

Although pre-specifying a configuration is not so common, it is relative easy to pre-specify growth profiles based on some theory or previous finding. For example, we can hypothesize certain growth patterns based on our expectation or previous findings. Also, it is important to note that in this case, we may mainly be interested in shape of the growth or change rather than difference in level. Let us use an example to illustrate.

	Time	Hypothesize trend	Observed trend
Table 12.2 Hypothesized and observed growth trend over five-time points	1	9.800	5.62
	2	9.996	7.46
	3	12.220	10.16
	4	13.066	12.36
	5	14.290	13.75

The example comes from the Motor Performance Study at Michigan State University. For the univariate growth modeling analysis, Park and Schutz (2005) used the jump-and-reach variable (JAR) that was repeatedly measured from 204 male children at five occasions from ages 8–12 year. They analyzed the correlation matrix using structure equation model and reported the linear growth model fit the data best, with the average jump growth of 1.02 per year from ages 8–12. Based on this finding, we expect children's ability to jump should be a linear increase with age.

In order to test this hypothesis, we collected data on 50 children of five age groups: ages 6, 7, 8, 9, and 10. This is not ideal since it is not truly longitudinal rather a cohort sequential design to save time and resources. Given the physical nature of normal development of children, cohort sequential design roughly approximates true longitudinal design of the same children. Thus, we scaled these jump data using MDS analysis.

There are two ways to perform this kind of confirmatory MDS analysis. The first one is to compare two profiles and test for growth pattern equivalence between hypothesized one and observed one using the method discussed above. The second one is to use maximum likelihood MDS analysis program such as *Proscal* (MacKay and Zinnes 2014) to test the same hypothesis. Let us start with the first method, which is relatively simply. Based on the means and average growth rate of 1.02 per year reported by Park and Schutz (2005), we pre-specified the linear growth trend as shown in the second column of Table 12.2.

We scaled the data using MDS analysis, and the result of the scale values are shown in the third column of Table 12.2. To test growth profile equivalence, correlation between the two profiles was computed, and $r_p = 0.98$, indicating that the hypothesized growth profile was supported by the data. It should be noted that the scale values obtained from MDS analysis were re-scaled to have a similar metric. But this re-scaling is not affecting the relative distance, nor the shape of the profile. Again, since we are only interested in shape of the profile, we are not concerned about the level and scatter of the profiles, which are affected by the re-scaling of the scale value. If we are interested in all three aspects of the profile equivalence, we should put them on the same metric before doing MDS analysis. But in longitudinal analysis, we focus primarily on shape and the initial value.

The second method of confirmatory MDS analysis is to use maximum likelihood MDS analysis (ML-MDS), which naturally fit for confirmatory analysis. In addition to testing shape,

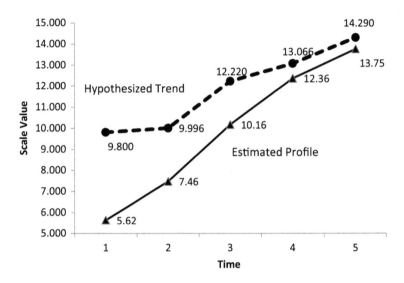

Fig. 12.2 Hypothesized and observed profiles

ML-MDS also provides for the testing of hypotheses concerning the variance structure of the profile among other things such as dimensionality of the space, metric properties of the space, the existence of a common space for proximity and hedonic rating, dependent or independent sampling and the structure of the measurement model. Typically, the question of whether a complex model is significantly better than the simpler model can be answered by using a likelihood ratio test or information criterion statistics.

In the current example, we used the same scale values in Table 12.2 as our hypothesized configuration profile, which was then tested against the estimated profile from the data. We tested the degree of similarity between the hypothesized growth profile and the growth profile derived based on the data. The results of the analysis using *Proscal* program indicated that the match between two profiles was very high, $r = 0.98$, suggesting the hypothesized growth profile was supported by the data. Fig. 12.2 shows the two profiles estimated using *Proscal*.

12.3   Conclusion

In this chapter, we discussed how to conduct confirmatory MDS analysis. As it may be apparent to you by now, the procedure and process of confirmatory analysis using MDS model is different from that of commonly used method such as structural equation modeling, although the concept of confirmatory analysis is identical. Most researchers are familiar with structural equation modeling approach to confirmatory analysis, but much less familiar with MDS approach. The take-home message for conducting MDS confirmatory analysis is that we are testing to two (may be more) configurations or profiles, with one of them being hypothesized or pre-specified. Then we assess the degree of similarity or equivalence between them using correlation, t-test, or F-test, depending on what aspect of similarity we would like to test. The process is simple and straightforward and much less complex, which may seem too boring or less exciting, particularly to research in social sciences or education. But we should know why we are conducting research from the first place rather than focusing on new or complicated analytical methods. If the methods fit the purpose of our study, they are appropriate, regardless of how simple or complicated they are. In this case, simpler methods may be better.

References

Borg, I., Groenen, P. J. F., & Mair, P. (2013). *Applied multidimensional scaling*. Berlin: Springer.

Carroll, J. D., & Wish, M. (1973). Models and methods for three-way multidimensional scaling. In R. C. Atkinson, D. H. Krantz, R. D. Luce, & P. Suppes (Eds.), *Contemporary developments in mathematical psychology*. San Francisco: W. H. Freeman.

Cronbach, L. J., & Gleser, G. C. (1953). Assessing similarity between profiles. *Psychological Bulletin, 50*, 456–473.

Gower, J. C. (1975). Generalised procrustes analysis. *Psychometrika, 40*, 33–51.

MacKay, D.B., & Zinnes, J. (2014). *PROSCAL* professional: A program for probabilistic scaling: www.proscal.com.

McCrae, R. R. (1993). Agreement fo personality profiles across observers. *Multivariate Behavioral Research, 28*(1), 25–40.

Park, I., & Schutz, R. W. (2005). An introduction to latent growth models: Analysis of repeated measures physical performance data. *Research Quarterly for Exercise and Sport, 76*(2), 176–192.

Chapter 13
Mean-Level Change vs. Pattern Change

Abstract Illustrate the similarities and differences between MDS growth analysis and growth mixture modeling approach using structural equation modeling. The key point is that MDS focuses on pattern with mean-level removed, while growth mixture modeling focuses on mean-level. Although the results from both approaches may be the same at times, two approaches may provide different aspects of growth or change. An example is provided to demonstrate these two approaches.

Keywords Growth profile analysis · Mean-level change · Pattern change

In recent years, statistical methods for latent growth modeling have been commonly used in educational and psychological research. In Chap. 11, we discussed how MDS can be used to study latent growth profile. One issue that has not been explicitly discussed is the level vs. pattern differences when modeling profiles (either longitudinal or cross-sectional). In this chapter, we discuss how MDS profile analysis focuses on patterns per se in the data, not on level patterns, and illustrate how MDS growth pattern analysis may differ with respect to modeling changes in level, as commonly done with other methods, given that all these methods have similarities in terms of model estimation, latent groups identification, classification of individuals, and the interpretation of growth trajectory. The goal is to show that MDS models changes in shape not in elevation, a differentiation should be made (Skinner 1978).

13.1 Differentiating Level, Scatter, and Shape of a Pattern

For the purpose of convenience, we repeat the equation of MDS profile analysis as discussed in Chap. 10:

$$m_{sv} = \sum_k w_{sk} x_{kv} + c_s + e_{sv} \tag{13.1}$$

C. S. Ding, *Fundamentals of Applied Multidimensional Scaling for Educational and Psychological Research*, https://doi.org/10.1007/978-3-319-78172-3_13

where m_{sv} is an observed score of person s on variable v, w_{sk} is profile match indices for person s on dimension k, that is, w_{sk} is a participant by dimension matrix, with the order of s participants by k dimensions; x_{kv} is a variable location parameter (i.e., scale value or coordinate) along dimension k, c_s is a level parameter, and e_{sv} is an error term. For Eq. 13.1, we have the constraints for scale values as:

$$\sum_v x_{kv} = 0 \qquad \text{for all k} \qquad (13.2)$$

This constraint specifically states that each profile is ipsative; that is, the mean of the scores in each profile is zero. Thus, profiles will produce profile patterns (scatter plus shape), but not the mean (i.e., level) of the profiles, which is reproduced by level parameter c_s. The implication of this constraint is that the growth profiles from MDS analysis may differ from those that are based on models explicitly using level information; that is, MDS profile analysis depicts growth patterns of scatter and shape, while the other growth modeling analysis depicts growth patterns of level. We will discuss this difference in the context of growth mixture modeling.

13.2 A Brief Overview of Growth Mixture Modeling

One particular kind of latent growth curve modeling[1] receiving more attention in recent years is growth mixture modeling (GMM). It is beyond the scope of this chapter to introduce the details of GMM. Those unfamiliar with GMM may wish to consult Jung and Wickrama (2008) or Ram and Grimm (2009) for a good introduction. Suffice it to say here, GMM is an extension of single-population latent growth models, combining latent class analysis and latent growth curve modeling into one coherent modeling system. It is particularly useful when the subpopulation is unobserved or unknown a priori and is designed to identify and describe qualitatively distinct classes of cases with respect to change in level, allowing different growth parameters across the classes. As such, it can be employed to test the hypotheses of (a) whether there are different change trajectories actually present in the clinical population and (b) if they exist, whether the trajectories are defined by different initial growth status (i.e., initial level) as well as later growth rates in level. Ram and Grimm (2009) specify GMM model as follows:

$$y_{it} = \Sigma \left[\pi_{ic} \left(f_{0ic} \lambda_{0ct} + f_{1ic} \lambda_{1ct} + e_{ict} \right) \right] \qquad (13.3)$$

where y_{it} is an individual's score y at time t. f_{0ic} and f_{1ic} are latent growth factors that represent intercept (i.e., initial score) and slope (i.e., growth shape) of latent class c

---

[1] As indicated by Ram and Grimm (2009), latent growth modeling is a generic term that include various similar growth modeling approaches, such as latent trajectory analysis, latent curve modeling, mixed effects models of change, multilevel models of change, etc.

to which individual i belongs. λ_{0ct} and λ_{1ct} are factor loadings corresponding to the two growth factors. e_{ict} is a time-specific residual. π_{ic} is the probability that individual i belongs to latent class c, with $0 \leq \pi_{ic} \leq 1$, and $\Sigma\pi_{ic} = 1$. Estimated posterior probabilities for each individual's class membership are derived as $\pi_{ic} = p(k_{ic} = 1|y_i)$, with the latent class membership indicators, k_{ic}, being 1 if individual i belongs to class c, and 0 otherwise. The objective of GMM is (1) to represent across-class differences in the initial score and the growth shape, (2) to determine the means of growth factors, and (3) to establish variance and covariance of the growth factors.

As indicated by Jung and Wickrama (2008), there are three main areas of GMM that attract much of the current debates: (1) identification of latent classes, (2) which model fit index to use, and (3) the problem of convergence. The first two issues are not unique to GMM since many other modeling methods encounter the same issues. In this regard, good research should focus on questions that prompt the clinical hypotheses. We need to judge the models by whether they conform to our theories. The third issue is more challenging since the computational load of GMM estimation is very heavy and mathematically modeling a sample distribution that consists of a mixture of many different kinds of sub-distributions is extremely difficult (Jung and Wickrama2008). As a result, some models are less stable or difficult to estimate. Accordingly, Wang and Bodner (2007) recommend using GMM in a confirmatory manner rather than exploratory manner in which the model may undergo many modifications to find a better fit.

13.2.1 Growth Mixture Modeling Via MDS

Since Chap. 11 discusses the analytical approach of growth and change via MDS, in this chapter we only focus on some key differences between MDS approach and GMM using a SEM approach. As discussed above, multidimensional scaling growth pattern analysis is an exploratory method that focuses on modeling change in pattern only, with level being removed. This is the chief difference between the two approaches. That is, a key distinction between GMM and MDS is that MDS does not accommodate level differences, while GMM can be used with a random intercept factor within-class to account for differences in level, with differences in shape being accommodated through class level differences. Although MDS analysis has the same objective as GMM, its methodological foundation is a geometric or spatial representation of relationships among repeated measures. As discussed in Chaps 10 and 11, dimensions represent profile, and thus a dimension from MDS growth analysis represents changes in pattern (i.e., scatter and shape) when the variable under study is repeated across time. In other words, in MDS models, each dimension k represents a growth curve, or an exemplar of a particular arrangement of scores of different time points, called a prototypical growth pattern or latent growth profile. This growth curve is quantified by a set of scale value estimates x_{kt} from the Euclidean distance model in MDS analysis. In a sense, this set of scale value estimates can be considered a set of polynomial contrast coefficients, which can be used for hypothesis testing in a subsequent analysis.

For convenience, we repeat the equation of the MDS growth pattern model in Chap. 11. The model is:

$$y_{it} = c_i + \sum_k w_{ik} x_{kt} + \varepsilon_{it} \qquad (13.4)$$

where y_{it} is the observed score for individual i at time t. x_{kt} is a scale value, as described previously. c_i is a level parameter or initial score for person i if the average scale value is centered on the first time of measurement. ε_{it} is an error term for person i at time t. w_{ik} represents the individual's profile match index that quantifies the degree to which an individual manifests the identified growth profile. First, MDS analysis involves estimating scale values from a distance matrix computed for every pair of time points, t_i and t_{i+1}. The distance data for time points t_i and t_{i+1} is the difference between the scores y_i at times t_i and t_{i+1} for person i.

MDS growth pattern analysis to modeling growth mixture, as we described above and in Chap. 11, has three main aspects that differ from commonly discussed GMM. First, the estimation of growth pattern or profile, as indicated by scale values, and the number of growth classes (i.e., growth profile type), as indicated by the number of dimensions, are different. For GMM, latent class analysis model is first used for classification of individuals and a latent class indicator variable is computed. The growth model is then estimated using this information (e.g., Asparouhov and Muthén 2012; Vermunt, 2010). MDS growth pattern analysis takes the reverse approach, first identifying the typical growth patterns or profiles and then determining how much each individual resembles a given growth pattern or profile. However, both approaches can be subject to classification error.

One practical implication of this difference is that the model building process for MDS growth pattern analysis is easier to implement as one only needs to specify a set of 1 to k dimensional solutions and choose a k dimensional solution that best approximates the data. The measure for model selection is *Stress* value (Kruskal 1964) or R^2, an index of the proportion of variance in observed growth profiles accounted for by the model. There is no need to specify a series of models with respect to growth trajectory and number of classes, as recommended by Muthén and Muthén (2001) and Ram and Grimm (2009) for GMM analysis.

Second, and more importantly, MDS growth pattern analysis typically models change in patterns rather than in levels that mirror the observed trajectories. This is because the growth profiles of MDS solutions have a mean of zero and are represented as deviations about the growth profile's mean of zero. Positive growth profile scale values signify scores above the growth profile's mean; negative scale values signify scores below the growth profile's mean. Thus, the MDS solutions display the patterning of scores in a prototypical growth profile but do not display elevation or level information (Davison et al. 1996). In most GMM analysis, growth trajectory is typically represented by a regression model, either linear or nonlinear, which indicates the change in level. This is a key difference between the two approaches as discussed previously. One implication of this distinction is that MDS and GMM analysis may result in a different number of growth classes/types. Specifically, when change in pattern displays the same information as the level, two approaches reach the similar findings. But if there are fewer changes in pattern than in level, then MDS growth pattern analysis may results in a fewer growth classes/types than that from GMM analysis.

13.3 Numerical Examples

Two hypothetical examples and one actual data are used to illustrate the points discussed in the previous sections. In the first example, we simulate a dataset (n = 500) with two latent classes that have only one growth pattern but have differences in growth levels. That is, given one overall growth pattern (an increased trend), the individuals in each latent class may differ in level with respect to the growth pattern, with some individuals having a higher growth level and some having a lower growth level. Figure 13.1 shows observed growth trajectories of 50 individuals randomly selected from this first simulated dataset. Figure 13.2 shows the estimated latent trajectory from MDS growth pattern analysis and Fig. 13.3 shows the estimated latent trajectories from GMM analysis.

As can be seen from Fig. 13.2, the growth trajectory from MDS growth pattern analysis reflects the observed overall patterns with differences in mean or level removed. Thus, one growth profile is estimated to represent the prototypical growth pattern in the observed trends. On the other hand, the growth trajectories in Fig. 13.3 from GMM analysis indicate two growth classes, which can be expressed as

$$\text{class} 1 : \hat{y}_{it} = 1.24 + 1.68time + 0.74time^2$$

$$\text{class} 2 : \hat{y}_{it} = 1.10 + 1.67time + 0.03time^2$$

These two classes mainly differ with respect to mean level, although class 1 seems to have a faster growth acceleration.

In the second example, we simulate another dataset (n = 500) that has two latent classes, each with its own growth pattern - one is linear and another is quadratic. Accordingly, the grow trajectory differs not only in terms of level but also in terms of growth pattern (i.e., scatter and shape). Figure 13.4 shows observed growth trajectories of 50 individuals randomly selected from this second simulated dataset. Figure 13.5 shows the estimated latent trajectory from MDS growth pattern analysis. Figure 13.6 shows the estimated latent trajectories from GMM analysis.

As can be seen from Fig. 13.5, two MDS growth patterns reflect the observed growth patterns with differences in mean removed. That is, two growth profiles are estimated to indicate the prototypical growth patterns in the observed trends. Similarly, the growth trajectories in Fig. 13.6 from GMM analysis also indicate two growth classes, which can be expressed as

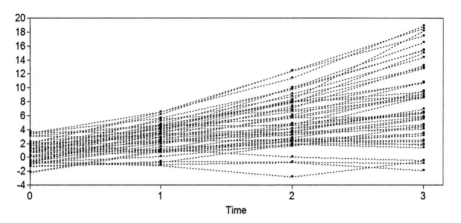

Fig. 13.1 An example of observed growth trajectories of 50 individuals randomly selected from the first simulated data with two latent classes but one growth pattern

Fig. 13.2 Estimated growth pattern from MDS growth analysis based on the first simulated data

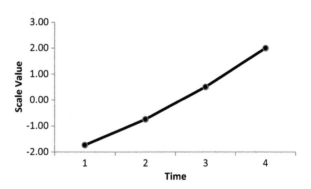

$$\text{class 1}: \hat{y}_{it} = 0.96 + 1.56time + 0.48time^2$$

$$\text{class 2}: \hat{y}_{it} = 2.29 + 3.69time - 1.28time^2$$

Thus, the key point is that both analytic approaches are correct in depicting the growth trends, but in a different way. One practical implication of this difference is that the growth trajectory from these two analytic approaches may manifest a different pattern as can be seen here, depending on the degree to which the observed patterns coincide with the level.

In this third example, we analyzed the mathematic achievement of 9549 children with the complete data across the four waves of a mathematic assessment, which contains items that assess basic skills such as counting, shapes, addition, fractions, area, and volume. Scale scores derived from item response theory (IRT) were used for the growth analysis. The data were based on the Early Childhood Longitudinal Study, Kindergarten Class of 1998–99 (ECLS-K) study, which were collected from

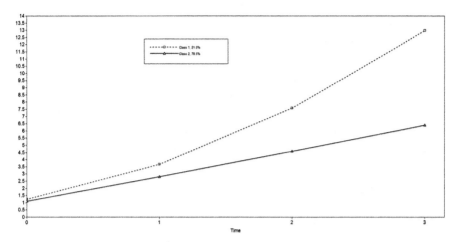

Fig. 13.3 Estimated mean growth trajectory of GMM analysis based on the first simulated data

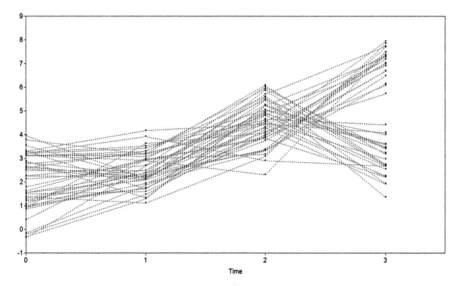

Fig. 13.4 Observed growth trajectories of 50 individuals randomly selected from the second simulated data with two classes, each with its own growth pattern (one is linear and another is quadratic)

a nationally representative cohort of children when they were in kindergarten (fall-1998 and spring-1999), during first grade (fall-2000 and spring-2001), during third grade (spring-2002), and during fifth grade (spring-2004) (Denton et al. 2003; Princiotta et al. 2006). Details of the discussion of ECLS-K can be found in the references provided.

The results of the MDS growth analysis is shown in Fig. 13.7, which depicted one growth profile corresponding to the one dimensional solution and revealed an

Fig. 13.5 Estimated
growth pattern from MDS
growth analysis based on
the second simulated data

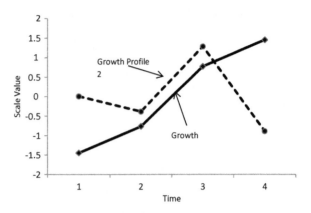

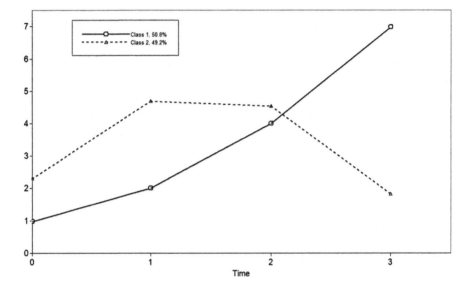

Fig. 13.6 Estimated mean growth trajectory of GMM analysis based on the second simulated data

Fig. 13.7 MDS growth
pattern of mathematic
achievement

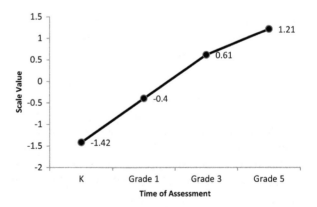

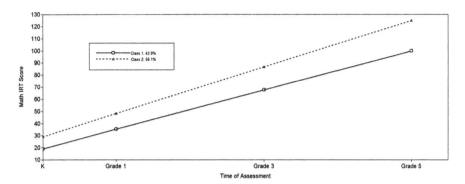

Fig. 13.8 Estimated mean growth trajectory of mathematic achievement

overall increased pattern of achievement over time. This growth pattern indicated a pretty steady rate (39%, 38%, and 23% from K to grade 1, grades 1 to 3, and grade 3 to 5, respectively), identifying an overall linear trend with a slower growth rate from grades 3 to 5.

The results from GMM analysis is shown in Fig. 13.8, which depicted the two-class solution. Essentially, there was one pattern of growth (as in MDS growth pattern) but with differences in level. We can say that Class 1 indicated an initial low developing group and Class 2 indicated an initial high developing group. But both groups had a similar growth pattern over time.

13.4 Conclusion

The purpose of this chapter was to illustrate MDS modeling of change in pattern, which may differ from change in level using GMM approach. Since the method of MDS growth pattern analysis is less well known, we discussed some major aspects of such an approach as well as some of its differences from GMM. Given that the GMM approach is more common in modeling growth, the significance of the chapter is that it discusses the MDS-based approach in the context of growth mixture modeling, showing that the MDS model can be a viable method for growth analysis that has been exclusively belonging to the realm of SEM technique. Researchers and practitioners should be aware of the utilities of MDS in modeling growth.

Based on the results from two simulated datasets used to illustrate MDS growth pattern analysis in the context of GMM, the following points were worth noting. First, the growth pattern from MDS analysis reflected the observed growth trends in the data with differences in level removed. When the observed growth mean trajectories did not significantly differ from patterns, as shown in Figs. 13.1 and 13.2, MDS growth pattern analysis seems to capture that pattern as a prototypical pattern in the data regardless of any mean differences in these trajectories. In contrast, GMM analysis captures the mean level differences in growth trajectory resulting in two growth classes. However, when growth patterns significantly differ from the growth mean trajectories, MDS growth pattern analysis reflects these different growth patterns resulting in two growth profiles. This is similar to those from GMM analysis as shown in Figs. 13.3 and 13.6. Thus, the MDS approach is modeling the patterning of scores without level information of growth trajectories. With the same goal of identifying latent growth trajectories, these two approaches focus on different aspects of growth trajectory.

Second, the focus of the MDS analysis on pattern rather than level may account for differences in number of growth classes/types. Since class membership is assigned after the growth pattern is identified, there was only one growth class from MDS analysis. In contrast, GMM analysis takes the reverse approach. The number of latent classes is estimated first and then the growth trajectory is estimated with respect to each class, resulting in two growth classes.

Third, one may naturally ask which approach is better or best reflects the reality? The response can be considered from two angles. First, since GMM approach and MDS analysis are modeling different aspects of trajectory, we should focus on what information is more important or relevant to know. Second, as Cudeck and Henly (2003) said, a realistic perspective of data modeling is that there are no true models to discover, and searching for the true number of latent classes is "pointless because there is no true number to find" (p.381). Thus, "the issue of model misspecification is irrelevant in practical terms. The purpose of a mathematical model is to summarize data, to formalize the dynamics of a behavioral process, and to make predictions. All of this is scientifically valuable and can be accomplished with a carefully developed model, even though the model is false"(p. 378). In this regard, MDS analysis provides another perspective in understanding the nature of the change.

Thus, one needs to realize that in selecting a growth modeling method, one should consider the desired information to be obtained from such an analysis. We hope that this illustration of MDS latent growth modeling approach can facilitate researchers in better understanding how MDS analysis can shed light on the growth trajectory of individual behaviors in relation to a GMM approach. Besides the pedagogical value of the chapter, we also hope that it can pique the interest of the readers to employ MDS growth analysis in their research.

References

Asparouhov, T., & Muthén, B. (2012). Auxiliary variables in mixture modeling: A 3-step approach using Mplus. statmodel.com.

Cudeck, R., & Henly, S. J. (2003). A realistic perspective on pattern representation in growth data: Comment on Bauer and Curran (2003). *Psychological Methods, 8*(3), 378–383.

Davison, M. L., Gasser, M., & Ding, S. (1996). Identifying major profile patterns in a population: An exploratory study of WAIS and GATB patterns. *Psychological Assessment, 8*, 26–31.

Denton, K., West, J., & Walston, J. (2003). *Reading—Young children's achievement and classroom experiences, NCES 2003–070*. Washington, DC: U.S. Department of Education, National Center for Education Statistics.

Jung, T., & Wickrama, K. A. S. (2008). An introduction to latent class growth analysis and growth mixture modeling. *Social and Personality Psychology Compass, 2*(1), 302–317.

Kruskal, J. B. (1964). Multidimensional scaling by optimizing goodness of fit to a nonmetric hypothesis. *Psychometrika, 29*, 1–27.

Muthén, L. K., & Muthén, B. O. (2001). *Mplus: Statistical analysis with latent variables*. Los Angeles: Muthén & Muthén.

Princiotta, D., Flanagan, K. D., & Germino Hausken, E. (2006). *Fifth grade: Findings from the fifth grade follow-up of the early childhood longitudinal study, kindergarten class of 1998–99 (ECLS-K)*. Washington, DC: National Center for Education Statistics.

Ram, N., & Grimm, K. (2009). Growth mixture modeling: A method for identifying differences in longitudinal change among unobserved groups. *International Journal of Behavioral Development, 33*(6), 565–576.

Skinner, H. (1978). Differentiating the contribution of elevation, scatter and shape in profile similarity. *Educational and Psychological Measurement, 38*, 297–308.

Vermunt, J. K. (2010). Latent class modeling with covariates: Two improved three-step approaches. *Political Analysis, 18*, 450–469.

Wang, M., & Bodner, T. E. (2007). Growth mixture modeling: Identifying and predicting unobserved subpopulations with longitudinal data. *Organizational Research Methods, 10*(4), 635–656. https://doi.org/10.1177/1094428106289397.

Chapter 14
Historical Review

Abstract Briefly discuss the key development of MDS models over time. Explain some new or possible applications of MDS analysis. Strengths and limitations are also discussed.

Keywords Historical development of MDS models

Up until the late 1980's, articles and books on multidimensional scaling (MDS) appeared at an ever-increasing rate, and MDS applications grew in a great number of disciplines, with the historical root in psychology. Because of such a large bibliography, it is hard to be exhaustive in tracking all technical materials on MDS as well as its applications. In the following sections, I present an overview of development of multidimensional scaling up to the late 1980's since most of the MDS developments occurred before this time period. Beginning in 1990, MDS may have lost favor with the advent and popularity of structural equation modeling.

There are quite a few writings on the history of MDS developments (e.g., Shepard et al. 1972; Young 1987). The following review is based primarily on Young (1987).

14.1 Four Stages of MDS Development

The First Stage: Metric MDS Model According to Young (1987), development of MDS models went through four stages. The first stage, started in the 1950's, is characterized by Torgerson's MDS model or algorithm (Torgerson 1952). The algorithm determines or constructs the multidimensional map of points by (1) obtaining a scale of comparative distances among these points, (2) converting the comparative distances into ratio distances, and (3) determining the dimensionality that underlies these ratio distances. In 1956, Messick and Abelson (1956) provided a better algorithm to Torgerson's original model to accomplish the same goal. The enhancement was made by improving the estimation of the additive constant, as in Torgerson's second step, that converts comparative distances to ratio distances based on firm mathematical grounds. These approaches to MDS have become known as metric

MDS in the literature since the observed distances are assumed to be equal or proportional to model-derived distance in a multidimensional space in Torgerson's algorithm.

The Second Stage: Non-metric MDS Model The assumptions of Torgerson's metric model are very restrictive (discussed in later section), and thus his algorithm is rarely used in its original form. This limitation leads to the second stage of MDS developments in the 1960s. Thus, this second stage is characterized by development of what is now known as non-metric MDS started by Shepard (1962) and followed by Kruskal (1964). Non-metric MDS requires less restrictive assumptions than a metric MDS model by Torgerson (1952). The chief difference between non-metric and metric MDS is that non-metric MDS requires only that the rank order of observed distances be the same as (i.e., monotonically related to) the distance estimates derived from the pre-specified MDS model.

Kruskal's Contribution It is worthy to note Kruskal's contribution to the development of non-metric MDS at this stage which will have implications for our interpretations of the findings. First, he introduced a least square fit function that objectively defined the goal of the MDS analysis by minimizing normalized residuals between a monotonic (i.e., rank order) transformation of the data and the model-derived distance based on multidimensional space. Second, he defined two optimization procedures that handled data that have equal distance between any two pairs of objects (called tied data): primary procedure (i.e., untie tied data) and secondary procedure (i.e., tied data remain tied). Third, his algorithm could analyze incomplete data matrices and be able to obtain MDS solutions in non-Euclidean distance space, such as the city-block distance space used by Attneave (1950).

Coombs' Contribution Another noteworthy contribution to non-metric MDS development is by Coombs' data theory, which states that relationships among data can be represented in a space (Coombs 1964). Although not directly related to MDS algorithm, Coombs' data theory is of central interest to MDS. Specifically, he suggested four types of data: (a) preferential choice data, when a person indicates he/she prefers a particular object or behavior (i.e. an adolescent girl prefers talking to her mother with respect to sexual behaviors); (b) liking data, when a person indicates whether he/she likes or dislike certain behaviors (i.e. a female may indicate she likes children while a male may indicate he likes playing computer games); (c) comparison data, when a person indicates which of the two objects is more of some attributes (i.e. a student may indicate that teachers are more helpful than students in school); and (d) similarity data, when a person indicates how similar the two objects are (i.e. an adolescent may indicate that smoking and drinking are the same with respect to deviant behaviors). All of these four types of data can be represented in multidimensional space. As we will see later in the chapter, different MDS analyses can be performed using these four types of data. For example, the MDS preference models can employ one of these types of data to study individual differences in behavioral preferences.

The Third Stage: Individual Differences Models The third stage of MDS developments involves individual differences MDS models. The basic idea of individual differences MDS models is that when we analyze data from individuals, we have two choices: (1) analyze a single matrix of data, averaging across all individuals or (2) analyze each data matrix if we believe that the manipulation of independent variables has had an effect on individuals. Individual differences models, so named, have been used mainly to investigate variations of data structure across individuals, such as to describe variation in person's perceptions across time, settings, or treatment conditions. Thus, individual differences MDS models are able to simultaneously analyze a number of individual data matrices, producing indices of individual differences with respect to certain behavioral traits, with individual differences being represented by dimensional importance indices (called weights) in a Euclidean distance space.

INDSCAL There are several individual differences MDS models. The most well-know model is the Weighted Euclidean Model, also called INDSCAL, developed by Carroll and Chang (1970). Several other researchers also contributed to this line of work such as Horan (1969), Bloxom (1968), McGee (1968), Tucker (1972), and Tucker and Messick (1963). However, the model developed by Carroll and Chang is most used because they developed the computer algorithm (also called INDSCAL) to implement the model, which turns out to be successful in many applications. Based on these developments, Takane, Young, and de Leeuw (1977) developed a computer algorithm called ALSCAL (alternating least squares scaling), which has been incorporated into SAS and SPSS, making MDS more accessible to a wider audience than before.

ALSCAL In a sense, the ALSCAL program can be viewed as a consolidation of all previous developments during the first three stages. It includes metric MDS model (Torgerson 1952), nonmetric MDS models (Kruskal 1964; Shepard 1962), individual differences models (Carroll and Chang 1970; McGee 1968), and multidimensional unfolding (preference) models (Carroll 1972; Coombs 1964).

The Fourth Stage: Maximum Likelihood MDS The fourth stage of MDS development involves maximum likelihood multidimensional scaling, which makes it possible for MDS models to be an inferential tool rather than a descriptive tool. This inferential nature of MDS analysis is based on the idea that maximum likelihood MDS allows significance tests to determine dimensionality, the appropriate models, the appropriate error models, and confidence regions for stimuli and individuals.

The most well-known maximum likelihood MDS algorithm is *MULTISCAL* developed by Ramsay (Ramsay 1991) and *PROSCAL* developed by MacKay and Zinnes (2005). In addition, there are many articles on maximum likelihood MDS and its applications such as those by Ramsay (1977), Takane (1978a, 1978b), Takane and Carroll (1981), DeSarbo et al. (1991), and more recently Treat et al. (2002), MacKay (2007), and Ver et al. (2009).

This brief historical review of the MDS developments provides a fundamental picture of where we are with MDS as a psychological and educational analytical tool. In here I did not discuss a great number of literature that dealt with various technical issues around the MDS, nor did I discuss the different applications using the MDS models. However, one can explore those issues and applications using the four themes of MDS developments as a roadmap. Moreover, one should realize that given about 40 years of development, MDS has reached to its young adulthood, as Schiffman et al. (1981) suggested. In other words, MDS has become quite a sophisticated analytical tool that is yet to be taken full advantage of, especially when we have access to computing power unavailable for MDS analysis 20 year ago.

14.2   New Applications of the MDS Models

Currently, continued efforts have been devoted to improving the estimation algorithms of MDS analysis (Busing and de Rooij 2009; Busing et al. 2005; Busing et al. 2010). On the other hand, the new applications of MDS models have been focused on latent profile analysis for both cross-sectional data (Davison et al. 1996) and longitudinal data (Ding 2001; Ding et al. 2005). Latent growth analysis via MDS models has been shown to be a viable alternative to explore developmental trajectories. At its core, MDS latent growth analysis applies the distance model to a set of time related variables and examines their configuration. Conceptually, the MDS latent growth model has similar analytic goals as growth mixture models (GMM) (Muthen 2001) and the group-based approach (GBA) (Nagin 1999)--to determine the optimal number of latent growth groups and the shape of the trajectory for each group that best fit the data. Then, outcome measures and covariates can be incorporated into the analysis with respect to the different latent growth groups.

In the MDS model, a latent growth class is called a "latent growth profile", and it is represented by a single dimension. The dimension is estimated from a distance model and consists of a set of scale values that indicate the shape of the growth trajectory. For instance, if a potential cubic trend exists in the data, the set of scale values estimated by the model would potentially recover that pattern. In a way, the set of scale values functions like a set of polynomial contrasts. Depending on the number of dimensions, one set of scale values for a given dimension reflects a particular shape of the trajectory for a given latent group. The number of dimensions can be determined by Akaike Information Criterion (AIC) (Akaike 1973) in addition to traditional Stress values (Ding and Davison 2010). Each participant can be assigned to a latent growth profile group based on probability of profile membership (Ding 2007). Moreover, MDS growth modeling can be used to explore the latent growth trend by using deterministic MDS analysis as well as to conduct a hypothesis testing regarding developmental trajectories by using maximum likelihood MDS analysis.

In summary, the key issues discussed are that the MDS latent growth model can be used to identify distinct forms of growth/decline profiles in the data, which may reflect the source of heterogeneity. The distance-based MDS growth model is flexible because it does not restrict the functional form of trajectories across different latent groups, and no distributional assumptions are required. This approach provides the opportunity to analyze potential latent profiles via continuous or discrete observed variables, and to include covariates in the subsequent analyses.

14.3 Strengths and Limitations

In this chapter, I have covered some of the major topics on MDS models and analysis. As I mentioned at the beginning of the chapter, the literature on MDS is quite extensive and it is not possible to cover every line of work on MDS. As a conclusion, I mention strengths and limitations of MDS analysis with respect to its use in psychological and educational research.

Strengths A main strength of MDS models is they can be used for analyzing various types of data such as row-conditional data, matrix-conditional data, and other types of preference data. These types of data contain rich information about individual differences and MDS models provide various ways to capture the information. In its application of longitudinal data analysis, it provides an alternative and complementary method to study growth heterogeneity in the population.

Second, because MDS models can accommodate more data types, it encourages researchers to think critically about the assumptions about the data. For example, in commonly-encountered data of person by variable matrix, does each individual use the scale (e.g., Likert-type response scale) in the same way? The other questions may be: How will a change in the wording of an item change participants' perception and liking of that item? Do male students and female students perceive mathematics concepts in the same way? How many different latent or subgroups are there in the data and how big are they? Which attribute of a construct should be emphasized in the assessment of that construct?

Third, the maximum likelihood MDS models can be used to test various hypotheses with regard to instruments as well as people. The application in this area is under-developed and has much potential in psychological research.

Limitations One main limitation is that interpretation of configuration of MDS analysis is impacted by similarity transformation of the configuration. Thus seemingly different but essentially the same configuration may be interpreted differently. For example, if we change the sign of the scale values along the dimensions, the configuration may appear different from the original one, which may lead to a different interpretation of the configuration.

Second, MDS has traditionally been viewed as a data visualizing method. However, data are not always visualized in two dimensions. Higher dimensionality, on the other hand, makes dimensional solution difficult to be visualized, which defeats its original purpose.

14.4 Future Directions

MDS has not developed into a mature analysis technique, as predicted by some researchers (e.g., Young 1987). The issues that need to be addressed include, but are not limited to, the following:

1. Covariates need to be incorporated into MDS models so that underlying structure of data can be better modeled.
2. Statistical procedures for assessing participants' ideal point with respect to latent group configuration needs to be developed. Rather than relying on visual inspection of participants' ideal point, some statistical criteria need to be used to objectively examine the degree to which an individual prefers a particular behavior.
3. Analytical method of assessing participants' preference is typically standard multiple regression analysis. It may be useful to incorporate logistic or multinomial regression to examine the probability of preference with respect to a set of behaviors.
4. In MDS latent growth analysis, the person-model fit index is based on R^2 statistic. But a better set of person-model fit indices needs to be developed so that we can perform statistical testing.

However, MDS models, particularly preference modeling and profile analysis, can provide a unique method for studying individual differences that cannot be revealed by a structural equation modeling analysis. For instance, in research of moral reasoning, MDS preference modeling may be employed to investigate, using the concept of differential preferences, age differences or developmental trajectory that represents an emerging desire to imagine one's good behaviors as internally motivated, but one's bad behaviors are externally provoked. In addition, confirmatory MDS using maximum likelihood method can be used to test specific hypotheses regarding latent profiles of individuals, as that can be done in structural equation modeling analysis. These analytical possibilities, along with many others, for example, studying participants' multiple ideal points, can further advance MDS models as a psychological and educational research tool.

References

Akaike, H. (1973). Information theory as an extension of the maximum likelihood principle. In B. N. Petrov & F. Csaki (Eds.), *Second international symposium on information theory* (pp. 267–281). Budapest: Akademiai Kiado.

Attneave, F. (1950). Dimensions of similarity. *American Journal of Psychology, 63*, 516–536.

Bloxom, B. (1968). Individual differences in multidimensional scaling models. *Research Bulletin, 68–45*. Princeton: Educational Testing Service.

Busing, F. M. T. A., & de Rooij, M. (2009). Unfolding incomplete data: Guidelines for unfolding row-conditional rank order data with random missings. *Journal of Classification, 26*, 329–360.

Busing, F. M. T. A., Groenen, P. J. K., & Heiser, W. J. (2005). Avoiding degeneracy in multidimensional unfolding by penalizing on the coefficient of variation. *Psychometrika, 70*(1), 71–98.

Busing, F. M. T. A., Heiser, W. J., & Cleaver, G. (2010). Restricted unfolding: Preference analysis with optimal transformations of preferences and attributes. *Food Quality and Preference, 21*(1), 82–92.

Carroll, J. D. (1972). Individual differences and multidimensional scaling. In R. N. Shepard, A. K. Romney and S. Nerlove, (Eds.) *Multidimensional scaling: Theory and applications in the behavioral sciences,* Vol I. New York: Academic Press.

Carroll, J. D., & Chang, J. J. (1970). Analysis of individual differences in multidimensional scaling via an N-way generalization of "Eckart-young" decomposition. *Psychometrika, 35,* 238–319.

Coombs, C. H. (1964). *A theory of data.* New York: Wiley.

Davison, M. L., Gasser, M., & Ding, S. (1996). Identifying major profile patterns in a population: An exploratory study of WAIS and GATB patterns. *Psychological Assessment, 8,* 26–31.

DeSarbo, W. S., Howard, D., & Jedidi, K. (1991). Multiclus: A new method for simultaneously performing multidimensional scaling and cluster analysis. *Psychometrika, 56,* 121–136.

Ding, C. S. (2001). Profile analysis: Multidimensional scaling approach. *Practical Assessment, Research, and Evaluation, 7*(16).

Ding, C. S. (2007). Studying growth heterogeneity with multidimensional scaling profile analysis. *International Journal of Behavioral Development, 31*(4), 347–356.

Ding, C. S., & Davison, M. L. (2010). Multidimensional scaling analysis using Akaike's information criterion. *Educational and Psychological Measurement, 70*(2), 199–214.

Ding, C. S., Davison, M. L., & Petersen, A. C. (2005). Multidimensional scaling analysis of growth and change. *Journal of Educational Measurement, 42,* 171–191.

Horan, C. B. (1969). Multidimensional scaling: Combining observations when individuals have different perceptual structure. *Psychometrika, 34,* 139–165.

Kruskal, J. B. (1964). Nonmetric scaling: A numerical method. *Psychometrika, 29,* 28–42.

MacKay, D. B. (2007). Internal multidimensional unfolding about a single ideal: A probabilistic solution. *Journal of Mathematical Psychology, 51,* 305–318.

MacKay, D. B., & Zinnes, J. (2005). *PROSCAL professional: A program for probabilistic scaling:* www.proscal.com.

McGee, V. C. (1968). Multidimensional scaling of n sets of similarity measures: A nonmetric scaling. *Multivariate Behavioral Research, 3,* 233–248.

Messick, S. J., & Abelson, R. P. (1956). The additive constant problem in multidimensional scaling. *Psychometrika, 21,* 1–15.

Muthen, B. (2001). Second-generation structural equation modeling with a combination of categorical and continuous latent variables: New opportunities for latent class/latent growth modeling. In L. M. Collins & A. Sayer (Eds.), New methods for the analysis of change (pp. 291–322). Washington, DC: American Psychological Association.

Nagin, D. (1999). Analyzing developmental trajectories: A semi-parametric, group-based approach. *Psychological Methods, 4,* 139–177.

Ramsay, J. O. (1977). Maximum likelihood estimation in multidimensional scaling. *Psychometrika, 42,* 241–266.

Ramsay, J. O. (1991). *MULTISCALE manual (extended version).* Montreal: McGill University.

Schiffman, S. S., Reynolds, M. L., & Young, F. W. (1981). *Introduction to multidimensional scaling: Theory, methods and applications.* New York: Academic Press.

Shepard, L. (1962). The analysis of proximities: Multidimensional scaling with an unknown distance. I and II. *Psychometrika, 27,* 323–355.

Shepard, R. N., Romney, A. K., & Nerlove, S. B. (Eds.). (1972). *Multidimensional scaling: Theory* (Vol. 1). New York: Seminar Press.

Takane, Y. (1978a). A maximum likelihood method for nonmetric multidimensional scaling: I the case in which all empirical pairwise orderings are independent-evaluation. *Japanese Psychological Research, 20,* 105–114.

Takane, Y. (1978b). A maximum likelihood method for nonmetric multidimensional scaling: I the case in which all empirical pairwise orderings are independent-theory. *Japanese Psychological Research, 20,* 7–17.

Takane, Y., & Carroll, J. D. (1981). Nonmetric maximum likelihood multidimensional scaling from directional rankings of similarities. *Psychometrika, 46*, 389–405.

Takane, Y., Young, F. W., & De Leeuw, J. (1977). Nonmetric individual differences multi-dimensional scaling: An alternating least squares method with optimal scaling features. *Psychometrika, 42*, 7–67.

Torgerson, W. S. (1952). Multidimensional scaling: I. Theory and method. *Psychometrika, 17*, 401–419.

Treat, T. A., McFall, R. M., Viken, R. J., Nosofsky, R. M., MacKay, D. B., & Kruschke, J. K. (2002). Assessing clinically relevant perceptual organization with multidimensional scaling techniques. *Psychological Assessment, 14*, 239–252.

Tucker, L. R. (1972). Relations between multidimensional scaling and three-mode factor analysis. *Psychometrika, 37*, 3–27.

Tucker, L. R., & Messick, S. J. (1963). An individual differences model for multidimensional scaling. *Psychometrika, 28*, 333–367.

Vera, J., Macias, R., & Heiser, W. J. (2009). A latent class multidimensional scaling model for two-way one-mode continuous rating dissimilarity data. *Psychometrika, 2009*, 297–315.

Young, F. W. (1987). Multidimensional scaling: History, theory, and applications. In R. M. Hamer (Ed.), *Multidimensional scaling: History, theory, and applications*. Hillsdale: Lawrence Erlbaum Associates.

Index

© Springer International Publishing AG, part of Springer Nature 2018
C. S. Ding, *Fundamentals of Applied Multidimensional Scaling for Educational and Psychological Research*, https://doi.org/10.1007/978-3-319-78172-3

Printed by Printforce, the Netherlands